The Coming Civil War

Tom Kawczynski

Contents

Section 4: Scenarios

Section 5: Practical Advice

This Book's Purpose—A Look Ahead

War is coming. In truth, it has already begun.

States are fragile things that only hold together through careful cultivation when two essential components are considered. People need to believe they share common cause with their fellow citizens, and most of those citizens need to share a common set of ethics about right and wrong, hopefully bolstered by an ambition that motivates all to work together.

Sadly, but quite intentionally, America is in the opposite situation in many ways. Despite a noble eleventh hour effort by the Trump Administration to energize a form of civic nationalism rooted in economic prosperity and wrapping oneself in the flag, even a booming economy and opportunity reveal themselves each day to be inadequate sustenance to the Left whose radicalization has been a project at least sixty years in the making.

To understand that story in full, my earlier volume Someone Has to Say It: The Hidden History of How America Was Lost is a great entrance, but there are many excellent books written which tell the same basic story. As means to take control, cultural Marxists exploited every division in our society, breaking unity along racial, gender, culture, and regional lines, to ensure the rising involvement of government in our lives. Surrendering liberty for tranquility, the Right basically ceded control over culture and the population of America to the Left in exchange for an implicit promise peace would be found the moment equality was achieved. With the settling of grievances from out-groups, some more legitimate than others, the expectation was that all would be happy.

٭ This supposition could not have been more wrong. In retrospect, it's not hard to comprehend why the Left, acclimated by a half century of submission by the forces of tradition and restraint, would come to expect they would always get their way. Why settle for halfway compromises when you can take the whole thing? ٭With schools teaching how our once universal values are now irredeemably corrupt, who can blame these leftists for seeking complete victory?

A key feature of leftist thought has always been radical idealism: the belief that Utopia could be realized if just enough people would suppress their own selfish desires to achieve a greater common good. Undeterred by the myriad failures which only expose what are presented as unrealized corruptions of the communist ideal, their love for equality drives them toward destruction of the very pillars of society that sustain a country.

The most stable states throughout history have consisted of a single people, almost always from a single ethnic background. People who share such familial background are more likely to exhibit trust toward one another, and crucially, are less susceptible to being divided along lines of resentment, where one race is played off the others. Although the Right is often called racist, the Left has spent decades perfecting the game of systematizing resentment of the minorities against the majority, sometimes called White Privilege or White Guilt. *

Once the majority was demonized and then demoralized, as they have been for many years, the attack upon the values which sustained the majority who build, bled, and worked to make America great was predictable. Christianity came under assault as a dogma of oppression used by the racial majority to hold down the potential of others, to be corrected through the mass importation of Muslims as well as encouraging atheism for those who eschewed religion altogether. And for those who remained Christian, only those who could toe the new politically correct line would be considered acceptable, where gays get married and every person worldwide is free to ignore borders. *

It's not that the Left doesn't believe in borders, but the dividing line for them is not a line in the desert that separates America from Mexico, but rather a boundary in their minds between the prestige and resources of an unjust past they seek to destroy, and which stands in the way of the fulfillment of their happy dream of all living happily in harmony. Or more accurately, toward limiting their march toward absolute control.

Moving rural folk into the cities where they discard their foolish notions of autonomy is no major concern to the communist who wants to bring people into conformity. Suburbs are an indulgent waste of resources for those seeking to compromise, and it is no accident you see centralization pushed everywhere.

If people will not vote for these ideas, then they will be shamed into supporting them and censored if they oppose them. As Marxism has little value for liberty, it causes those on the Left no remorse to destroy those who oppose their plans, and the ruthlessness with which they proceed is abundantly clear in how they treat those who dare to extol a politically incorrect truth. Losing a job as I did is the least of their punishments, as they actively work to ensure you never fit into their society again, and the number of times they have gone so far as violence is a matter of historical record. * ANTIFA *

Once you understand what the Left offers and believes, it becomes clear as day there is no compromise with these ideals for people who believe in a more traditional way of life. Liberty is fundamentally at odds with the control regime they endorse and trying to settle things peaceably by meeting them halfway is akin to treating just part of your body during some terrible infection. You might buy a little more time, but at the cost of absolute certainty that the same problems will come back even more virulently next time.

I fully realize in writing this volume how extreme my words might seem at first glance, especially to those who have only been hearing the primary public narrative, where America is doing great and we live in a time of great optimism. In many ways, this is very true, but as has been the case for an incredibly long time, the wealth we enjoy in this country has hidden these core divisions which have festered at the heart of the empire which quietly supplanted the republic.

To make the case why this division will only grow and fester until resolved through some more permanent means, we're going to look first at the values which once united us and see how these have been corrupted to such a degree that we now often work against our own best interests.* The core four values of morality, responsibility, identity, and liberty are the bedrock of any state, but the essential unity of these values has been shattered here in America, leading to a situation where we have inertia driving us forward as different sides are planning to take control to remake and redefine America.

As proof of this concept, close examination of the various elements of government that exercise power is the right place to start. Consider the ubiquitous Deep State as exhibit one, where we can see daily how the bureaucracy works in opposition to the elected government. The Deep State promotes the very opposite ideas of the Trump Administration, and some of its functionaries have been indicted for having worked to ensure—as certain FBI agents did—that Hillary Clinton would be elected.

A more just media would correctly label this as tampering at the minimum, but more honestly such actions would be described as treason. But the Fourth Estate has often been a Fifth Column and understanding the major institutional actors who are most influential in American society outside the government is just as vital. So often, these are the people who buy policy, and in exchange, receive massive amounts of financial support from the government for their various endeavors and businesses.

Beyond the parties themselves which have their own layers of corruption, what becomes clear is that these actors have agendas and people pulling their strings also. Most lean Left, but a few lean Right, and once you start looking at the conflict through the prism of how each is trying to remake society either to spawn a progressive future or protect our storied past, the scope of the ongoing conflict becomes staggering.

These actors set the backdrop against which the rest of us as individual citizens must live. Beneath the facile identity we share as all being Americans, we define ourselves in many ways, most of which are increasingly at odds with one another. Most importantly for this thesis, these different divisions line up in such a fashion that if any one of these conflicts boils over, several other issues will arise at once.

I call these the Color Wars. While the name possibly conjures up race as the first suggestion, ethnic identity is only one line along which conflict can emerge. Frankly, I think it is only the third most likely with other divisions being even more pressing.

The division of Red versus Blue has reached such a boiling point ideologically that many families cannot have dinner together during a holiday meal without breaking into arguments, fights, and occasional histrionics. Maps and migration show how Republicans and Democrats are moving apart not just in terms of core concepts, but in real space, where they occupy increasingly separate spaces and exist under different governing regimes.

But such conflict today is even more damaging because unlike in earlier America where significant political control happened at state and local levels, the centralization of government the Left achieved has forced one size fits all solutions onto a country which is not built to receive these. As the Right has realized this and finally started fighting back on the same basic terms of imposing their culture as a reactionary movement, the Left is now aghast to be experiencing the same defeats the Right has swallowed for several generations, and they're mad as hell.

After the 2016 election, the cities feel like they're being punished, and the rural areas of the country finally feel respected. Both are right, ironically, and the second division that is yawning wider in America is between those who live in the few big urban megalopolises and the many other Americans who choose to live apart from the cities. Different lifestyles and different pacing give way to widely divergent values. Whereas the city generally wants more government, the country only wants to be left alone.

Just as with partisan affiliation and geography, ethnic and cultural factors are lining up along certain boundaries with increasing speed. Excepting white liberals who have gentrified their neighborhoods in many ways to buy themselves out of the parts of diversity they cannot admit to themselves they don't like, what we find is white folk are heading out to the suburbs, exurbs, and country to live a

11

pro-American life that is less diverse, more traditional, and conservative.

Blacks continue to be overwhelmingly leftist and urban, and Latinos though less uniform, trend the same way by a better than 2:1 margin. Asians are more of a mixed bag but are also starting to reveal the same basic leftist trend, proving the argument that immigration only ever benefits the Left, and hinting that cultural conflict along partisan lines will likely descend into racial strife as well.

As this anger grows and the conflict spreads into even more areas of our lives, making it less possible to simply live without politics getting in the way, the two sides are already visible to those who are willing to connect where their interests align.

Whether the battle develops along ideological, regional, racial, or cultural lines, the alliances are basically as follows: Right leaning white people who tend traditional and rural will be facing left leaning diverse people who tend progressive and urban. As the enmity grows, these camps will become ever more uniform, and the solutions that are proposed will shift from the idealized language we currently use toward more pragmatic policies designed to benefit one coalition at the cost of the other.

While life doesn't have to be a zero-sum game, when you have at the heart of your society groups of people who want different things and do not want to talk to one another, the opportunities to walk things back from the abyss disappear and through some means or another, these differences will have to be solved.

We're going to look at some of these options ranging from the civil to the extreme, operating under the assumption—which is being proven daily—that neither side wishes to, or frankly can go back to some consensus accessible to all their partisans. Is separation or some form of secession possible, or even preferable to conflict? We can't know these answers, but we need to be honest with ourselves and ask.

While I suspect strongly most people reading this book at the time of writing will understand why I present the argument in these admittedly stark terms, for the sake of history and in hopes a wider audience might become exposed to my thoughts if only for their own security, you need to consider one important fact: Let us assume for a moment that 90% of America is content to just live their lives normally, going to work and taking their children to school and sporting events, and wants no part of any conflict, let alone one as disruptive as I'm projecting. If that estimate held true, that would mean 5% of Americans are roughly lined up on each side, approximately 15 million citizens, ready for a fight and unwilling to back down.

The American Revolution only had about 3% of the people participating in that fight. Yet, it forged a new nation. The First Civil War saw 2% of the male population die, with under 10% of the men actively engaged. We've become accustomed to the idea that 50%+1 equals governance, but this is a historical aberration which is

13

complete folly to trust. When enough people get mad and are willing to do something about it, it only takes about 1 in 20 to disrupt things enough to reset everything. And frankly, we're likely well past 1 in 10 now, with the only restraints having been the strength of the existing police state, the fears of those who would be combatants to act, and the lack of organization on either side on these stark divisions.

As an activist, historian, and someone who spends his life at the center of these things, take heed this tsunami is already rolling from sea to shining sea. Be mindful of what is happening, and I will conclude this book with practical advice for people ranging from the engaged to the indifferent to help protect and bolster yourselves and your families.

I always make very clear that my loyalties lie to the Right and to the traditions and people that spawned this great nation. But I am also loyal to decency and dignity, which is why I share openly what is coming, whereas people like Antifa plan and plot their violence in private. Although I have many thoughts about how to best preserve what made America great which might occupy a future volume, our story today is about the fight ahead, why it is happening, and how to survive.

If I save just one decent life through these considered yet dangerous words, it will have been worth all the effort. But my hope is we can save much more than that if people become informed and are honest about the dangers ahead.

Section 1: What Was Lost

This first section of the book explains how America became so divided that a simmering civil conflict threatens to break out into hot war. The rise of government and the demand that a singular cultural solution be applied to the entire country has pushed people onto irreconcilable sides increasingly antagonistic to one another.

After a cursory review of recent history, four core values which will need to be defined for a victorious faction are identified:

Morality: *A shared set of beliefs to motivate and guide society*

Responsibility: *The expectation and reality that citizens will adhere to these beliefs*

Identity: *Recognizing honestly who will and will not conform*

Liberty: *Using this newfound unity to live in prosperity and freedom.*

In concert, these represent the beginning of a cultural renewal which, with mass adoption, will represent victory in the civil conflict, whether these values emerge through consensus, compromise, or after conflict.

Chapter 1: How America Was Transformed: A Brief History

At their core, most Americans are incredibly decent people, and this being the case, even those who are less savory often act the same way. We want to believe the best in people, to take an optimistic vision of our future, and to trust rather than fear. We have been welcoming for centuries, and in many ways this has done us well in attracting the best talent from around the world to join this incredible effort.

The problem is having so many good people around means America also exerts an irresistible allure for those whose intentions are decided less pure. Those who wanted to remake the world made the obvious connection that America, especially post World War II, was at the center of the global future, and decided to corrupt our destiny. Cleverly, using language designed to allay suspicions, and using causes couched in the veneer of social justice, our wealth was siphoned off to create global institutions that work actively against our national interests and our kindnesses have been exploited as weaknesses.

One chapter is not nearly enough to make the case that took me a book to write just a few short months ago, but what needs to be understood for what follows to make sense is that the people controlling the political, economic, and cultural scene here in the United States have for a very long time sought to accomplish the fundamental transformation of America that Obama spoke about during his eight years in office. We are to be made into something very different than we once were, no longer sovereign and free, but instead subservient to the "greater good" which communists dislike calling by name.

The economic and political case began in the 1910's when the government voted itself power to tax the people directly, to have a central bank control national finances, and took its first steps toward perpetual war under the guise of humanitarianism. The latter is especially important in how America evolved because we have tacitly accepted the idea that our wars are not the traditional sort of imperial acquisitions, but rather are in defense of universal values.

Most importantly, big wars mean big budgets and a bigger state which can do much more to transform society. It's no accident we average a war about every decade. This is a convenient way for all those who believe government should be used to transform people into compliance with their beliefs to keep the faith. Whether the wars are great like the World Wars, or minor like our incursions into East Asia and the Middle East, during each conflict, the government gained more resources and power from the people who have sacrificed their wealth and autonomy.

In concert with the warfare state, FDR catalyzed the welfare state, and through a big boost from LBJ, we now have a cradle to grave regime that basically subsidizes people through their lives. We also have, in the Democrats, a party which encourages this dependency in accordance with their leftist thinking that a person who needs a thing will support the politicians who provide it to them. Such cynicism runs counter to the American ideal of independence and success, but it turns out to be incredibly effective in ensuring voter loyalty.

When finances fail, culture jumps in the gap, and the Left utterly dominates culture throughout America today. The universities are bastions of politically correct thought where people are paid to churn out tracts that support the party line. Ranging from obvious subjects such as sociology, where thinly veiled Marxism is taught as truth, even the hard sciences are not immune from their influence. Try publishing a thesis skeptical of climate change—a scheme designed to move money from the First World to the Third World—and you'll see no job openings available.

The media works hand in glove with academia to push the Leftist idea of radical equality, always speaking positively of those who are deemed social victims and never wasting any opportunity to demean the traditional culture and people of this nation* No Republican can do right, and no Democrat can do wrong in their eyes, and yet, when we look behind the curtain, we see the media is owned by just a very few companies whose leadership pushes these communist ideals.

It might sound contradictory to what we are conventionally taught to think of big business as being in bed with big government, as we're told these two entities work against one another. But this is a populist myth going back to the turn of the Twentieth Century. Honestly, large corporate entities realized long ago that controlling government was far more efficient than fighting one another, and so we see the revolving door between business and their regulators across many industries.

That's why up until the current administration, no one cared if jobs were shipped out of the country. A devil's bargain had existed for decades between the money people on both sides. Far too many Republicans were happy to support anything that elevated profit margins, even if it hollowed out chunks of this nation into unemployment, decay, and sometimes despair. And the Democrats didn't mind policies that brought in cheap labor immigrants to whom they could preach their gospel of envy and dependency. ✶

For as much as there are differences between the Right and the Left, it's worth noting the people who run these parties share more in common with each other than their partisans, and the corruption racket they have run with our country for decades has served not the interests of ordinary Americans, but instead an emergent global elite.

They hide behind gated fences and transnational institutions, starting with the bankers first and foremost, but expanding outward into foreign policy and other areas, speaking with cool reserve as they casually expend our lives and energies for their causes. They control our wealth, they open our borders, and they fund politicians who vote for the wars that push people all around the world, disrupting the lives of regular people who spend years working harder and harder just to keep up.

Thankfully, some of these efforts are coming to light now, and I personally am glad the Trump Administration is revealing each day new ways in which America was placed in thrall to interests which were not our own. On this level, many people are being awakened, but the cultural conflict may be even more important, and it is there I fear we are in the deepest trouble.

At heart, civilizations and countries exist as the realization of some ideal, backed by a concrete group of people. For Western Civilization, it was white people who were seeking to improve their lives through knowledge in tandem with a commonly shared wisdom and morality. For a few hundred years, things were going mostly well, and then the clock turned to 1900.

Wars and other calamities destroyed the moral confidence the West felt in its people and its civilization. We stopped fighting for our traditional Christian faith after seeing so many of our own die, and instead, we succumbed to hedonistic relativism. It didn't happen all at once, but as we embraced a material ideal of comfort and secularism, we stopped fighting against those who had very different ideas.

I'll always give the Marxists credit for being brilliant in packaging their ideals to appeal to the widest possible audience, and when you look at what the Sixties spawned, the idea of free love, universal tolerance, and the brotherhood of all men would sound great at first glance if you could pull everyone together. We spent sixty years trying to realize this most righteous vision, and we have learned a few things.

People aren't blank slates. Bring people from a different culture, a different part of the world with different truths, and there will be discord. Two people can both perceive themselves to be acting morally, but when morality itself is different, then division and eventually conflict ensue. Faced with having to make choices, our society has learned again and again to make a virtue of indecision, agreeing only to destroy what once served as core principles, to instead say anything goes.

Men and women have been taught that we are now to be one and the same, both working, and neither serving as parent. Children are now raised by proxy, whether by the schools run by the state or by the television blasting certain messages. We have learned to care for stuff more than people, because that was safe and inoffensive. We have been brought so low as to stop caring for ourselves and believing in ourselves, and we have let our civilization slip away. Others wanted it more, and we simply watched as they entered, content to reside in little enclaves of thought, and existing until a quiet end would come.

But the Cultural Marxists wouldn't even allow this death with dignity, and as we see so painfully clearly today, their jihad to wreck all we once held dear to enact their final communist vision will not wait. Not content to wait out the dwindling majority, they started forcing policy after policy upon us, bringing people in by the millions each year from the Third World, and labeling Christians and men who loved liberty as terrorists. Perhaps from their perspective, it might be true, because a communist fears no man so much as one who has a higher authority than the state.

These are the people who control what goes on the radio, on the TV, who try to censor dissenting visions away from the Internet, and who have access to money in quantities so vast they can literally print all they want. Their goal is the eradication of all our traditional values, of the sovereign citizen, of natural authority ranging from the family to the priest, and of reason itself: because truth doesn't serve their purposes.

I don't know how you meet people like this halfway. They certainly aren't interested in acting by half measures either, other than each step bringing them closer to the fatal goal the Russians, Chinese, Venezuelans and others had inflicted upon them to the tune of millions of dead. History has shown communists have zero inhibition about killing people in massive numbers to realize their dreams, and while we were focused on being comfy, they took control of much of our country and the key institutions that shape ideas.

We let it happen. There were actors who deserve infamy who will certainly come out in the fullness of time, but the reason they succeeded so thoroughly is because we stopped caring to defend and articulate beliefs of our own. Some stood up, but they were unwilling to fight with anything more than words, and so they were backed into tidy boxes, whereas the Left used every ounce of control they took to push their insidious agenda.

22

It is only now that their victory is almost complete the Right has awakened to this crisis with perhaps enough urgency to act. Whether we will or not is an open question, but after the Trumpian revolt, the global project to push transnational institutional communism is in jeopardy because too many Americans dissent and refuse to play a part.

Please understand the people who have built this international order reject natural law, so they do not like sovereign citizens. They do not believe people have inherent rights or sacred liberties. Most frankly find God anathema and believe in no higher authority than themselves and the heartless arithmetic they serve. So, while they have happily plundered America of blood and treasure which we were foolish enough to provide in copious quantities, they have no love or need of our nation or antiquated concepts such as those enshrined in the Constitution and Bill of Rights. ✶

In their calculation, America needed to be taken down *OBAMA* in order to realize the global project, and as you see the first glimmers of a national effort in opposition to that, a positive limited effort struggling to overcome the bureaucrats who betray us all at every opportunity, it becomes clear the Left would rather collapse America than see us oppose the new world without borders where everyone intermingles under a controlling network of agencies. No guns, no resistance, no free speech, and no problems is what they want. ✗

Only we stand in the way of the fulfillment of this Orwellian vision, and as each day's hysteria on the news reveals, the powers that be are working overtime to push the

Left into revolt to topple America into a conflict that will remove us from prominence on the world scene. Should they win, our rights are gone. Should they fail, the rest of the world will have consolidated against us, save those few brave nations trying to fight themselves free of the same entanglements that brought us low.

This is where we are today, and it is one hell of a dilemma for a person who cares about this country and our historic values. No matter what we choose, any path but submission and surrender only leads to greater conflict, so this makes us consider the first important question: What are we willing to fight to preserve?

Individuals and families will have to answer this question in the coming months and years in a much more meaningful way than has been required in generations. The easy days are coming to an end, and while the economy is booming and we're enjoying an Indian Summer for our embattled nation, these questions will only become more pressing in the days ahead.

Assuming we decide it is worth the cost and risk to not just preserve, but revitalize both our civilization and our country, I humbly submit four values essential to the survival of a healthy state which we've lost and need to regain, each of which we will have to fight to reclaim, and all of which can only be restored with great cost.

Chapter 2: Morality—The Importance of Culture

There are two types of glue that hold society together. The first are bonds of blood, natural and fortified over generations by a common people with a shared ancestry. The second are bonds of culture, rooted in mutually expressed beliefs defended by institutions and passed down across generations expressing aspirations for the future, understanding of the past, and the morality that serves a person transiting the present to exist as part of that greater whole. In concert, these make up the nation.

Morality is at the heart of every society as it asks questions not just about behavior, but also about our greater purpose in the universe. Most often emerging from religious beliefs, up until relatively recently in the West generally and America specifically, this meant the most valued morality was Christian, but these central precepts were under-girded by older values emerging from our martial ancestry.

From Christianity, we learned faith, hope, and charity –, concepts crucial for a high trust society and which served us very well so long as we were circumspect about who was admitted into the nation. For in these promises, there was an implicit agreement of reciprocity, like a medieval vassal to a lord, where if support would be provided for all who needed assistance, then industry would be expected from all who could offer support to the group.

From each according to their means and to each according to their needs has been warped by Marx and the communists into a catchall whereby the state has taken responsibility for everything, but the basic concept that people should be invested in one another, voluntarily, to provide mutual support is as basic as civilization itself. Charity is the recognition of mutual investment without compulsion, something that allowed us to brave the many different challenges of what was once an untamed land with faith help would become available.

History demonstrates faith is at the center of most great endeavors, for what else could motivate people so thoroughly as the hope to please the divine, to make purpose in this life through showing one's own deeds? Although there is an implicit tension between faith and good works, it was in this relationship we built up first the Enlightenment and then the many frontiers that coalesced into America. With a sense of mission and purpose to bring civilization forward, our destiny truly was manifest, and we approached our duty with a sense of purpose and gratitude.

Lastly, hope stems from an active sense of purpose and gratification of belonging to a larger group. We've become so atomized that we have wandered in a million different directions without some uniting purpose from which to draw inspiration. We've been conditioned into a bland sort of indifferent efficiency, the least common denominator which is all that is left in an age where relativism is enforced, and so we exist in a place beyond hope just waiting in frustration.

As means to fulfill these functions, our morality also added four other key precepts sometimes called cardinal virtues to the theological instructions to which almost all

Americans once subscribed: Prudence, temperance, fortitude, and justice were expected in how men and women would govern themselves. With patient minds, avoiding indulgence, personal character, and a sense of fair play, a decent people were able to build a great nation because we shared these common values, having been overwhelmingly of European descent up until the betrayal of 1965.

Such values represent our European heritage but let us not neglect the uniquely American aspects of thinking we've added for ourselves from years of working this land. Add innovation, creativity, the urge to explore, and the will to overcome, and it becomes easy to see why America achieved hegemony. In the balance between pragmatism and optimism, we have ever found our future, and such thinking is what has propelled us toward success since the launch of this republic.

The problem is we've lost these values. Not everyone, but the new cultural matrix which was imposed upon us through our schools, our media, and increasingly our government itself, was one of victimhood and relativism. Instead of the older concept in America wherein success was an opportunity to be seized, now large portions of our people embrace a more cynical idea of being perpetually part of an imagined underclass. It didn't take long for such predictions, helped by government subsidy, to become self-fulfilling prophecies, leading to a chasm in the population.

The Sixties were especially devastating with their nihilism as they sought not only to unmake traditional values, but the institutions that backed our traditional beliefs were ruthlessly attacked. Families were torn apart with women's liberation where mothers now traded their timeless gift of raising children for a paycheck instead. Churches were vilified and then blackmailed by tax implications, becoming either silent, or parties to the state welfare apparatus being constructed. As people stopped gathering, the civil society which once cared for people with love and charity morphed into an indifferent bureaucrat sitting at a mandated counter.

*But this should have been expected because the dirty secret of the relativism the Marxists love so much is that tolerance is just another word for indifference.*A tolerant person is really saying they care so little about what those around them are attempting, they will not stop them under any circumstances unless they either directly threaten the other person or seek to impose their beliefs on another. Everyone can believe whatever they like, but just never enough to do anything about it. It's unsurprising the massive apathy we now experience has been the result, as everyone is now alone in their own world and we cannot relate as we once did so instead we simply pretend to be connected.

Put differently, in a moral society, people believe in a shared purpose greater than themselves because there is an agreed upon culture that emerges to accomplish some greater end. There is a transformation that occurs as the nation engages to realize unity, the opposite of this so-called diversity promoted as the virtue of tolerance. We are told there is no cost to bringing in people from many different places with wildly varying beliefs, but it is painfully obvious this is another politically correct lie.

If my truth is different than your truth, we may disagree. If you put large groups of people who have a different truth, like Islam, into a country where there had been a dominant truth centered on radically different principles, like Christianity, such disagreements will eventually rise to the level of direct conflict. That's why there were jihads and crusades, and why family groups and extended kin in Europe as well as other areas came together to form nations on ethnic terms, choosing to link their kin beneath a set of common beliefs and then enforcing those for mutual protection.

Here, we've intentionally torn down the institutions that bound us in mutual morality, and asserted value to be arbitrary, trusting quite naively that wealth alone will serve to mollify our human instincts for how we should live. As the rising conflict between groups illustrates, such secularism is proving inadequate to integrate people who have ever been driven by desire far more than wanting simple material satisfaction.

As we've watched our country diverge, there are several different moralities now in play. There are people who try to subscribe to the traditional model which built America into a great nation, seen more commonly as one moves outward from cities, with the contrasting approach emerging from the cities. "Anything goes" is the idea in urban spaces, with the idea the government will fix things, and even if such responses will ever require further revision, at least they make promises to fulfill their false vision of justice.

Envy has been co-opted as the key weapon at the heart of cultural Marxism, which basically is a theory that divides people by whatever means possible, figuring that each contradiction allows one more step toward bringing the state into compliance with the imagined larger agenda: Centralization and control. Dialectical reasoning isn't the most entertaining subject, but it's important to recognize just how frequently the Left creates a problem to offer their preferred solution in response.

But the vacuum the Left offers morally can be filled only by the resentment they've been pushing with increasing angst against the majority. The people who built America were kind and perhaps foolish enough to share fully of their generosity and labors. By contrast, to listen to the leftist drivel, morality is defined as taking from those who have more, as such a situation of inequity could only have happened unjustly and redistribute all that is earned to those groups who are perpetually oppressed and dispossessed.

America once created free thinkers and individuals, but now from the poorest in the ghettos to the best educated at the Ivies, the same basic concept of plantation thinking has been accepted where we now only exist to give what we stole back to the victims. Never mind the details that the alleged infractions are often centuries old, and never mind also the capacity of individuals to better themselves, cultural

Marxism never worries so much about production. Instead, it moves swiftly to consider using force, moral or physical, to convince people to surrender their assets and energies to their cause.

We face this corrosive morality of defeatism today, and up until this point, we have not been able to articulate a national solution. Our national identity, such as it is, remains around patriotism and symbol but the loss of a common purpose is the ugly heart of the schism now widening. When we stopped believing in ourselves and our values, stopped passing judgments for fear of being called names, we gave up control over not just what we would think, but what our children would be taught to think.

To reclaim morality on a personal level is as easy as choosing to identify those values which lead to the best life, both in our families and in our communities. As a recommendation, small towns often have some of these features remaining and if you are lucky enough to find the right place, you might find out what you've been missing and can skip a few steps. But for the man who wants to be moral today, be ready to be attacked and brought down, because the people who run this system do not like moral judgments. They would reserve such jurisdiction for solely themselves, because their culture is about control, not liberty.

Morality matters because it gives people hope and purpose, and because men who believe in something will fight to protect what they love. We lost sight of that for a while, but as the contrast heightens between relativism on

31

the Left and reason on the Right, the contours of the intellectual argument currently rising become crystal clear.

Chapter 3: Responsibility—Citizenship as Duty

Once a person has <u>a moral compass</u>, ideally shared by most of their fellow community members, only then can the second missing element in a happy society and nation be recovered: <u>Responsibility.</u>

Compare the America of 2018 to the expectations of 1900. Back then, a family most likely produced the food they needed to survive, had no government agencies to bail them out, and lacked the technological conveniences we now enjoy which insulate us from the world. Yet, for the myriad challenges our ancestors faced daily, such adversity taught them discipline, the importance of planning, and patience.

Now, <u>we expect instantaneous gratification in</u> all we do in our lives. Technology puts the world at our fingertips so much so that some people can't even walk to the fridge to feed themselves. If one is unhappy, whereas in previous times a person might have tried to change their society, we are now encouraged instead to find a <u>happy pill</u> to correct ourselves into a better state. If we are without means, and especially part of one of the historically designated groups for protection, government will throw money at people, families, and even whole tribes for their welfare.

Seeing as we are so well protected, it's easy to understand why people have developed this unique luxury of practiced indifference. Our wealth has been so extravagant that those who have the most means to change our nation can buy themselves into posh enclaves where they only see anything irritating in passing. Such opulence allows one to exist above the consequences of one's actions to our society, and as a result, the failure to exist responsibly crosses all social classes.

It's a global phenomenon, but most heavily and dangerously practiced in the West. Around the time World War II ended, the decision to move toward a global bureaucracy kicked ideas which had been under consideration for decades into high gear. With the rise of first the United Nations and then the various financial institutions like the International Monetary Fund, World Bank, and Bank of International Settlements on one flank, and organizations like the G7 and then G20 on the other, alliances were made across borders whereby the elites could work with one another to suppress all their respective nations for their joint class interest.

Such arrangements were nothing new to the European leadership who proposed these institutions, as there was a long history there of seeing the people as merely pieces to be used in a greater game, a philosophical tenet the Marxists coming into power gladly accommodated. Nor was such action unfamiliar to Asia where authority was long dominant, or Africa and Latin America where military force was often used to take charge of countries whose ability to function could be compromised. But America was different.

We certainly weren't alone in having a national mission, a manifest destiny, and a belief in our people and our cause: to spread liberty and tame frontiers of both the land and the mind. We also weren't alone in having those who had the most in our society overlook their countrymen of blood and land, and instead embrace radical idealism. But we were betrayed by those who decided to look for a better future for themselves by transforming those beneath them into something less capable to ensure perpetual servitude.

It is an ugly thing to share, but there's no better explanation for why migrants, and by that, I mean invasions of young men who espouse a very foreign religion, are being encouraged to percolate throughout the West. Our elites want their own people distracted, demoralized, and ultimately diffused to create some sort of competitive advantage. Whatever the public rhetoric, these people have prepared far too well to justify ideas which are clearly unpopular and exact a great cost on the impacted societies for this to be explained as some naïve accident.

America has our own version of this, where we bought into a line about being unable to make things for ourselves any more, where our elites sold us on the need for cheap labor to have inexpensive goods. That conversation goes back to the 1950's and 1960's, right about the time we opened our borders with the passage of the 1965 Hart-Celler Act that made immigration a lottery for the lucky.

I think about California, the state that produced Nixon and Reagan, and wonder how bringing in millions of Latino immigrants, as many illegal as legal, could possibly be a benefit. Just look what that has done to the Golden State, which now has the highest poverty rate of any State in the country. A combination of feckless Marxists led people who subscribe to Reconquista ideologies in hatred of this

*

NOT TRUE

?

nation, our history, and the majority of our people.   It happened to Colorado.   It's happening to Arizona.   And then, probably, Texas will be the biggest prize.

All of this happens because the elites are irresponsible about what they leave behind, thinking only for the profits of the day, and not for the welfare of succeeding generations. Linking back to the dominant secular morality, these people think they're acting morally by giving away the country to those who never had a turn to be on top, and by wishing away the hateful presence of their own people. At least, that's the line enough of the elites use to convince people—whose hearts are often better than their minds –to rationalize self-destructive tendencies of <u>misplaced altruism</u>.

But it isn't just the elites who are to blame, especially here in America, where we have an active citizenry. For a very long time, people have been willing to accept government taking leadership in many areas that are leagues away from where the Constitution grants sovereignty, because they either didn't want to fight or were content to surrender their personal responsibility to others.

(? *INTERNET-*

I reckon it no accident that society is structured in such a way wherein we are always provided a reason to be busy, and rarely have time to simply think and reflect. For those with children, amplify this statement one hundred-fold. We might care about things outside our homes, but there's always another job to be done, especially now that both parents are expected to work, and we never have time for other issues. Most people are probably glad, or at least relieved, someone else is there to take care of the problems.

Except, let's think of some things we've accepted as problems which are best served as government responsibilities. Start with education where most American students now are propagandized through their formative years as a state service which we pay for regardless of whether our children attend or not. If you have kids and you haven't read through the textbooks they're provided, you might want to take another look. They're not teaching what you would expect if you're not paying attention.

How about the back and forth fight over health care? How did everyone like having to pay for the privilege of not purchasing some overwrought government plan? Through both public solutions, and through mandated subscription to insurance companies' private solutions, we are constrained in our options and forced in our choices. In such a large system, how can any outcome be expected other than to reduce us all to numbers and statistics? For the greater good.

All of this comes from our failure to exercise personal responsibility. When we shift away from mindfully supporting those we know out of genuine concern, the problems of people stop being human issues worth time and energy, and instead become another deduction from our paycheck. Frankly, that's where we are today, where under the deceit of tolerance, we functionally practice institutional indifference and pretend it is some great virtue.

Perhaps that is why so many people are unhappy, because for all the superficial connections we experience in our daily lives, we struggle mightily to form bonds that allow us to do things of consequence. We distract ourselves through a million clever devices and tricks but having observed people living their own purpose-driven lives of simplicity and interconnectedness, I cannot help but feel we're missing something deeper by taking our responsibilities so narrowly.

To introduce the concept, I purposely avoided talking about political participation, but a time is coming when this is going to change. We've become very accustomed to thinking of politics as 50% + 1 decisions where our only obligation is to vote, but that isn't going to be enough in the future. The world will belong to passionate people who make our fate their responsibility.

How one goes about that is entirely up to them, but I have observed a nationalist spirit rising on the right and a communist one emerging from the Left. After years of existing within a well-centered and moderated view which was policed by financial interests who found it useful, the center has cracked and now those who are willing to do more than cast a ballot are jumping into the fray to shift their respective parties.

If you win primaries, run candidates, and get involved politically, your influence in politics will become more than your neighbor's.

When you grow your own food, own land, and know your neighbors, your ability to not just influence politics, but survive bad policies, also grows.

Whether you're political or apolitical, the rewards of taking responsibility are manifest, and the costs of not exercising judgment are plain to see. Once people accept the easy promise that anything goes, they will behave that way and social ties erode.

I sometimes have this argument with civic nationalists who want culture to be enough to hold this nation together, who think lofty ideas hold people together more thoroughly than kin and blood. Even as I admire how civics once succeeded and built America in many ways, we must admit we lost our tools. We gave up the culture of achievement, of opportunity, and yes, responsibility in exchange for misplaced guilt.

Now, we live in a house that needs to be rebuilt, both morally and pragmatically, because we've rewarded so many bad behaviors, entitled so many undeserving people, and then brought in those people most likely to push even harder against what we used to believe. I understand why foreigners might want to come here, and I hold them blameless, because choosing not to look out for our own our own people was our own failure.

Assuming we can re-establish ourselves on a solid moral basis and we are willing to take greater responsibility in our lives, who are our people and how do we help one another? Because if we identify the wrong people as our own, it will not be very long before all we can offer in peace will be taken in strife—as has already happened.

Chapter 4: Identity—Finding Where You Belong

A great deal of time, energy, money, and effort are invested to convince people that we are all the same. Our ideas are said to be interchangeable, our heritage compatible, our cultures can co-exist, and differences in appearance are purely aesthetic. It's propaganda that theoretically benefits everyone to accept, to keep the peace, and so it has proven remarkably resilient in the face of overwhelming evidence to the contrary which can be readily observed.

Let's dispense with the preliminaries and observe that different people are different. Not everyone is the same. Men and women are different. People who hail from different parts of the world are different, their genomes having favored certain traits over generations adaptive to very divergent environments. Their culture often follows in close linkage to these traits, making a virtue of whatever traits are most manifest. This is true for people from Europe, Asia, or Africa.

Identity is also regional. Up in New England where I live, people speak a certain way and consider it a sin to have their lawn beyond a certain pre-determined height. But were I down in southern Appalachia, such Yankee thinking would be seen as a needless infringement. Perhaps there is a reason why a place settled primarily by English people—as the Northeast originally was—would have values akin to what might fit England, whereas areas first colonized primarily by Scots and Irish would have a wilder streak.

Other examples abound, but the point is that we have different identities which make this country unique, and these work in concert along both ethnic and cultural lines. Even though people do not like to talk about these differences, and there remains an incredibly strong social stigma for doing so, especially for groups deemed reactionary or regressive, look where people choose to live and how so many choose to be in places with people akin to themselves as proof of the importance of these differences.

Such thinking is natural. We're hardwired to want to support our families, despite incursions of Marxist propaganda against such natural inclinations. And when we look for help, we first look to people with whom we can relate. First and foremost, we will look to family starting with parents, siblings, and then extending outward to kin and clan. Our circle then widens from blood to the extended community, where if values and trust are shared, there exists a network to work in concert to solve issues.

This model sustained most of human history, including the American model, and it is the foundation for nearly every state in existence today, excepting a few arbitrary creations of the post-colonial era in the Third World, and a few empires that have a single dominant group subjugating others. Nations built upon ties of blood and family grow to share ties of culture and language most easily. Such nations prove resilient as memory and tradition become part of a common ancestry. Therefore, we see people whose states can sometimes be disbanded for centuries re-emerge as the same people, as the Poles did in Europe or most spectacularly, as the Jews did in Israel.

America wants to be different, and to some extent we are. We have always tried to envision ourselves as a people apart, of no nation and of all nations, driven by a mission. Whether one defined that as freedom or conquering the frontier, there was a wider variance of what it meant to be American and based upon a successful Nineteenth Century that was part luck, part providence, and much hard work, we took certain lessons that we could integrate people into our culture who came from different backgrounds.

The problem is the people we originally took weren't all that different. The clear majority of first and second wave American immigrants were European in origin, which means they basically accepted reason as a governing principle, limited government, personal responsibility, and Christian morality. Languages were an issue, but there was a clear sense that English would dominate and be the sole means of public discourse, and this ensured integration would happen. Furthermore, there were no handouts given to these settlers.

America recognized that even immigration of similar others with different languages was becoming a problem, and we shut our doors to outsiders in 1924 specifically because we were taking in more people than we could readily integrate. This is a sane and reasoned approach most countries undertake without any further explanation. A country is not just a set of laws, which can be followed or ignored, but also the people who live there and their willingness to meet expectations and follow a common moral compass that guides them to construct a shared future.

In earlier writings, I used the term folkism to describe the larger ideal, which is that a nation is truly its people, connected by kin and family, and that such bonds are far more stable and enduring than those of ideas. Proof of the concept is self-evident as we see how our diverging views of what constitutes justice in America is tearing this state apart with increasing speed each day. An empire built upon truth can only last so long as that truth remains unchanging, and we long since abandoned our core beliefs that led us across our continent. Now, we will contest one another to find a new truth, but in this moment, we might also discover our nation.

Or, we might discover as some observers have shrewdly noted, America has several different nations. Having traveled, I can observe for myself that New England, the Mid-Atlantic, the Southern Coast, the Deep South, the Upper South, and the Midwest all have very different mores, modes of being, expectations, and a sense of internal unity. The exact borders might be blurry, but as centrifugal forces amass to force compliance with the central authority, regional identity becomes more powerful. But where America previously handled these impulses through having a weak Federal regime, now we have made decentralization an unlikely option.

Ideology is another form of identity. Red states get redder each day and blue states get bluer. When we look at data in a more granular form, at the county level, what becomes clearer is that America is a very conservative country that has a few very progressive enclaves in the biggest cities and a few coastal regions. So, we talk about popular votes and numbers, but what the maps show is two countries sliding past one another like ships in the night.

Worse still is that as this pattern reinforces itself, people feel permanently disenfranchised. Try being a Democrat in Texas or a Republican in California. Your state basically exists to limit your ideas. And we see that happening increasingly at the national level, where the GOP plays the geography game and the Democrats try to win a numbers battle by using immigration to change the demography of the electorate to one that favors them.

This brings us to the next and probably most important component of identity, which is race. It's a funny topic because everyone in America knows it is real because of how the Left incessantly complains about white privilege and blames everything they can on institutional bias, and yet enforces a double standard that is both awe-inspiring and utterly ludicrous. In America, racial pride is seen as an absolute positive for anyone Black, Latino, Asian, Native American or even from more obscure origins. Ethnic pride is promoted publicly, along with advocacy networks for each of these groups, and issue groups which openly advocate for money to be given to each of these racial groups—as causes in and of themselves—just because of who they are.

If you dare to breathe even the same exact sentiments for white folks, you'll be branded as the worst racist, Nazi, and tyrant ever out there. If you don't believe me, Google my own name, read the quotes attributed to me, and look at how I was editorialized into being a zealot. Why Whites are so despised and opposed by major media—and the people who control it—is a topic with which you should familiarize yourself, but which is beyond the scope of this book. One hint though: You'll begin finding answers when you look at whom you aren't allowed to criticize. You'll need an open mind to reconsidering much of the history you have been taught to see the pattern, let alone accept the conclusions.

Regardless of the reasons why whites have been chastised, the simple reality remains we are now in position where we are legally inferior to other groups in this country. We do not have the same legal protections against being fired for racial discrimination. We are not eligible for special consideration when applying for Federal contracts or to send our children to college. In fact, we are actively discriminated against to such a degree that we cannot simply say we are a group of people in this country that affirm our own self-worth and want to look out for the interests of our people, just the same as any other group.

This censorship regime is maintained through a combination of learned silence, educational engineering, and the rigid enforcement of high social costs for speaking out. We sometimes call this the politically correct police, and frustration with the clear and evident hypocrisy of those who push these ideas led to Trump's election and reveal the heart of the division in America. While race is one prominent example, the Left has undermined traditional identity in all its forms: White, Christian, straight, and rural as all being unworthy to survive and has targeted these forms of identity for dissolution and destruction.

Such language may seem harsh but consider what we've seen in the past few decades. For many years, Americans were told by the Left that if we treated all people equally and tolerated their lifestyle choices, we could all live peacefully without interfering with one another. Some could argue we even reached that point sometime near 1990 where the issues that bother us today seemed to have been resolved. These problems came back because upon achieving equity, the Left continued consolidating control and sought dominance. For the equality they sought was never an equality of opportunity or legal status, but they rather sought to impose the communist system of absolute equality of outcomes that both haunts and ultimately always destroys them.

People are not interchangeable and do not universally fit into our system. Some people will make better Americans than others, and I'd submit to you that those who share our common ancestry and faith, all other things being equal, are more likely to blend in. Unfortunately, we've adopted the opposite strategy since 1965, taking anyone from anywhere lucky enough to get picked, trusting we can just dump more ingredients in and it will all work out fine.

The Left knows better. They bring in new people from the Third World to destroy existing identity through strife, to encourage state development in response to problems they create, and to bring in new voters. Because as unpopular as it is to admit, the best predictor of a person's vote—their political expression—is their race.

The Right now knows this also, although they haven't come to terms with it. How the Right chooses to deal with identity, how honestly and quickly it makes this identification, will be key to its survival. Not because they want to shift away from their preferred narrative of individualism and liberty, but because failure to do so will result in a demographic collapse of the previous majority and the victory of the Left for the foreseeable future.

These are difficult and complex questions which will require a degree of sensitivity that I think should be rooted in a basic principle: People should have pride in their own identity, respect for the circumstances of their birth, but be held to account for choices their beliefs lead them to make in their lives. Each of us can and should be proud of our heritage, for all races and ethnicities, because identity builds community. But we need to understand we are not alone in that belief and try to at least understand and acknowledge others will feel the same.

The alternative of pretending we're all the same is failure, because not only do we have less in common each day, but we're also losing the ability to talk rationally about that very gap, which is why we see anarchy replacing liberty.

Chapter 5: Liberty—An Ideal Under Assault

Liberty presumes you can make better choices about your life than those around you can make for you. Such a statement seems incredibly simple and powerful, but we live in a world where fewer people believe it each day.

Let's avoid politics for just a moment to consider something more common and less controversial: A visit to the doctor. To become a doctor is a highly regulated profession, requiring years of study, professional certification, and what they may prescribe is highly regulated by both the government and insurance companies. Only a doctor can assess what remedies may be considered for your health, and pharmacies tightly control what pills are available, ranging from extreme treatments to something as mundane as antibiotics for regular illnesses.

We're told we need experts to make decisions, and without impugning the good work done by the medical profession, this is but one example in our specialized world where we're told we don't understand how to manage something that impacts our lives, and to let another make decisions on our behalf. While people may find the example of medicine more acceptable given the risks involved, the essence of liberty is accepting greater personal responsibility and greater risk in exchange for greater freedom of action.

We see this freedom further constrained each day. Is it any accident judges behave like they own absolute authority when the entire legal profession conducts itself as an impenetrable guild designed quite intentionally to keep outsiders out and to obscure the comprehensible to maintain power? We see the same thing in academia, where research has given way to academic dogma worthy of medieval Catholicism, where there are truths defended and authority taken away from you, the individual.

One hundred years ago, America was not this way. Believe it or not, most people could do most tasks needed to survive on their own, and with that actual independence, liberty flourished as people had no desire to sacrifice their self-determination. But with the industrial economy and the assembly line, we all became cogs in a machine, enjoying greater wealth and material comfort, but at the price of the freedom of action we once cherished. Americans became a bit more like everyone else, and that's one reason why leftist thinking became more compelling.

With few exceptions, we now live in an interdependent world where few of us understand all required to live on our own, and with those who do largely choosing to live a more modest lifestyle. I have the good fortune to know some of these people and have seen how happy they are. The freedom they derive from greater self-sufficiency has great value to them, so it's worth asking whether our conformity to a system based on efficiency, cooperation, and integration is making us happier. It seems to me that the price of peace is a studied indifference where we're told we can all have what we want so long as we accept that everyone else will get the same ... and to not look too closely at the contradictions this inevitably must spawn.

It's a strange concept of liberty in the current year, but the bargain seems like we can have it all, if we only agree to keep our own little universe to ourselves and not project or impose our values outward. It's great to care, but not too much, or you might offend. In the current thinking, that would violate the liberty of others. So, we all pretend to be nice, only acting like we care, and go through our lives feeling disconnected and like there could be more but knowing better than to voice that dissent.

Speaking only for myself, I can imagine a better world easily. I imagine one with clear moral values rooted in our best traditions, mindful of nature, and applying reason. I see people standing up for one another on this basis, building culture from these core beliefs. And yes, I can imagine people like me, who think as I do, coming together to build something larger—maybe another trip to the stars or to cure some horrible malady, perhaps like the Chronic Lyme Disease that ravages my wife. But we are not allowed these bigger dreams because liberty is now defined too narrowly, giving such precious discretion to people who frankly are likely to use it only for licentiousness.

Natural law isn't something you hear about too often these days, but there was once a common belief that rights were God given and government was not to infringe upon them, with the Bill of Rights being the most perfect expression of such ideals. But the Left, vacillating between godlessness and Islam, certainly doesn't accept such thinking as they see the natural relationship between man and the state as one of submission, of being an entity to be corrected and molded by the state rather than as an independent being who is free through divine intent. The changes demanded by the Left would render the very idea of liberty moot, but because we're not supposed to assert morality or culture, this argument gets silenced.

We should talk about it much more often because for liberty to serve as anything other than anarchy used to usher in a strongman, we need to understand how to protect our freedoms. The most basic point, which should be obvious, is that we need a group of people of size and determination to defend these beliefs. Jefferson spoke ably when he reminded us that the defense of our liberties would require perpetual sacrifice. In our age of comfort and convenience, we've forgotten his wise admonition about the tree of liberty being watered with the blood of patriots and tyrants.

Even as citizens, we've come to the lazy assumption that showing up to vote means we have fulfilled our civic duty. This is not even close to enough, because if one has paid attention to most elections in the last fifty years, we have most often been given a choice between two candidates who expressed minute differences with one another and frankly, neither of whom even seemed to represent an American national interest. The Clintons, Bushes, and Obamas—supposedly representing two opposing parties –, were all just as happy to ship jobs abroad and use our men and women as cannon fodder, but because we voted as best we could, we comforted ourselves and said that was enough.

Being a former politician, I'll say what most politicians know but few will publicly voice: people largely get the government they deserve. They get corruption because they prefer a voice that offers compelling promises rather than hard truths, and because they do not hold to account those who defraud the people. They choose not to offend, and so they get ambivalent government, which spends trillions of dollars, but ultimately makes very little positive impact in people's lives. If people accept this as enough, it will continue this way.

For better or worse, although the mass continues churning along indifferently making cries of peace rooted more in fear of the unknown than in some greater principle, things are changing. We see both sides mobilizing, or as this book makes clearer, multiple converging interests gathering, such that we're going to have a conversation about what liberty means in this new epoch.

The Left would define this as freedom "from," wherein no one faces any persecution or judgment, save for impacting another, but at the cost of government running all our lives. The most generous interpretation of the Left's freedom would be a kinder world, but also a hollow one where all we have are pretenses, and our conformity will be enforced to ensure no threats of individual autonomy could interfere with the central planning. Liberty would still be used as a word, but its meaning would be inverted compared to its historic intent.

If the Right were to win, it would be messier, because individualism would be involved, and the divine would not be discarded. We would have freer people who sometimes argued and disagreed, and who even sometimes fought, but there would also be greater potential for exploration, as liberty would be defined in the search for truth, reason, and betterment rather than in tranquility and conformity. The freedom to do things would be reserved to the people, and government, out of respect and fear of the people, would be restrained.

Whichever side wins this battle, given the struggles forthcoming, it's likely authority will be focused and centralized for a while. This is a natural human desire following what will most likely be a very messy and decentralized battle. Whether that struggle remains on the political level with which we are familiar and comfortable, or whether it descends into full blown military conflict—a possibility far more realistic than most Americans are prepared to imagine—what should become clear over these preparatory chapters is that the divisions are real and the bonds that once held us together are gone.

I've read of a useful way to describe this circumstance, called the Fourth Turning. The theory favored by Dugin and others argues that generations go through cycles wherein they must relearn lessons once known by earlier people because everyone who lived certain struggles has already died. Under this theory, it works out that every fourth generation serves as revolutionaries whose descendants then rebuild, maintain, and deconstruct in that order. Having experienced a lifetime of seeing values that were sacred to this country dissolved, I cannot tell you how many people I know personally who are ready to do whatever it takes to get back to this being a good and just country.

I have no doubt those on the other side have just the same passion. We want different outcomes, have different truths, and exist as different cultures with people with different identities. Perhaps the last remnant of the old America that we share in common is the willingness to fight for our beliefs. But our historic vision of liberty is what is truly at stake.

Now, the prelude to this conflict has already begun. Where the Left had taken much of state and society from the Right, the inevitable reactionary/nationalist response has come with Trump and a dedicated push against the politically correct dominant culture which has been massively disrupted by the Internet. Before we get into the many sides of this affair, to make clear what is already happening, we need to understand the players on the board of our society and just who controls what.

It's a mess. And it's only getting worse.

Section II: The Players

Group I: Government

In the second section of this account, we investigate the major players who shape American society and cultural life, teasing out their sympathies, affiliations, and interests to imagine how they will behave under normal situations and as stresses intensify within our domestic culture.

This first group covers the various entities within government, identifying five key agencies that will shape how the state holds together and responds to the civil crisis. The three obvious branches of the Executive, Legislative, and Judicial branch are all covered, and considering the upset Trump victory, these are bastions of the Right whose strength will intensify absent external events for at least the next few years.

In contrast to the three formal branches of government we have the permanent Bureaucracy, the residence of not just the infamous Deep State, but the many civil servants who actions and inaction will undercut the ability of the elected majority of the Right to unmake the leftist agenda which they had advanced unchecked for many decades. Although nominally responsive to the Executive branch, their actions demonstrate they are clearly acting in revolt against the Republican line.

Lastly, the military is considered as an entity of last resort, asking where their loyalties lie in different conflicts, most prominently if the civil service should seek to unseat a sitting President, and how they might respond if civil unrest rises to levels of actual violence.

Chapter 6: Executive—Our Shifting Kingship

Although the Constitution begins with Congress as the first enumerated branch of government, having nominal control over the purse strings of the Republic, today so much power, wealth, and authority has been granted to the Executive and the President specifically that any discussion of who controls the American destiny must begin at 1600 Pennsylvania Avenue.

It's worth noting the Founders specifically sought a weak executive as leader of the nation, imagining the President much more as the magistrate and figurehead of a modest government which very importantly did not have access to a permanent and bloated income tax coffer with which to engage upon any enterprise it so chose.

Throughout the 1900's, with the tacit support of all sides, the Presidency moved in the direction of something much closer to that of an elected monarch. Congress willfully abdicated its responsibilities by passing mandates which automatically would be funded each year as entitlements, ensuring their veto essentially was reduced to a paper protest. Worse still, with the passage of the War Powers Act, the President was given unilateral authority to declare war, provided the Congress was informed, transferring powers of the purse and statecraft all to the Executive Branch.

It is no exaggeration therefore to say Presidents matter, but what we can observe happening in these early years of this new millennium is that the Presidency has come to be used as a cudgel by the party in power against their opponents. Whatever one's opinion, it is undeniable we live in a sharply divided nation where at any given point in time probably around forty percent of people feel disenfranchised.

We began the aughts with the election of George W. Bush in a highly contested and disputed election where Al Gore was defeated by a vote within a very small margin of error in Florida. It's highly probable cheating was involved, as frankly both parties engage in different methodologies well known in political circles, but not expressed publicly, to work the numbers. Democrats stuff ballots and allow illegals to vote, where Republicans tend to prefer to gerrymander districts and limit turnout. Behind such hijinks, the country was torn apart and only with the intervention of the Supreme Court, in what was widely seen as a partisan decision, rooted as much in expediency as any legal precedents, ruled in favor of George W. Bush.

The Democrats went insane, as they have during the rule of every President since Eisenhower. It's worth noting their recurring strategy in conjunction with their media allies is to paint every Republican who reaches the highest level as either a complete idiot or an evil fascist, and interestingly sometimes even both despite how those would seem to contradict. The fun thing about being on the Left is you don't have to have reason behind an emotional rage-driven argument, which we saw as virulently with the younger Bush as we saw with Reagan before him and as we see with Trump today. But conversely, complicit with their media allies, every Democrat is painted as being polished, smart, and deliberate, a sign of the progress of the people.

To say the media is unhelpful in pulling America together is an understatement, and this book will give them the fair judgment and condemnation they deserve. However, what matters here is to illustrate how Bush, more a neoconservative than a Republican, was able to shred the Constitution with the glowing consent of the people and the legislature to pass the Patriot Act and create the suitably misnamed Department of Homeland Security, which seems most effective at confiscating snacks and water bottles from would-be travelers while simultaneously ignoring private airports which are much more likely to serve as the point for another attack.

As attacks continued, both the result of American foreign policy adventurism and the inefficiencies of our law enforcement, wars began, and tragedies recurred. Although this is terrible for both the liberty and psyche of the American people, it is great for the state, as the demands for justice and/or retribution ensure the Presidents can play wherever they choose. This is how Bush was able to glibly start the $7 trillion-dollar misadventure, and we still find ourselves stuck in Afghanistan, Iraq, and more quietly throughout the Middle East, and why Obama continued the fight through to today.

With the election of Obama, we saw a radical shift from a President who paid lip service to traditional values, even as Bush worked to allow many people into this country as cheap labor for his Chamber of Commerce friends who had no such principles, to one determined to fundamentally transform this country. And to his credit or detriment, Obama achieved a great deal in this direction.

He, more than any other President before him, illustrated the model of how when one takes power, they put their political opponents on the defensive. When Congress agreed with him, he passed legislation like the Affordable Care Act which basically fined people for refusing to buy a service. When Congress refused to help, he simply passed Executive Orders, the newest fashion of government by fiat. Given a complacent judiciary and an incompetent Congress, Obama continued to push his agenda to remake American culture.

Refugees were brought into the country in increasing numbers, border security was lax, and we were preached the import of diversity and inclusiveness. When criminals shot police, the response of the Justice Department was to create community policing guidelines whose purpose was to constrain authority and empower the disaffected. In all that he did, Obama never forgot he came from and represented the coalition of the ascendant: A slice of white progressive liberals leading along all the minorities. Obama pushed the plantation mentality—and promised to redistribute as much wealth as he could while never failing to lecture at or apologize for the American majority which built this country.

The Left saw their dream of a diverse, tolerant, progressive America coming into being. The Right saw this as communism at the gates, seeing as traditional values were being criminalized as with bakers being sent to jail for refusing to bake cakes for queers, and how children were being sexualized into transgender madness. The divide deepened, and the Presidency was clearly becoming a prime-mover, not just for war and economics, but as the center of the culture wars through enacting policy via executive orders with a mind to the judges who appointed themselves above all the other branches.

With such angst and with a lack of congeniality on both sides, the Right finally jumped into the game to punish their opponents with the utterly unapologetic figure of Donald Trump. Violating all the norms of being genteel and submissive to which Republicans had paid lip service for years, Trump is avowedly pro-American, and populist in his affections, even as he embraces gaudiness in so many ways. He took a verbal machete to the power centers of the Left: The media, academia, and their politically correct doctrines which he rightly identified as being designed to silence any debate or discussion. The coastal elites saw this man as a buffoon, but the people living in flyover country—as it had been derisively called for years—finally saw a singular opportunity to take back the America they once knew and did so in astounding numbers.

When Trump was elected, the elites rightly perceived this was the center of the country and all those who didn't live in the progressive and wealthier enclaves taking a shot at their leadership. Despite their very real differences, Bush and Obama, as most Presidents before them, shared a belief in the neoliberal orthodoxy of free market economics, international institutions and that America should be constrained within a set of global arrangements for the benefit of world stability. Who benefits is a question which was not asked nearly often enough. Anyone who has been in the Rust Belt can share the details of how all our manufacturing abandoned the heartland for cheap labor sites abroad to justify profit margins. This certainly caused much pain to many Americans, predominantly white people in the Midwest—the Trump voters.

So now the Right has control of the Executive branch, and what a difference it is making! The economy booming as taxes have been reduced and unwarranted government interference in life sliding away. Across all classes and ethnicities, statistics suggest opportunity is growing, and yet what is interesting is that the core of the Left is only becoming more violent and angry, with their rage clearly going beyond quality of life issues. Instead, they are mad because they are out of power, and because the project which Obama kicked into high gear through Executive Orders is being erased.

It's important to understand that in cultural Marxism, which is the dominant mindset on the Left, politics becomes a zero-sum game. They play to the resentments of out-groups, using envy and ambition in equal measure, embracing politics of identity for every issue, and employing the resultant fear to motivate people. For a very long time, the Left has deliberately collected every group who stood against the mainstream of society from gender to race to religion, an odd hodgepodge of people united primarily by their opposition to the status quo. And now their special status is being threatened.

So, they want to fight. Trump, facing an administration at every level replete with people sympathetic to the Leftist cause, is stuck fighting his own bureaucracy which seeks to thwart his every action. The entrenched career bureaucrats imagine themselves literally as some heroic resistance, as if from some fantasy novel or Hollywood movie. If nothing else, it's a clear sign of how far our cultural norms have degraded that we see such fights, but it also shows why the culture war is bigger than even the most powerful man on Earth.

Trump is an important beachhead for the forces of tradition and continuity. He is an interesting contradiction in being almost a mercenary to the cause given his own peccadillos, but is nevertheless moving the Court to the right, removing America from foreign entanglements, and trying to destroy the entitlement mindset. At the time of this writing, it's uncertain how successful or lasting such efforts will be, but what they show is the possibilities implicit in controlling the Executive.

I have zero doubt that if Hillary Clinton were President, any of us who exist to the right of Trump would currently be targeted as thought criminals, much as was done to Dinesh D'Souza. Under a Hillary Clinton administration, what we have seen happen in kangaroo courts after the Unite the Right rally in Charlottesville, and in a hundred less controversial places, would be multiplied dramatically. Whereas Obama had the IRS going after the

Tea Party, at least having somewhat neutral leadership means there is a respite during which the Right can organize.

Looking ahead, however, the Left is utterly determined to impeach Trump without any regard for evidence or facts. That, coupled with the desire to cover up their own misdeeds with the illicit uranium sale to Russia, is why that false narrative continues to be propagandized by the media, and why you see voices like Maxine Waters being given disproportionate air time. The Left must be built to a froth because their centralized command and control theories require them to take charge and hold command of the Executive to impose laws and policies which people would never willingly choose.

With control of the Presidency, nominal control of law enforcement follows., We will consider the Federal bureaucracy as its own separate branch, a situation which while not legally factual most accurately describes the current behaviors of many of the three letter agencies and their top lieutenants. Having the authority to act with the power of government remains important. Efforts to control the executive will thus only increase as we see strife widen as both sides want control of the many resources available to the President, the least of which is not the bully pulpit.

Consider this: Should the conflict ever rise to the point where people are willing to fight, it will come upon the President as Commander and Chief to rally the military against those seeking to leave or depart. One can imagine California seeking to depart over abortion restrictions or

Texas leaving over infringements of the Second Amendment. Each of these would be in response to very different leaders, and yet, seeing the core values diverge between our states with no recourse to act differently, it becomes easier to envision how if one side rallies a workable majority, they will come down on the other and could force the issue. Certainly, that played a major role in why Lincoln chose to escalate the conflict to the actions at Fort Sumter, for historical comparison.

Both sides understand the stakes in a way the moderate voter has not yet begun to comprehend, and that's why you will see no more legitimate presidents, highly contested elections going forward, and zero compromise. The Right feels they gave as much deference as they could to Obama and the Left showed no such forbearance. Which isn't to say they liked him, because they loathed him and all he stood for, but they tried to honor the traditions, which he basically ignored in using fiat dictates to govern. So now, both sides need control of the Executive, and neither wants the other to have it.

The Right controls this branch for the time, but it's worth remembering the Left has always been better, which is to say more vicious and complete in exercising authority, and their overwhelming supremacy in culture and the permanent bureaucracy go a very long way in blunting the force of what can be achieved at present. How the elected government regains control over its own bureaucracy will be one of the key battles in the prelude to this wider conflict.

Chapter 7: Legislature—Our Absent Congress

Congress was not supposed to be a rubber stamp. It was designed to be the strongest branch of the Federal Government, to exercise control over the finances of the nation, and to represent the interests of the various states and the peoples therein.

Why it no longer does this is a complicated story that has at least two major factors, and potentially many more. But we must understand these factors as part of the complex interplay between the public and private actors who operate America. This book will necessarily seem circuitous at times in describing these relationships, but that's because the checks and balances of who manages whom have become an almost incomprehensible mess. This is the nature of a well-funded and often out of control bureaucracy that funds a number of wealthy private sector offshoots.

As implied by the network connections with Congress, one easy answer to why our legislative branch doesn't work is because they're all bought. With few exceptions, there are not many members of Congress who can afford to promote a line that's independent of the orthodoxies of their parties. And these party orthodoxies in turn reflect compromises required by the well-funded interests who support each party, or, in many cases, both parties.

Let me share some details outsiders might not know, but which are familiar to people who have been involved in the political election industry, and which exist for both the

House and the Senate but are far more pronounced in the lower chamber. My numbers might be a little out of date as I've been out of the game for a few years, but I'm certain they have not gone down: To win a House seat, on average, will cost upwards of one million dollars spent in advertising. To win a Senate seat, expect that number to rise above five million dollars, running even higher in densely populated states. Your average person does not have this sort of money, and absent some sort of celebrity status brought independently to the consideration, doesn't have the name recognition to break through to win a competitive seat.

While there certainly are wave elections like the Tea Party candidates of 2010 for the Right where marginal candidates are carried into office on a passing wave of public anger, even these are dampened by the staggered nature of Senate elections in which only one-third of seats are contested at each election, and the way maps have been drawn for many years to heavily favor incumbents on both sides. People unfamiliar with the process are often unaware that state legislatures draw the lines by which Federal Congressmen are elected, and the bizarrely shaped districts which result in so many states are the result of agreements between incumbents of both parties to protect their respective seats by stacking the area with partisans most likely to re-elect them.

Of course, the dominant party will set up the districts in such a way as to maximize their potential winnings, with the Republicans generally being better at this than Democrats. But putting all the opposition in one area serves both the interests of the dominant party and the incumbent politician of the minority party who now represents a district with 80% of the voters agreeing with their viewpoint. Electoral districts drawn in such a way also serve to limit the impact elections can have, which is why despite there being 435 seats in Congress, informed observers realize only about a hundred seats are ever likely to turn over in any given election cycle.

Couple that with the reality that Senate seats overwhelmingly tend to stay true to a state's partisan identification, which increasingly is becoming more solidly red or blue, and the number of Senate seats even potentially at stake falls to about a third. Assuming equal distribution across the six-year cycle, that means at most ten Senate seats would be in danger of flipping in a wave year election.

All of this "inside pool" is designed to illustrate one thing: Being a Congressman has lucrative possibilities with little risk, so those who get into office find many ways to stay there. They game the system to get into power, and provided they have resources, they distribute wealth to those in district and those who were friendly out of district to remain. Frankly, these patronage networks are safer and more reliable to the office holder than populist messaging which can shift quickly and radically, and this explains why we see so little functional action from the Congress.

To take this one step further, their own rules in legislating are also used to delay and retard the progress of many other actions, as members make the rational personal decisions to move cautiously. As they well know, voters are more likely to come after you for the thing you do they don't like than to vigorously support you for good things you've done. It's like a marriage, where twenty years of devotion can be ruined by one fling with the other side if caught.

And that brings us to the other point which is how political parties have become the dominant means of identification. Congress was supposed to represent the interests of the states, which is why Senators were once chosen by the constituent state legislatures, but now all are popularly elected. So instead of the States having a direct advocate, now all the states functionally serve only as part of a conveyor belt system for would-be officials to work up their party ladder.

It's a dangerous thing to have division be the heart of the Republic, and George Washington warned very clearly about these dangers in his Farewell Address. He understood that if two versions of truth diverged enough, war would result. Just as it did over the issues between the North and South in 1860, we are reaching a similar point between the Republicans and Democrats today, surrogates for broader coalitions to preserve our ancestry and traditions versus transforming America.

These are the structural impediments which reward intransigence from Congress. But the system of primary elections is yet another. Unlike general elections, primary elections have lower turn-out so that those activists who are most devout in their partisanship and most fervent in their beliefs are most likely to vote in them. The hyper-partisans have learned to game the primary process, electorate, so the only reasonable expectation is that Congress will reflect primary voters, becoming more radicalized, more partisan and less able to work together on points of agreement.

What does this mean? The Republicans will continue to control Congress most years in the near term due to their wider geographic distribution. This will no doubt irritate the more populous Left. Expect for them to apply the strategy they used in Colorado, are currently using in Arizona, and will soon attempt in Texas. Specifically, they will bring new people who are committed Left-wing voters into those states where they will convert their numbers into a functional majority in key districts. When that happens, given who votes for which party, the Republicans and Right will likely never regain control of Congress. It's also worth noting that on those occasions when the Left has taken control, they have shown little restraint in expanding the scope and budget of government, in accordance with their desire to use the state to control people.

It will come up in more detail later, but I cannot stress strongly enough how important it is to look at how demography shapes governments in a country, and California is the perfect example of how repeated amnesties and immigration caused a state that once had Nixon and Reagan as governors has become a socialist playground. The institutional GOP is loath to talk about these things as they fear being branded racist, but the numbers don't lie in reporting White people vote very differently than minorities, and the last Presidential election proves the point and indicates the emergent pattern.

Until about 2030, since Trump is setting up rules for the census which will exclude illegal immigrants from consideration in apportionment of representation, it is likely the Republican advantage will persist, but by 2030 birth rates, immigration, and changing affiliations will probably mark the end of the Right as competitive, much less dominant unless there are major cultural shifts before that time. For such reasons, this book envisions the cultural clash must come by the 2020's if this situation is to change. But the Left's dominance in culture and education is so complete, it is difficult to imagine how the Right can preserve itself as anything other than a majority quietly acquiescing to become a dwindling and despised minority unless conflict intervenes to change these bastions of leftist power.

For all these predictions about the future and how the Left would enshrine their cultural beliefs if they could hold Congress in concert with the Presidency, we should assume the House and Senate will remain under control of the Right and consider how the two houses of Congress might act to help the cause. The most likely answer, honestly, is they probably won't do much because of the corruption and entrenched interests who own the individual members, or who at least can make their lives very difficult if they oppose the beliefs of their benefactors.

An important tension which will have wide ranging implications is if the free market bloc which dominates the congressional GOP finds value in the nationalist proposition the Trump faction is pushing that greater profits are to be had under a tariff friendly regime in America, as opposed to maximizing profits through cheap labor havens abroad. For the common man, it is perhaps a dismal reality to share, but if the rich people are getting poorer, the nationalist revolution will not last past this Presidency in anything like the form we see emerging today.

What's interesting is the new Republican orthodoxy will necessarily dump the old elements of fiscal conservatism as those thinkers on the Right who see the larger picture try to figure ways to convert their control of formal government into some advantage to change the picture going forward. From about 1980 onward, the theory was to try to convert minorities to Republicans based upon an ideology of individualism and opportunity, but as Obama illustrated most aptly, such approaches failed. Conversely, Trump succeeded by maximizing White turnout. While such a strategy was uniquely effective in 2016 where the Democrats misjudged their coalition's enthusiasm to support another White candidate, this technique will soon have issues. Although few will say it publicly, people realize these lines are coming into being, so we can expect new language to emerge, probably in a cultural context, to avoid saying Whites are trying to retain control.

The Republican Party will live or die as the White voter does. It doesn't like that, and it will kick and scream this isn't true. But it's not about who they bring in so much as who votes for their policies, and if Trump's model shows legs, the GOP will have no choice but to lead the Right to defend the identity interests of the majority. Either that, or they will fail, and be replaced by someone who does. Just as Trump was able to essentially usurp the GOP based on nationalism, the only future path to electoral victory on the Right will follow a similar trail.

Should the Congress become nationalist, and Republicans learn to effectively use power to maintain a workable majority, it's possible the one place they could make a real difference is immigration reform. The two ways to reshape the future are to change who is coming into the country and to change who is having children. If America were to adopt policies whereby it rescinded the 1965 Immigration Act that set up the visa lottery and brought in so many Third World people, refused any amnesty, and perhaps even selectively removed people who are not citizens whose views run counter to the Right, or alternatively, bring people in from Europe or other places who might be sympathetic, the math could change. The Left would see this as clear as day, however, and would go into insurrection with all their allies at the mere suggestion of such policies.

The second path is subtler, but family planning makes a big difference. I could imagine a shift from paying people to have children out of wedlock, a policy we subsidize, to a Right leaning America instead paying families to have children and not paying out of wedlock mothers for children, but instead for birth control or even go so far as voluntary sterilization. Such ideas sound crazy in the current context, but the Europeans are experimenting with them now, and frankly they fit the nominal leftist critique that we are beyond our environmental carrying capacity.

The Congress certainly won't go that far any time soon but should Trump win in 2020 and get his people in power, it's very possible this is the path those seeking peace will push to try to change the equation about who will hold control in the future. The problem is the Left knows this as they've deliberately played and won the immigration game to remake America for sixty years, and they will use every ounce of influence to play sympathy for these invaders. If there should be any mistake from the Trump regime or any future nationalist Right figure, there will be hell to pay.

The Left would rather fight than see America preserved for Americans, as demonstrated by how Nancy Pelosi defends the humanity of bloodthirsty gangs for MS-13, and how leftists will portray billions for a border wall to be a budget buster, but that spending hundreds of billions on social services for people here illegally is an act of humanity. Whether they believe their own BS is an open question, but the cynical thing is both sides really do use these people migrating as a political football.

To be clear, these people don't belong here. It's also equally true in many cases that our misdeeds abroad, either via government or corporately, played a large role in moving these people around the map. Whoever is in control, we need to be much wiser about how we act in attacking regimes. For instance, had Gadhafi retained power in Libya, Europe wouldn't be nearly as flooded with invaders today. It is the strangest coincidence how the Left's

73

humanitarian interventions so often push humanity north into our countries at the same time they transfer national resources south. Look for the Left to become even more globalist as the Right, however reluctantly, finally takes on nationalist stripes in defense of the existing American people.

Chapter 8: Judiciary—Activism Amidst Legalism

The Supreme Court is another institution that has lost its way. As envisioned, the Court was supposed to stay above the political fray and the political circus to serve as a neutral third party. In fairness to the Justices, their failure was inevitable as government waded into areas of personal life for which the Constitution was not designed to comment, and so like everyone else in America, their views became colored by the respective ideologies different Justices embrace.

The Right calls its philosophy originalism, which is the practice of reading the Constitution as exactly written and making judgments in a light that reflects the understanding of the Founders or those writing a law at the time of its enactment. Sincere to the intent of the law, this philosophy ends up essentially being conservative in nature, and reflects the current majority on the Court including Justices Thomas, Alito, Gorsuch, and to a slightly lesser extent, Roberts.

The Left calls its philosophy the living Constitution, which is how they justify judicial activism by subjectively transforming laws from their written intent to fit modern circumstances in a fashion often driven more by their own desires, coyly phrased as public desire. It is also how they seek to remake law to realize justice as some sort of abstract value they define outside the laws written by the Congress. Justices Kagan, Ginsburg, Sotomayor, and Breyer fit this mold.

As is abundantly clear except for recently retired Justice David Souter, who has long been seen by the Right as a dismal failure of selection by Bush, the legal philosophies of the Justices reflect the political ideologies of those who appointed them, and again represent two very different views of what law should be. Should it be the job of the judiciary to adhere to the laws as the originalists require, or does the Court have the right and responsibility to legislate from the Bench, interpreting law and describing proper usage by some larger social ethic?

Here we see as clearly as anywhere the difference in how the Left and Right fundamentally view government. The Left has little issue with judicial activism, actively promoting the concept to constrain the ignorance of the other branches, so long as it is executed in a way that advances their agenda and ideology. Whatever lip service the Left pays to law, remember their preferred method of dealing with laws they don't like—like those that require deportation of people here illegally—is to ignore those laws blithely, publicly, and proudly, as with sanctuary cities.

Perhaps because the Right has a natural respect for authority and tradition, it has always felt more constrained by the words and intent of laws, and so looks at the laws as passed as being valid specifically because of the process and details included. You will rarely see people on the Right espousing their valor in flouting existing law, but instead see them quietly encouraging people to follow rules and structures. It's a telling difference that demonstrates that how things are done matters much more to the Right than it does to the Left, who cares solely about the results.

Seeing this, those on the Right realized that losing the Court would lead to even more rapid cultural degradation. Where the Court had consistently worked against the popular will to force more integration of unassimilable people, more acceptance of degenerate behavior, and limiting people's power to show discretion based upon conscience and judgment in their life, this had begun to shift from the Rehnquist Court onward as a precarious 5-4 majority leaning rightward has held.

With the recent retirement of Justice Kennedy, all these tensions are being released, as his was the key vote that upheld legalized abortion, who enacted gay marriage, and who served as an unpredictable swing vote. Many conservatives who disliked Trump voted for him for this single reason: To ensure someone who shares their values and beliefs would be selected to ensure the Court rolls back these activist stances, and instead allows the people through their legislatures to determine what will and won't be law. In Kavanaugh, Trump has rewarded their support with a suitable pick, who has set the culture warriors of the Left into an absolute frenzy.

The Court, properly functioning, should not inspire such zeal from either side. But the misuse of the Justices, a habit the Left has practiced faithfully since at least FDR, when he infamously tried to expand and stack the Court to enact socialism without any constraint, has created a situation wherein the Left uses the judiciary as a veto on popular sovereignty, and the Right sees the Court as a last line of defense against the imposition of the new and foreign culture being pushed ever more strongly.

As bad as things are, I can only imagine how crazy the Left would go if someone like Ginsburg passed, with the promise of a 6-3 Right majority being enough to ensure a generation of control over what can be pushed over the will of the American people. They won't accept that either, not when they've been in the habit of seeing activist judges stymie the Right for so long.

Just using the current moment as I write in July of 2018 as an example, we see not just Supreme Court judges, but judges across the register from the Federal Courts to State Courts and lower levels issuing injunctions left and right to constrain the Federal Government from all sorts of actions. Most recently we have seen judges in Hawaii using the novel judicial doctrine that previous comments made by the President, which indicate a bias, somehow invalidate his legal authority. This attempt to stop Trump from exercising his clearly delineated Constitutional authority was recently overturned by the Supreme Court itself in yet another 5-4 decision. In other words, the Judge decided that since he didn't like what Trump did, he would invent a reason to shut down the policy and tie things up if possible.

As much as the Right has held a finger hold on the Supreme Court, strengthened now by the improbable election of Donald Trump, the Left has packed the lower courts for years, and the rulings they've made have done much to advance the cultural agenda they support by consistently attacking traditional institutions like the Church and freedom of conscience in favor of giving legal preference to the out-groups preferred by the Left. It's hard to see equality existing under the law when the protections that extend to certain protected classes are denied to the majority, an issue which has not been lost on the Right, and which has been upheld by a contentious interpretation of the Fourteenth Amendment, among other issues.

The Left likes playing lawfare, and with the skill of people who well understand bureaucracy, uses the courts to tie up and bankrupt opposing causes in civil litigation and selective enforcement. It helps that lawyers, as a class, lean overwhelmingly to the Left, which makes sense because it creates many more clients for them to have everyone be a potential victim, and because the independent streak and deregulatory tendencies of the Right are a threat to their business.

I think it no accident the laws have become so voluminous and cannot help but also believe the citizenry is misrepresented when laws become so complex only experts can interpret them. The lawyers have become the guild masters and the judges arbiters in a process increasingly removed from justice and equal consideration, especially considering that in non-criminal trials, the prohibitive cost of even participating in a legal case serves as deterrent and threat to those who would otherwise try their case.

This is changing to some extent as Trump and the Republican Congress have been working in concert, quickly by DC standards, to put new judges on the judiciary to fill many vacancies. It will be interesting to see if an influx of originalists changes how the courts behave, but the problem is broader than who is in power, but rather the inflated powers we've assigned to the judiciary. Although it believes itself above the people, the struggle to assert popular sovereignty through both bill and referendum above what the judiciary believes is appropriate will likely only increase tensions between branches and their partisan controllers.

In the broader thrust of the civil conflict emerging, the high likelihood the Supreme Court will be working against the Left for a generation now in constraining their activist impulses, and the likelihood the lower levels of the judiciary will be decreasingly sympathetic will probably cause their radicalization to happen much more quickly. From their perspective, their cultural monopoly may be put at risk through government action against their supremacy, and so waiting to act is a major liability to be avoided. What form their direct action might take remains to be decided, but as a first step, look for them to take control of certain friendly states and push hard in a direction counter to the Federal direction.

California is the best example of several that demonstrates a state which may ignore Federal mandates and see how far they can push against the Supreme Court. It remains to be seen if the Right, whose time out of power in DC has brought them to appreciate decentralization, will allow this, and perhaps offer returning power to the states as a possible compromise, or if they will instead push for Federal authority to be recognized. Given Trump's tendencies and the nationalist impulse, the latter seems somewhat more probable.

In the meantime, cases which were considered to be "settled law" are going to come before the new Justice who will be appointed just before the midterm election. Should the Court choose to follow its originalist interpretation of the Constitution instead of taking the public policy perspective of endorsing precedent and case law, a full-fledged riot may ensue from the forces on the Left, especially from feminists about abortion and gays about marriage. While the Court will likely not prohibit either activity, their returning these powers back to the states will be a devastating setback and will galvanize at least some places to fight vigorously in a culture war where they show no quarter in demonizing the people on the Right who simply want the right to refuse.

Battles like this are eminently predictable on the near horizon and given how engaged and passionate the combatants will be, I therefore argue our current economic boom is only going to provide more funding for this far nastier and unresolved conflict brewing now at the surface, and threatening to engulf us all, as it has our government.

According to the textbook, there are only three branches of government, but as anyone who has analyzed this or is paying attention to the news today realizes, there are at least two more actors who have enough freedom of action, should they choose to exercise it, that we must consider them: The bureaucracy and the military.

Chapter 9: Bureaucracy—Artificial Selection

It's hard to get excited about the bureaucracy. As an aside, even this chapter feels like a chore to write, but like the details on a legal contract, it's incredibly important not to look at just the high-level picture of laws and policy that are passed, but to get down to the level where policy is enacted and enforced, which is the bureaucracy.

Long ago when I was a younger man, I worked for a court as a clerk and had several colleagues who demonstrated the power of the bureaucrat. Although every case would be heard in legal order, it was not uncommon for people to visit the Court to try to get their case handled at an earlier date or in a more favorable venue. Now, the person who made these decisions had no formal authority other than to schedule cases, but for those who were nice, they found themselves getting what they wanted more often than not. For those who came in throwing a fit about being a taxpayer and citizen, they often ended up going last, their rage building to a lovely cherry hue. There was never any investigation or major coverage of how business was conducted, but as you can see from this little anecdote, the bureaucracy is incredibly powerful in what it chooses to do or not do.

Expanding this example to a larger level, the best example of selective enforcement might be the interminable Mueller investigation into Trump and Russia. Bureaucrats instinctively know how to prolong and extend any action they so choose by adding pieces and delaying results until the moment where they can hurt the most. So, by this logic, a lifelong bureaucrat and hatchet man like Mueller, whose previous resume includes the highlight of leading the FBI through the failures of 9/11 and the sanitized report produced by the 9/11 Commission, is almost certainly purposely just serving as an anchor designed to restrain Trump's range of actions. Never mind that Mueller has a lifetime legacy of failure—he has learned to take bullets and keep walking imperviously, key attributes for the man behind the scenes who only occasionally and reluctantly comes forward.

One could wonder why an investigation of equal intensity and fervor has never been launched as deeply into any of the many potentially fraudulent acts assigned to Hillary Clinton, a deeper look into Benghazi, or asking why Loretta Lynch was meeting Bill in that infamous nearly hour-long meeting that just happened to accidentally occur in Phoenix to talk about "grandchildren". The problem is the bureaucratic state protects their own, probably because corruption and graft are the only way this ill-considered system can function, and because at heart, those at the center of the action have a sort of vague contempt for the idea they should be accountable to the people writ large.

Because they see themselves as an entitled class in many ways and their own sort of guild, a tendency true from a bean counter at the IRS to the most dangerous Federal Agent at your choice of alphabet soup agencies, the people who implement government policy overwhelmingly lean Left. Like any rational group of people, they support those who will use and expand their functions, and they know the leftists have never met a government program they didn't like and will always believe they know best, which means ultimate job security and opportunity. For those with real power, they use their positions within the bureaucracy to curry favor and create networks within the private sector to ensure additional perks including kickbacks and future job opportunities.

These people are always worried, because they understand the nature of the game and in many ways, they have the most to lose. If they were aware, the public would never accept such power and graft being taken by people who were supposed to be faceless entities in the background. Thus, it is no accident that the strongest resistance against Trump, and specifically against the nationalist version of the Right, comes from the bureaucracy, and more specifically the Deep State.

It's a term we use often but define obliquely. The Deep State is really a network of connections that exist between a series of government agencies, international institutions, certain think tanks and prestigious universities, and well-funded corporations. In their own conception, they are the people who make America run, what Eisenhower aptly termed the military-industrial complex who make money from the interminable wars and who bring jobs and trade back home. They are the architects and agents of the globalist plan, and they have allies in most countries, especially in the West, who share their same goals and aspirations.

Worth noting in this definition is how the influence of the Deep State expands far beyond the government itself, even though its power is rooted in the bureaucracy. It usually manifests its power in the form of reports written to Congress that inform the laws on obscure subjects that get zero public interest but are worth hundreds of millions or even billions financially for key players. When required, the Deep State emerges as the voice to identify the threat of the day, after which our impressive war machine is whipped into action and we find ourselves in yet another war, in some suitably obscure country that usually happens to have some vital geography or natural resource. All wars are now humanitarian, but it's funny how we only deliver relief to those with something to offer in return.

It's apocryphal, but if you want to read something to teach the Deep State mindset, find an old book called "The Report from Iron Mountain". Although it is derided as a hoax, a claim only some believe, this short profile is a report which purportedly was commissioned to have academics and businessmen figure out the best way government could control the people and provide for stability. The story is breathtaking in its calculation and cynicism, but if you can't conceive of the Deep State properly, try to imagine people who look at the general population like a child might look at an ant farm. It's fun to watch the ants dig, but at any moment, it all might be wiped away to be rebuilt.

To be fair, I don't subscribe to their basic worldview, and I would be remiss to deny there are bureaucrats who do dark things because they think it necessary to protect

America and the world. Some of these people are correct. Since we have no transparency, it's hard to say who is telling the truth and who is lying. And although we all want to know what is happening, it's even harder for me to admit publicly we can't.

Having served in government in multiple roles, there are projects which don't make sense until they're complete, and to launch them at the wrong time would be fatal. There are also things people don't understand about the mechanical needs of how government works that they would not want to understand, and the proliferation of too many laws, competing jurisdictions, and contradictory suggestions forces anyone in government to sometimes skirt the rules. In a positive sense, think of it as when someone crosses a double line to pass a tractor driving 15 mph in a 55 mph zone.

The problem is we are forced to trust people whom we probably cannot, and since the Left has built the bureaucracy, they've stacked it with people who share their basic worldview. This has become so evident since Trump came to power, where they imagine themselves at their desks as parts of some grand resistance where they're subverting the very republic that sustains their livelihood. But they don't see it that way, and thanks to their friends in the media, they'll likely never face that moment of intellectual reckoning.

So, what we will see is policies half-enacted or not enacted at all, and people ignoring new directives with which they disagree, or politely practiced confusion. People who have sometimes upwards of twenty years' experience can do much to slow down the cogs of government, and the other thing they will do is look the other way whenever they can to their benefit.

All this said, there is a darker side to the Deep State we must discuss: these people know too much and can do too much. The NSA presumably can learn every detail about anyone. The CIA has a track record of assassinating people who become too inconvenient. We know FBI agents actively discussed fixing elections in America. All these are a matter of public record, and yet we don't think about the consequences. Do you believe agencies which work to preserve a certain position for America in what is truly an ever-evolving new world order would let the momentary voting preferences of the American public disrupt their efforts?

A magic bullet fired into Jack Kennedy was the first warning this would not be permitted, and I've always found it fascinating how happy LBJ was to give the agencies and the defense establishment free rein. Other examples abound, but it's worth realizing these agencies have the ability at any time to radically transform our government. When the former directors of Federal agencies actively agitate against a sitting President like Donald Trump on social media, threatening that he will be made to pay for questioning their actions, you begin to realize how foolish we were to hand our hen house over to the worst wolves for protection.

Liberty and freedom cannot exist when people whose existence is seldom publicly known have such power, and that's why we see a state at odds with itself such that nationalism—love of one's own people—is rebuked, because it serves as a threat to a status quo upon which many powerful and well-connected people have built their lives. I don't even want to speculate what sacrifices were made to gain such dominance, but these people are out there. They want their old America back: Where the parties echoed one another, and they ran the show.

How far they will go to achieve this is anyone's question, but it is clear the bureaucracy is its own independent actor. The textbooks might say they are run by the executive, but their size, scope, and capacity for independent action ensure they are in many ways the most powerful branch of government, un-elected, and beyond public exposition. The catch is they are also the most constrained, as any systemic change could cost them everything, and knowing this, they will fight doggedly to protect the status quo. We see this contradiction emerging today and with such, this conflict is only accelerating.

If the bureaucracy keeps working to undermine the efforts of the existing administration, the roiling culture war will only be further stoked as the procession of leaks and innuendo substantiate the claim the current government is illegitimate. And no one knows better than lifelong bureaucrats just how deeply and annoying a paper cut can really damage someone. It won't kill anyone, but each day is another lost as one's hands are hampered and one's concentration is impaired.

The Left knows the bureaucrats are the last friends they have in government. So, we can expect media to shower them with encouragement and plaudits while they are described as "brave resisters." Turning the government against itself is very short-sighted, but for people who see the bureaucracy as a global network, they can sincerely believe that America's absence would be good for their global project. It's a terrible thing to envision, but if the cost of having the machine grow just a little bit bigger is to take down a President and his pesky supporters who think government should listen to them, there will be entirely too many people who will happily support trying to disabuse us of this antiquated notion.

Given this mindset, one of the first fronts in the civil conflict will be whether the Right can regain control of the bureaucracy to realize its own mandate to deconstruct the state or drain the proverbial swamp. Although one would think criminal actions would be one way to reduce the level of corruption, the problem I suspect is that so many bad actors are interlinked that to expose certain shady actions would functionally cripple whole elements of the government. Can America survive taking down entire agencies, in terms of the shock it would cause, the vulnerabilities that would be opened, or most ominously, in terms of the retribution that would rise from desperation? We can't really know and trying to work through this morass is likely occupying much time for Trump's Administration with very delicate and uncertain ends.

A frank assessment is that it may not be possible to unmake this house of cards without destroying the state in the process. Therefore, informed observers rate a governmental collapse as becoming a rising possibility, especially if pressure is applied at certain crucial points. As much as the thesis of this analysis is how we will be set at war against ourselves, it's important to keep in mind there's always potential for contradictions within the system or external actors to cause the same dismal cascade we're imagining.

Chapter 10: Military—Could Might Make Right?

When countries fall into decay, it is common historically to see someone rise from the ranks of the military promising to restore pride, honor, and stability to the chaos of a late decadent period. Given that the military consistently enjoys higher respect than any other branch of government across many ideological lines, it's possible to imagine if things continue further along these darkening roads, the appeal might exist for someone to play the role of a modern-day MacArthur in America and make his try across the Rubicon.

Although America has a long record of the military playing subservience to the elected government, with the tradition to defend the Constitution well entrenched within the rank and file of the different service branches, it's worth considering what sorts of activities could cause the military to consider action to be within their purview.

One thing that quickly jumps to mind is when un-elected actors, such as the Deep State which we covered in the preceding chapter, start taking illegal actions to shape elections and perhaps go so far as to unlawfully seek to remove a sitting administration. In such an event, the President might well seek military assistance to survive this functional coup. Having traditionally paid homage to the requests of the Commander-in-Chief, a clandestine war between military intelligence and operatives against those assets run by the CIA is not so difficult to imagine. There have long been stories where the military in the field ended up fighting undercover Agency assets, especially abroad, so this would be an extension of an existing turf war.

Where the generals and admirals stand is at the heart of the question, and though they would like to feign being apolitical, it is a well-known truth those who rise to the higher ranks within each branch only do so with tacit approval from DC. Anyone higher than a mid-ranking officer must have their promotion approved by Congress, and when stars are involved, to think there is no understanding about duties and responsibilities seems a bit short-sighted.

Given that most of the current senior brass were elevated during Obama, one wonders if they're more sympathetic to the Left or to the country in general. It is unfair to suggest one must lean rightward to love this country or serve, yet all those senior officers who retired during Obama (and many of whom endorsed Trump in 2016 quite publicly in their retirement) makes me wonder if loyal functionaries were being put in place who would serve the interests of the national security state by following orders rather than the Constitutional oath all officers swear. We can't really know, but it matters deeply.

In terms of assets, if it can hold together and avoid foreign entanglements, a major problem which only escalates during any appearance of civil conflict, the military has the logistical and manpower potential to provide great aid and stabilization here at home. Beyond the legal issues of posse comitatus, that the military is not supposed to be used to control the domestic population, what purposes would the military be willing to serve?

I cannot imagine there would be any major outcry against providing relief and support to people who need assistance, and both the regular military and National Guard do so regularly and with great courage during natural disasters and hurricanes. But it would be a different matter if there were ever partisans representing two or more sides having active conflict with one another. Under normal government operation, such affairs would be assigned to Federal law enforcement, but given how compromised the FBI has been proven, would they act and if they did, could such action taken against patriots be considered illegitimate or perhaps part of a coup itself?

Would the military intervene, and would it do so in an organized way, or would paralysis at the national level due to unrest, foreign issues, or uncertainty cause the military to potentially break their own chain of command? Such thinking sounds far-fetched given how things operate today, but we see the first signs of these divisions in how certain governors are willing to employ the National Guard to defend the border where others are highly constraining their actions. Should there be, for instance, a Latino uprising in the southwest, I imagine California and Texas would instruct their respective forces to act quite differently, and absent a compelling Federal voice to unify them, it's not hard to see these units beginning to behave in a divergent manner.

Admittedly, it would take a certain sort of political crisis for these scenarios to come into play, but the military's own planners have long concluded that a breakdown scenario in America will quickly fall into chaos with the government being stuck defending certain key areas. Most prominently, the I-80 corridor between Chicago and New York, the well populated but resource dependent cities of the East Coast, and a few other scattered megalopolises like we see in California and Texas would be key assets to secure.

Assuming that rioting is happening in the cities, and as these areas lean broadly Left and the military self-identifies by a better than two to one margin as leaning Right, will the soldiers remain or will units defect to support the country and rural folk against the cities, joining their ideological brethren? It's hard to predict absenteeism, but the more the government struggles to keep together, the more likely it will grow, especially if the soldiers find themselves at odds with the directions from above.

To make the case specific, given their stated preferences, it seems much more likely the military would stand behind Trump to protect the administration than some post impeachment sham regime offered up by the Deep State. If the Left rises, which seems somewhat more likely at the time of this writing, the military might help with suppression, although the higher-ranking officers are in doubt. If, during a later Democrat administration, there is a revolt by patriots—probably caused by restrictions in gun ownership—the question becomes much more chancy to forecast.

But these are questions which must be carefully and deliberately considered, because as order breaks down, the emergent reality will be that authority will align to those who can enforce their will. There will be positive aspects to this, where those who can feed and care for others will gain social currency, provided they can defend their operations, but also negative aspects where without the viable and organized potential for force, any insurgencies will struggle to survive.

In this formulation, we see one key that we can identify moving forward in how close we are to potential conflict. Law enforcement has been withdrawing from their authority, due in part to violence in cities. There is also a lack of political support for enforcing the laws, as we see in city after city. Due to "disparate impact" such that non-Whites tend to be prosecuted in higher numbers (due to higher per-capita crime rates), the only solution has been selective non-enforcement to get the crime numbers down. The crimes still occur, but the law is only enforced in the more extreme cases. In addition, there is a "Sanctuary" insurrection against Federal immigration laws. All combined, what is happening is that through their combined control of city hall and violent activists, the Left is actively undermining the ability of the state, at the national and local level, to maintain control. As this happens, and as the persons who represent law enforcement continue pulling out, the question of using the military will only grow as the

Deep State has abdicated their impartiality through demonstrable bias, therefore rendering themselves unusable to the Right.

One of the unique aspects of how this unrest is proceeding is with great restraint from the forces of the Right who are far better armed both individually and institutionally, but who struggle to organize due to a natural respect for hierarchy that keeps them bought into the existent system. In contrast, the Left is seeking to catalyze their people into flash mobs to act extremely quickly, using media and activist allies and a preferred cultural narrative to use their better collective skills to undercut the credibility of the Right's values and their elected officials in government. Watching how the Left is responding, they're certainly succeeding in rapid radicalization.

Given all the potential confusion about who has what authority, that's why a very probable outcome, at least initially, is that the military may try to exercise discretion to remain removed from any larger conflict. This would fit their training and cultural inclination, but it will only last until certain bases and facilities end up, if they do, throwing in with one side or the other. Should either Left or Right have the authority of the Federal government in a fashion reasonably conceivable as Constitutional, the military may back them, but if multiple entities, especially on regional bases emerge, then all bets are off. It would seem logical that bases would make arrangements with whatever ruling authority arises in their area, or alternatively, they may take control of their near environs and go into lock down mode.

No one knows, but these questions could prove decisive if America goes to war against itself.

Lastly, in the event of chaos in America, the military will face another choice. Given the unhappy reality that we have played world's policeman since at least the end of World War II, any prolonged issues in this country are likely to serve as an invitation for foreign powers to seek to settle their own issues. Imagine Chinese expansion into Taiwan or Russia adding another chunk of the Ukraine as but two possibilities. Will the military deploy to honor treaty obligations in defense of foreign lands, or will they return home, worried for the welfare of their own family, friends, and relations?

Furthermore, how would their involvement be impacted by the very high likelihood that agents representing several foreign governments would invariably get caught up in these fights, helping different sides, not to mention any actions which could impact our border nations of Mexico and Canada, assuming they are not caught up in the wider conflagration? The military will have a lot on its plate, questions far beyond the simple mission statement they enjoy now, and no one really knows what to expect.

All we know is the military could do much if it had the inclination and they're very aware of the underlying tensions. Look for America to begin withdrawing our forces from foreign outposts as opportunity allows, for cost savings certainly, but also in anticipation of a wider conflict. America First as a policy is not just upsetting to the leftist partisans who agitate, but to the globalist nations who bankroll their operations, many of which would be happy to see the U.S. reduced many notches in the standing of nations.

Section II: The Players

Group II: Private Sector Interests

Despite the immense power wielded by the American government, it is well understood such agency is largely exercised at the behest of the moneyed interests who fund elections, campaigns, and the entities which promote policy.

Any such review must start with the impact of banking, considering their control of the money supply and the demonstrated servitude of the American government to their interest which we saw on full display during the bailout of 2007. Acting as centrifuge for the weakening status quo, look for the banks and their affiliated and dependent industries like law and accounting whose social status is dependent upon our corrupt system, to seek to restrain actors as much as possible, but eventually throw in with the Left as centralizing forces sympathetic to globalism.

Big business is more of a mixed bag with extractive industries and productive industries more sympathetic to the idea of national development, but the largest American information-based sectors would almost uniformly to support the Left by enabling censorship to reinforce the cultural hegemony the Left has through more traditional institutions and forms of communication.

Lastly, though an appendage to this chapter, the impact of foreign powers is considered as they act much the same as a corporation, looking to America as a market for opportunity, but also potentially as a thorn against expansion. China represents a distinct threat, much more so than Russia, but each is likely to intervene in opposition to the other. The impact such conflict may have on Mexico and Canada is also briefly considered.

Chapter 11: Banks—Much Interest, Little Principle

They say all wars are bankers' wars. The reason being that there is no more lucrative human financial activity than the war cycle, provided people survive at the end of the fight. The banks make money on the loans they put out and the debt governments amass in advance of the conflict. They then help fund the fighting, either directly or by buying up war bonds, and issue more loans to convert infrastructure into war production. The weapons cost a ton of money also, and when the fighting is finally done, then they finance the rebuilding of everything that was expensively destroyed. Provided their hands don't get dirty, it's pretty much the perfect scam.

The connections are not so obvious in the current age, but it's no accident the first place worth considering as a separate entity once we expand our review of actors and institutions beyond those in government is the banking sector. Their influence over American politics was aptly demonstrated just a decade ago when both parties rushed to bailout the banks and their affiliated entities over the collapse of the mortgage bubble, a crisis exacerbated heavily by reckless financial products like derivatives. Those with the most resources were also the best protected.

Starting at the American level, which will have to be expanded upon because of the international connections and shared motives of banks, the Federal Reserve is a very strange entity that is poorly understood by the public at large. This institution which functionally controls the

American money supply is not a government agency, its stock is privately by the larger banks, and through actions like quantitative easing, the Federal Reserve has literally been able to create money from thin air. I've long believed the reason this trick works is because not going along has potentially even worse consequences and because so long as there are tangible dollar bills, the concept of fiat money is too abstract for people to mentally latch their minds around.

Since they control the money supply, through buying and selling money to get it off or on the market, they also control a great deal of the political scene. If the Fed wants to help protect a friendly politician, they might choose to allow a looser money supply, keeping the discount rate at which the Fed lends to banks at 0%. Such liquidity allows economic growth even under poor policies provided inflation is managed properly, and it's worth noting the Fed for years under Democratic rule for Obama purposely kept the rate flat. They also did the same for much of Bush's reign.

The moment Trump got elected and started changing the fundamentals of the economy from a globalist orientation toward something more nationalist, what is clearly the beginning of an economic plan to ensure America is a producer as well as consumer, the Fed started raising their interest rates. Such activity makes it more expensive for Americans to sell goods abroad, causes credit to tighten to slow economic expansion, and perhaps most importantly, represents a real threat to the housing market as mortgage prices will move in parallel with the rate hikes.

A conventional economist will say the central bank is acting responsibly in doing this by making sure it does not allow the economy to grow too quickly, by constraining the benefits of the recently passed tax plan and deregulation regime to a manageable pace. But that definition seems a bit strange because then the central bank basically exists to make sure America doesn't prosper too much under lighter regulation, and that when the government increases regulation that would hurt the economy, the bank exists to make them look good. It's almost like the whole concept is vaguely socialist in orientation, an assertion Andrew Jackson risked death to shut down when it was implemented in his era.

Teasing that out a little further, the symbiotic relationship between the banks and the rise of government has been laid out by many, including in my own earlier volume. The bank allows the government to print as much money as it wants to enact any policy item, and in exchange the state provides cover for how much the economy is being inflated by using tax dollars as collateral for development. With this arrangement, formalized in the United States with the passage of the Federal Reserve Act and Sixteenth Amendment in succession, the handshake between the big banks and big government was complete. It would take time to grow into the massive state and financial empire we see today, but the pathway was wide and open.

When we talk about power in the world, we often talk about money because of how we all recognize those who can buy influence can shape everything. Imagine if you had enough money to buy every newspaper in the country, control every TV station, fund every university endowment, and never have your name attached explicitly. When you consider the central bank literally makes interest off lending to the Federal government, a trillion-dollar enterprise, and has the admitted public capacity to release money at will, the prerogatives of those who own the shares of these banks must be considered as having great weight.

As it turns out, the banks are the beating heart of the globalist project. At every corner, you see them working to integrate economies globally, offering loans to poor countries at exorbitant interest. To illustrate just how wide their reach has spread, the current central banking system includes branches in every country except three: Iran, Syria, and North Korea. A thoughtful observer might note that the Federal government agitated most strongly against these nations, up until at least very recently, and conclude that humanitarian or security interests might not be the real motives for such agitation, and instead there could be the old-fashioned profit-motive.

Now, although these banks work nominally for separate interests, they reconcile through entities like the World Bank, the Bank of International Settlements, and the International Monetary Fund. Up until very recently, these entities were basically controlled by the Fed, the Bank of England, and the European Central Bank based in Frankfurt, which represent the most influential entities in the gathering. The same people who sit on these boards go to places like the World Economic Forum meetings in Davos,

Switzerland and Bilderberg Group meetings, summoning politicians to tell them what will and won't be financed and planning out the world.

We talked about how one of the crises not just in America, but around the world is that our elites have shed their national aspirations and instead imagine themselves as part of the emergent global over-class. As we look throughout the private sector, this will be a recurring theme, because in addition to the Left/Right paradigm which is most commonly used, those trying to pull the strings look at issues from a globalist/nationalist perspective instead.

To paint a picture, it's the sort of well-funded person who lives in New York and spends more time in London than in Albany, jumping from city to city, chasing numbers. They see governments as tools to be manipulated, something done surprisingly easily throughout the world, and always keep their eyes on the bottom line. Far more invested in their own circles than any nation at large, in as much as they are ideological, they usually tend Left because they're universalists—it's just that their form of exploitation is subtler than the brute force solution the Marxists most commonly apply.

Now, given the power of the banks beyond the central bank, they sit at the intersection of other powerful sectors. There have long been connections between the Central Intelligence Agency and Wall Street. It's generally believed that the banks launder black money for intelligence operations and keep quiet. In exchange, the agents ensure no one threatens the existing system. In this, the banks are at the top of totem pole, but such an understanding is at the heart of how American corporate economic imperialism was managed throughout Latin American and other parts of the world: Fist in glove.

In the larger context, one can frequently trace the sorts of uprisings and instability that cause global migrations back to inopportune investments. Whether by funding wars, collapsing states, or any of several other actions, banks are at the center of not just economic circulation, but that the movement of people as well. When they pushed for Libya to fall, perhaps because Libya was considering a rival gold backed currency to replace the petro dollar, that just happened to open the door to all the migrants now invading Europe. The crisis in Syria, heavily caught up in oil pipeline politics, has similar characteristics.

I know this chapter can seem somewhat disconnected to the larger narrative, but the key takeaway is even as we're sizing one another up for a brawl on ideological terms, America must be remembered for also serving as a piece on a grander chessboard. We are, in the struggle of nationalism versus globalism, the queen of the rebellion, the most capable piece with the widest range of actions, but nationalist options have been deliberately constrained by both those without and those within. To ensure we remain non-threatening, it's probable those who run the banks and who could live as easily within one national border or the next would contemplate sacrificing America to remove our pesky ideas of natural law, national self-determination, and an armed and freely sovereign citizenry.

From their perspective, we were useful as shock troops fighting war after war to establish the New World Order our own politicians helped create, but having served that purpose, we are now only valuable to the extent we remain compliant. We can be poor, or we can be rich, but we cannot be free and independent, because if America goes nationalist, then what other countries might follow? Could the whole European Union project which is slowly dragging that whole continent beneath bureaucratic rule be threatened? Quite possibly. Which is why trusting the bankers is dangerous.

Day to day, we see what banks can do to make person's life easy or hard. They control the money, and given that reality, it's worth noting the world we have today reflects what they want. Shallow, obsessed with profit and materialism, and without any notional opposition. Banks would support any side, amorally, provided they can control the money and collect interest on us all. That's their price, and while America has paid it for at least a hundred years now, casting off their yoke is a dream for many.

Some argue Kennedy was killed for trying to move in that direction, but while we cannot know for certain if that was true, we can reasonably expect that as the Right rises, the banks will be no friend of ours. As stated earlier, they fund a world of lesser people because they want control, and such a drive makes them a class apart. Let us only hope we have the good sense to identify these threats and not fall to their temptations.

Chapter 12: Regulators—Living for the System

If the bankers are the profiteers of the current system, then in many ways their foot soldiers and vassals are the hordes of people employed in the various legal and financial institutions that make up their empire of numbers. Lawyers, accountants, insurance agents, underwriters, and people who don't peek too high above their desk abound in skyscrapers and office buildings to ensure every dollar and cent are correct.

I've never been able to fully get past the irony of this system, to be 100% honest. At the top, we have bankers who make money from thin air, who either go alone or work with politicians who pass policy based on sheer idealism. Neither are truly accountable, and from this imagination trillions are brought into existence that can shape the whole economy. Yet, the moment the money is imagined, then there are thousands of different constraints, rules, and regulations applied immediately. Perhaps all this is done to create the compelling illusion which makes the money so valuable, and perhaps also this just gives people whose acquisitiveness exceeds their abilities a chance to buy in and cash out. But what continues to strike me is that the whole thing is made up.

Since from the previous chapter discussed banking, let's start with the accountants and insurance companies. Building upon the core relationship of status quo America, the connection between big business and big government, they work to pass regulations through the Congress which historically have favored big business or well-connected businesses. A great example of this is Sarbanes-Oxley, a compliance bill in the early aughts against financial malfeasance, whose compliance requirements just happened to shake out like this: The price of following these rules was devastating to small businesses and less prosperous entrepreneurs but could easily be handled by corporations which had their own compliance and accounting division. Helping the big at the expense of the small generally fits the government mindset and works within their economy of scale model.

Consider how many people are employed as auditors, accountants, and in tax preparation, following rules designed to confuse and obfuscate. It's no accident the IRS came into prominence at nearly the same exact time as the Fed arose, because these are all interlinking parts of a larger structure. Not only are they connected, but they're used to command compliance and to keep an eye on what everyone is doing. We spend untold billions chasing paper around in circles, trying to prove how legitimate each transaction is. People spend their lives in these traps, all when the top just makes the original funds from thin air.

But the fact the whole system is based on fictions is not obvious, because if you do comply with all the accounting tricks, and maybe learn to play them yourself, then you encounter insurance next. In some ways, it's the perfect synthesis of Leftist thinking with globalist greed where a person is forced to spend money to comply with a government order. It's one thing for someone to voluntarily seek to cover oneself against unpredictable calamities, but what we have now is something fundamentally different in how compulsory it has become: A lever of control, insurance is used to constrain people.

If one is tempted to resist, then the lawyers come along. In the eternal question of which group is least liked in society, there has been a long running contest between the bankers and the lawyers. Both take copious amounts of money and work at their own leisure. Both will bankrupt you given the opportunity. Yet, where bankers try to simplify everything to numbers, lawyers tie society in a maze of words, a clever trick to protect their guild and their influence.

Lawyers lean almost universally to the Left because they generally tend to believe life can be regulated better with precision and direction, and because they think regulation is the better form of organization. They also benefit from having a more complex regulatory environment because that creates many more opportunities to draft, revise, and interpret new laws. These people specialize in making what is natural complicated, and to make the complex even more so.

When the Constitution was designed, the Founders had the idea to make the document as simple as reasonably could be achieved, and in just ten amendments, the Bill of Rights served as a brilliant, expansive, and yet mercifully brief enumeration of the rights reserved to the American citizen. They did this because if barristers were needed to understand the rights of the people, it would be expected those rights could be hidden, lost, or undermined. They understood that when law is simple, people will understand and follow it, and will be protected by it in turn. When law is complex, that is an invitation to corruption.

Look how many more laws we have on the books today for any and every subject. And yet, we live in what is certainly one of the most corrupt ages in American history. Sadly, the worst forms of corruption are also the most legal, as we all hear stories daily of how different companies and entities play with national jurisdictions to protect and hide money and wrongdoing. The lawyers facilitate such malice, all perfectly legal, so long as those with means become a part of the global network. And once one's assets are caught up in this arrangement, why would one ever oppose these legal actions for something as pedantic as nationalism, liberty, or group identity?

The bribes, corruption and elite status offered for being part of the globalist network are how we lost so many of those who were once part of us to become something else. More Left than Right, they moved beyond their simple national idealism, and their dreams became smaller and more cynical. Their scope is global, but reductionist, in trying to force people to become less, to be easier to control by becoming less distinct from one another. Under the current system, these are the wealthy and the gatekeepers, and they are fighting to maintain their comforts and prerogatives.

In terms of the impending conflict we imagine, we see how lawyers are being employed to conduct lawfare at

111

many levels to prevent and forestall changes. This will come out more in the chapter on nonprofits, but the very model of the legal practice which encourages pro bono work for what are sometimes questionable causes is suggestive. Lawyers, if the standard scenarios are followed where laws remain applicable and there is no breakdown, can and will gladly tie up any civil action for years at great cost to all involved.

We see litigation increasingly being employed as a weapon by the Left to destroy opposing activists. Through a combination of civil and criminal actions, at both local and national levels, possible through their ownership of lawyers generally and the bureaucracy in most places, the Left can pull someone into the legal process and one cannot quit until one is utterly spent or surrenders. I think the unfortunate case of General Flynn is only one prominent example where the cost and anguish of an interminable process seemed enough to persuade him to surrender.

It's hard today for a single person to resist when there are so many rules that we supposedly commit three felonies per day without even realizing it. And while the government wouldn't be so obnoxious as to enforce all these rules constantly, what it has created is a position where the citizen is in constant peril because any of us can be turned into criminals without cause. The lawyers seem fine with that, especially if we're not in a legally protected group. This is a concern that will only grow, because we've seen elsewhere how this sort of selective enforcement becomes a powerful weapon when wielded adeptly.

Yet for all their power at the outset and in our current society, those who have gained the most from the system as it is, would also be the least valuable in many ways should an actual fight break out. How valuable would their encyclopedic knowledge of the law or regulations prove in a fight? Considering how so many of these people are the urban gentrified liberals, it's worth wondering how the urban poor would treat the wealthy among them when the intermediaries of law enforcement vanish. As they've lived in their costly enclaves with conveniences and superficial empathy to the poor, will they be able to work the leftists in the street or will they be the first targets?

A long-standing prediction I've held, especially if the government ever proves incapable of enforcing its will in a given area under emergency status, is those who live in the poorest neighborhoods will raid and take control of these areas first, and for those bean counters and paper pushers who don't get out early, they might very well end up stuck. The Right will have little desire to rescue people who have little practical skills and I can't imagine the Left will see them as very helpful either.

If resources are plentiful, the best I can imagine is they'd be tolerated, or perhaps kept around for their ability to ferret out hidden reserves. But if not, we will see a trend repeat which happens again and again, which is those that serve the banking regime often find themselves as the evidence to be swept up when things go awry.

While I'm sure there are good people in these professions whose service has been honorable and decent, it's hard to muster much sympathy for people who get wealthy off a system designed to constrain our liberties and essentially run hustles off either ignorance or revolving interest. Given how well they've lived, how rich they became while they saw that the rest of the country was being sold out, there just likely won't be much sympathy to be had for their plight.

If they realize this, look for them to push hard to counsel moderation and restraint at all times, because the one thing they don't want to see is any disruption to the gravy train that sustains their lives. They will gladly throw reams of paper at anyone explaining what is and is not possible, and if one is foolish enough to seek their permission, then it will just become a trap from which escape is not possible.

Maybe that is the right place to escape this layer of bureaucracy. Legitimacy of a regime sometimes seems like nothing more than offering the right distractions, and whatever else one might say of the conflict emerging, at least a real choice is being offered and a struggle worth fighting as opposed to the grind in which we've been captured for decades. People seem to sense we can be more than this and get more from life, and whatever emerges, neither side seems likely to want to follow these sycophants to the status quo.

Chapter 13: Corporations—Influence and Indifference

Reams have been written about the role corporate influence has on government with the relationships varying much by sector and interest. Even though this is not the most dynamic topic to research, it's worth understanding as thoroughly as possible if only to see better why we get the government we do, and how policy is crafted many times directly to satisfy the specific interests of large corporations. For our purposes, we will visit several particularly important areas where business intersects government, and we will pay attention to transnational corporations.

To explain why, I'll share a story from my time in local government, which scales up rather nicely. Every now and again a business will come to a given town offering an opportunity but looking to exact a cost. This was not during my brief administration, but it was well known in the town where I live that an entrepreneur came to town offering to build a box factory that would have employed upwards of fifty people and would have been a multi-million-dollar investment. In exchange, they were seeking a tax break for ten years to offset the development and infrastructure cost. Now, the town hesitated and ultimately did not accept the appeal for various reasons, but plenty of other towns were willing to accept such a bargain, which made sense financially over the long term for both parties. Small businesses didn't like the unfairness of such a deal, but realistically, from the government perspective, the eventual new tax base as well as new citizens and increased employment were compelling arguments.

Businesses exist for one purpose: To make money for their owners. Whatever else they say and whatever else they may even believe; the profit margin is the life and purpose of the business cycle. Even the most altruistic person cannot afford to indefinitely take losses. Smaller businesses are generally more responsive to the public because each consumer has greater contribution to profitability. But as a company grows and gains substantial market share, each consumer makes less of a difference to the bottom line, and responsiveness becomes less important. Corporations have a drive to become larger and inhabit the biggest space in the economy that is open and appealing to them, but as they grow, just like with government, they become lost in their own bureaucracy, dogma, and corruption.

There is a strange parallel precisely to what we see in government where even though these entities are composed of people who have values, are members of their communities, and hold certain beliefs, they become so miniaturized within the vast entities in which they work that they are swallowed by the rising amorality of the purpose. For government, it is to take power. For business, it is to make money. And as these two entities are large enough to dance with one another, it's no accident the cycle at the heart of the current American as well as global economy is putting money in each other's pockets. Unfortunately, citizens have become little more than a backdrop to this essential relationship.

Just as governments express shifting interests, corporations always seek new opportunities. Protected by the legal fiction that their officers and shareholders cannot be held liable for any but the most egregious criminal offenses, and even then, only sometimes, they tend to probe and explore without too much mind to the broader social consequences of their actions. They embrace the global mindset that borders merely represent different markets, and with such thinking, they have no problem seeing themselves as ethical actors when they pay slave labor in one country, which might very well be an advancement over local wages, and then sell for insane profit in a host country, even though they shut every factory down that sustained families in a first world country, as in our own depleted Rust Belt.

To put it bluntly, free market ideologies pushed by the global consensus elite have caused CEOs to believe their own BS about being ethical actors. They're not. They are creators and disruptors to a certain degree, especially in emergent sectors, but the real market heavies are just there to make select people rich, provide a return on investment, and do so with minimal interruption. Charity, such as it is practiced, is the benefit of having a tax write-off with a marketing component, which is why every corporation gives to breast cancer research, a highly valuable cause no doubt, but also almost universally surveyed to be the most popular and least offensive choice. Hollowness reigns.

Examine the biggest sectors. For most of history, beyond banking which we've already profiled in depth, their partner in crime was energy. Everyone needs power, and the value of gasoline remains vital to world economic operation. Until about the last ten years, you could predict reliably the wealthiest corporations would be firms like Exxon Mobil, Shell, Aramco, and other petroleum heavy industries. They rove the world looking for opportunity, hiring their own personal mercenary contractor armies in many places, and often have more wealth than the countries in which they operate. Though they play nicely in America because they rely upon our consumer market, never forget these are companies who dictate terms elsewhere and especially where government corruption is rife, can often do so with surprising ease and accommodation in resource rich, but civically challenged countries.

In terms of the political struggle, one would think they would lean Right if only because of the willingness to open resources for extraction. Trump's actions to open up ANWR (Alaska oil), approve the Keystone and Dakota Access pipelines, and to remove many EPA regulations used deceptively to encourage further shale and clean coal development are welcome to this sector. Certainly, their employees are also seeing major benefit, although the external politics gets tricky because foreign countries do not want to see U.S. competition as an energy exporter, disrupting the delicate global balance between supply and demand.

It's important to consider their prerogatives, however, because if America is to walk an independent path, we need to think ahead to a time where the only energy we can get is what we already have. Whether we remain united or split in segments, that remains just as true, and those resources in an odd way make competition more likely. A calculation is constantly being worked by both sides of how a fight can be picked which will lead to victory, and as part of that, being able to meet one's energy needs is huge.

Corporations, existing above and beyond this model, with the assumption the rule of law will continue unabated as it mostly has for the past two hundred plus years make investments on a generational basis. But as revolutions in the Third World have shown with Venezuela most recently, corporations such as Citgo Oil and entire industries can be nationalized practically overnight, and represent a great source of wealth and support for the state. If the contractors employed by the corporation are insufficient or the assets immobile, corporations will certainly be a target to consider as events play out.

What is interesting is the sector which has eclipsed the reliable energy sector for financial standing has been information technology. Best exemplified by the heavies of social media and search engines in Google (Alphabet), Apple, Amazon, Facebook, Netflix, and Twitter, these entities were the primary growth areas in the American economy pre-Trump, and you'll notice each is designed to both share and collect information. Because their perspectives are public, these entities claim their policies are mainstream, but we've seen firsthand that they actively support leftist causes and seek to marginalize those on the

Right, perhaps because of their global market driven outlook.

Although it is the smallest of those mentioned, Twitter is the most obvious example of such bias. It has long been known that traditionalists and conservatives suffer discrimination from Jack Dorsey, an unrepentant liberal, who uses the platform he must attempt to shade the culture war by assigning legitimacy to those on the Left and denying platform access to those on the Right. The censorship regime has become clever in the modern age, and sometimes the way it manifests is more in "what you are not allowed to see" than in "what you are not allowed to say."

Books that present a certain point of view only slightly to the right of this current text can find themselves banned from Amazon, whose owner I would note runs the Washington Post, one of the most vocal and frankly dishonest critics of the Trump Administration. Netflix just hired the Obamas to produce content for them—a kickback or a cultural embrace—perhaps both. Apple has long blocked anything politically right of center with even a whiff of controversy from being posted on the App Store, with a perfect example of how Gab, my preferred social media whose sole commitment is to free speech without censorship, has been blocked from making their application available specifically because of their unwillingness to silence community content by blanket means.

We'll separate Google out from the others, because search engines are very tricky. I'll give you an experiment that will prove the point. An alternate search engine used

120

by many people concerned about privacy is called DuckDuckGo. Look up a nonpolitical topic on both search engines and the results may vary slightly but will be basically similar. Now, try a politically charged term, especially one right of center, and you'll almost certainly have a different result. What Google's supposedly impartial algorithm will show overwhelmingly, especially on that first page, are results opposed to the Right, representing sources they deem legitimate, but which could as easily be called compliant. By contrast, you will quite possibly see much more varied sources using DuckDuckGo or any other alternative.

The war we're talking about has already begun with the first battles being fought in information warfare. It's no accident DARPA (Defense Advanced Research Projects Agency) was at the heart of creating the Internet, because it was designed to ferret out information and destabilize regimes. Why do you think ISIS accounts were kept open at the same time conservatives were shut down? It makes you wonder who benefits, a question we all must constantly ask. But in the American civil context, this war has been roiling for several years now. The insurgent forces of the Right, working from havens such as the infamous Chans (4chan.net/pol) were being incredibly effective, winning victories both with Brexit and Trump's election against massive media scripting and efforts.

The strategy being employed to stop these advances is subtle and clever, and we see it on YouTube (now a Google brand) and Facebook. Community policing, third party observers (including the infamous, deceitful, and criminal SPLC who is funded by foreign money), shadow bans, and selective and arbitrary demonetization schemes are all designed to silence, hide, and intimidate the Right. The Left thought their command of culture was complete because their control of institutions was overwhelming, but just as the printing press took down the dogma of the all-powerful Church, the disconnect between the reality being experienced by so many and the happy propaganda being pushed fueled a maelstrom of discontent that elected Trump and spawned new movements such as the Alt-Right, explicitly and violently counter-culture.

The Internet corporations, looking to keep themselves in charge, and to solidify their spots on the block as the new guys and top dogs, have done their best to ingratiate themselves with the global consensus by seeking to marginalize and demonize the discontents. I lived this as millions of dollars in national media resources were used to attack me personally in a small town of under one thousand people for just stating that Islam doesn't work here, and people can freely associate. This phenomenon gives us a hint of just how those tech billions are spent, and it should be disturbing, because the Left is working hand in hand with these tech leaders to try to censor us.

A warning of the future comes from Europe where the EU is working at this very moment to pass new copyright laws designed to eliminate the use of memes by outlawing anyone from using images but their owners. While such laws will inherently be unenforceable, and will only encourage further anonymity, what they create is the sort of legal jeopardy behind free speech where a right is essentially and intentionally being criminalized to take control. Lawyers are at the ready to do the bidding of the system, and the people will inevitably get screwed.

Fortunately, our protections here are more robust thanks to the First Amendment and the Right's control of parts of the judiciary, but it would only take two justices and one Democrat President to lose these forever, because we have seen again and again how they choose politically correct speech over free speech, preferring control to dissent. It is worrying how these businesses gladly go along with this agenda. The world has shown with its money that it values information more than all else, and it has put its faith in the hands of people who are inclined to financial amorality, and whose personal preferences lean toward the totalitarian.

Almost as much as demographic replacement fears, the Right understands the Left is trying to force cultural compliance through complete command of the information sphere. Apart from those insurgent forces that have managed to break away a small chunk of the Internet space and telecommunications, big money and big business are working to squash nationalist and particularist views of culture, especially from traditionalists. Seeing the rising criminalization of speech and thought, not to mention the long term rise of more effective AI, these actions are pushing the Right toward battle now with the assumption the future will not treat these vital sectors kindly.

Other sectors such as medicine, agriculture, and transportation will also matter, but these tend to be less ideological, though each loves to work within a larger government framework, and apart from some of those involved in logistics, the tendency for each will be to support the stability of the status quo.

The important exception to these emergent industries is in the manufacturing trades. Although these businesses historically leaned leftward especially for the employees involved in the traditional trades, a seismic shift is happening in partisan affiliations with the Right's direct embrace of nationalism and manufacturing in this country. Where the old neoconservative and neoliberal consensus across party lines had shipped jobs overseas for decades, gaining full speed in the 1980's and after passage of NAFTA, the American renewal happening in manufacturing is revitalizing long moribund sectors of the economy and states within the Midwest and Northeast which were hardest hit.

These owners understand the Right has worked to make America a place for domestic production again, and their employees after spending years living on the margins, are prepared to defend keeping jobs at home. It should be interesting to see how this plays out in the next election or two but look for the industrial areas of the nation to shift rapidly rightward and consider these assets as the business beachhead against the dominance the Left enjoys in information and other sectors.

Chapter 14: Foreign Influences—Is America for Sale?

This chapter is a bit of an orphan which could warrant its own section, but I chose to include foreign actors in the section with private party actors because governments are more like businesses representing separate interests than any other category. The motives of foreign actors are driven by power and influence, which is related to money but somewhat different. But these are the means and methods by which they work within the United States.

Although foreign corporations play a very large role, for the purposes of simplicity, we're going to assume them to either be independent agents acting on their own profit motive which tends to be trust for most western corporations and a few from Asia, or as subservient to the state interests which is true for other Asian entities, especially those operating in China.

There is zero doubt that any foreign nation worth their salt acts actively through both legal and illicit terms to shape the discourse in America and to attempt to curry favor. The most obvious is in some ways the most disturbing in that foreign governments have for many years lobbied for preferential trade and purchasing status within America, employing lobbyists for this purpose and often receiving assistance from the State Department, the flagship of the Deep State.

Before my latest foray into politics, I worked in purchasing for a sizable government contractor and as a result, had to familiarize myself with where we can buy products around the world. You would think that American projects would have as a basic requirement the desire to purchase goods made in the United States, but as it turns out, there's no functional disadvantage to importing from any of dozens of foreign nations, at least not in the eyes of the GSA or the military. They might list a preference for American goods, but as reward for friendly governments, who often get paid by the State Department and then use that money in return to buy influence in DC to bolster their positions, a refrigerator from Bangladesh has the same rating as one from Des Moines. It doesn't seem right, but people don't usually bother to read the small print.

In Washington, there are tons of deals made like this all the time, where the very size and scope of our government presents many opportunities for foreign powers, focused and deliberate in their intentions, to act. To be clear, many of these countries are acting solely in their self-interest to improve their own status without any deliberate harm intended to America, yet we have little ability and until recently, desire, to ask questions if decisions we're making serve to America's gain.

Rather than just focusing on minutiae, let's look at one of the biggest problems America has today which is our national debt. Currently sitting upwards of $21 trillion dollars, which is equal to slightly more than one year's projected GDP (Gross Domestic Product—the aggregate value of all the goods and services produced in America in one calendar year), nearly 45% of this debt is held by foreign powers. The largest chunks at slightly over $1 trillion dollars apiece are held by China and Japan respectively, but there are many players who own treasuries and other securities.

Up until recently with the more robust run of the dollar and demonstrable economic growth, the debt was becoming an albatross which countries who had sizable assets in U.S. denominated notes could use for leverage for preferential status in other areas. That threat remains, though slightly lessened for the moment, and to explain why this situation is so dangerous requires a bit of clarification for those less familiar with finance.

At some point in your life, you may have possessed a US Savings Bond. You could buy a note for $25 and after a set period, it would mature and deliver a predesignated rate of interest. You offered a loan to our government, and they agreed to pay you back, which you would receive if you waited the full term. If you redeemed it early, the government would only pay you the face value or a portion of the interest, depending upon the specific terms. But, in redeeming this early, the government then runs short of the revenue needed to conduct its operations and must issue more debt.

As a brief aside, one could ask why the government doesn't solve this problem by instead printing more money to satisfy the outstanding debts. In fact, this happens quite frequently and such inflationary measures which make the money in your wallet have less purchasing power, are called quantitative easing. The problem with this approach is the currency will inflate rather quickly, and other central banks basically have been doing the same for a decade, keeping the global economy afloat through a bubble they assiduously maintain based upon mutual ownership of debt and agreeing not to look too closely at how they're basically buying the economy along by shifting the cost onto their average citizens by killing their purchasing power.

If that sounds illogical to you, consider how much more things cost to purchase year to year even though we are told how technology and logistical improvements are making goods and services cheaper and more accessible. They're not lying about technology in most cases, but they're hiding that the banks are essentially siphoning those gains into their financial mismanagement. As much as anything, people should be angry about how our wealth has been stolen, but other books cover that far more comprehensively than I can recount here. Read them to get informed.

For our purposes, that debt which is overwhelmingly foreign owned has value and represents a way to influence our economy. If China or Japan were to cash in their substantial holdings prematurely, the American government would have to find a way to honor those treasuries, and they would likely choose to do so by either offering more debt, offering some collateral—a property or good with real value, or by offering considerations. For example, it is possible that we tactfully ignore the $507 billion-dollar trade deficit we amass each year in exchange for China not cashing in the American debt that it holds, and even more insidiously, for not offering an alternative for global exchange to the fiat dollar? Many have speculated about this possibility for a very long time.

Debt becomes a liability for nations just as it does for individuals, because it is an expense without any rate of return. The deeper in debt a nation goes, the harder it is to escape, and such debt is the primary means by which the global elites enforce policy. There is a willingness to embrace allowing as much debt or debt forgiveness as a nation requires—always enough to survive but never enough to quite reach independent prosperity—in exchange for following the rules and a guaranteed rate of return. Such action is considered good economics, but if you remember the money is made from thin air at the very beginning, you might see just how crazy this global pyramid scheme has become.

However, these things are paradoxically true because everyone behaves as if they are true. So, even though it is just paper, the dollar is incredibly valuable, and people sacrifice their lives and countries fight over its value. America fights war after war in the Middle East to ensure oil can only be bought with dollars, using the stick to silence any dissent. China and Russia often tease the idea of bringing back gold backed currency to offset that strength, which would collapse the dollar and expand the ruble or yuan, but which would cause the same run on their gold supply that is supposed to have bankrupted Fort Knox and was the reason why America went off the gold standard. It's a crazy world in finance, but state actors play this game and keep each other in check by such forms of financial mutually assured destruction.

It would be better if America could escape these games, but we, depending upon your perspective, made the decision to entangle ourselves to either keep the peace or take control of world policy after World War II. Everyone agreed to use the dollar and in exchange, America would serve as guarantor for a global order of peace and prosperity, backed by American might but paid for with American blood and the willingness to not use our competitive advantage to the fullest, but instead to rebuild the world.

Looking back with hindsight some seventy years after World War II, it's true these actions kept conflict to a relatively manageable level especially in contrast with the beginning of last century, yet we should ask whether this worth the cost to America? We paid to rebuild Europe who now lectures us about how all we do is wrong. We granted most favored nation status to China, who is building a military and economy to challenge America in the Pacific. We took in more refugees and migrants than any other country in the world, who reward our kindness with anger and hostility seeking to remake America into a place more like the homes they fled. Was our altruism misplaced?

This question is at the heart of the struggle. The Left would say these commitments by America were just and required, seeing them not as sacrifices, but instead as reparations against injustices upon which they see our power as having come and gone. They see the struggle we undertook to rise to the top as unjust, viewing the world idealistically rather than as realists.

By contrast, the Right sees a world that we built, and which hates us for having offered our best, and taken so much upon our shoulders. We've had our values questioned, our people replaced, and our jobs off-shored, and now we're told to shut up and simply go away. It's a hell of thing, the audacity of those coming in to power. One wonders how far just a little gratitude and some of that infamous tolerance coming our way might have gone, but we shouldn't expect it from the Left nor should we expect it from other nations who seek to aid their own rise and expansion.

As we shift from a Eurocentric world toward the Pacific, we move away from the collectivist pathology that afflicts white civilization generally where we are willing to give away all we possess to realize some humanist ideal, to face committed ethnic realists who are materialists. China, Japan, Korea, and India all have very well-defined ideas of who are members of their nation and who are not and have no compunction about working toward those ends.

Of these powers, the greatest challenge will arise from China. The oldest continually existing civilization in the world, marked by talent and ambition, China also has major problems. The one child only policy designed to constrain their rising population combined with sex-selective abortions means they are disproportionately male. Furthermore, the Chinese Communist Party has kept control by promising continual wealth. Yet, their famed manufacturing, due to their own progression, is shifting abroad to cheaper labor markets like Malaysia, at the same time as automation is making manufacturing more cost competitive than it has been in decades for First World nations that have long relied on China. China is attempting to transition more toward the model followed by more advanced nations but given their constraints on free speech and intellectual assets, this is hard for them absent some uniting national ideology. Look beneath the Communist slogans and you'll see raw nationalism, but you'll also see the same ethnic resentment against White people we recognize here from the Left simmering ever more hotly.

As Taiwan has become further removed in terms of thought and action from China, the Chinese have moved more deliberately into the South China Sea to reclaim their forgotten province. Now that China's military is improving, they are now agitating against neighbors making claims against islands held by Vietnam, by Japan, and others. The Tiger looks ready to pounce in many ways, and to escape the ring surrounding it, China must see the United States either weakened or to withdraw. The only problem is China needs Americans to keep purchasing their goods to keep their own economy afloat, which is why the impending trade war between our nations is fraught with peril.

Even though the Chinese are nationalists, they understand very clearly that their rise is constrained by American power. Subtle in their actions, they work within the international community to pay lip service to bigger ideals using language of national sovereignty and platitudes about Left social policy, presenting themselves as a model for European bureaucrats who wished they had such freedom of action. At the same time, it makes every bit of sense for them to work with the forces of the Left to destabilize America by calling upon common cause to communist, or as they are obfuscated in this country, socialist ideals. Should China choose to make common cause with the Left, a relationship thought to have begun back when the Clintons were seen to be soliciting donations from the Chinese, then it would represent a major threat to American stability in the status quo and a major force multiplier for the leftist forces.

Such strategic analysis is not alarmist if one admits the Chinese people arriving, predominantly on the West Coast, but also throughout the country, retain mixed loyalties. Look not just at San Francisco, but at Vancouver in Canada where Chinese have come by the millions, or in Mexico where ties are rapidly warming, and you see the beginning of a strategy to make the Pacific into a future friendly lake for them. While America can resist this now, thanks to our military and financial strength, it's impossible to ignore our most radical agitators all seem to come from out west. It is quite telling how far to the left the Pacific Coast has gone while the remainder of the country is mostly drifting rightward.

In the breakdown scenario, it's easy to imagine Chinese support for the Left, especially if American forces are over extended or uncoordinated. Assuming California was the center of the Leftist effort in a two-sided conflict,

Chinese support could include supplies, munitions, food, weaponry, and diplomatic recognition. Given the geography of the Rockies, that would represent a major stronghold, and there is a growing fear among those on the Right regarding the people who live out west. Given that their philosophies are universalist and communist already, would they not choose their beliefs over their fellow citizens in seeking a fight? Many would proudly answer yes.

In terms of major powers, it's unlikely most Europeans would be able to do much more than sit and watch, and potentially provide some aid and relief, most likely to people leaning leftward in the east. An exception to this could be the Russians. While Russia is no friend of America, they also will not want to see China be given such a free pass, and you could reasonably expect some assistance to be given to nationalist forces in terms of armaments and resources, especially once the American status quo regime is removed as a threat and a hindrance to Russian policy in places like the Ukraine.

Even though I jumped to the most extreme scenarios, less violent outcomes would likely follow the same patterns. All countries will oppose a united America, and should we divide, Left areas will draw Chinese influence and Right areas will draw Russian influence. That those two countries would allow such entanglements to draw them into direct conflict seems unlikely but could happen if their own expansionism draws other countries into larger conflicts with them in their own territory, in which case the American unrest could devolve into another World War. I could imagine NATO forces seeking to repel Russia from Belarus or Ukraine, or Japan leading a coalition to help sustain Taiwan under attack, in which case this gets even messier. It is more likely, however, that other countries will simply re-arm and watch Russia and Japan expand, building new alliances while America works out our own conflict. Afterward, a new balance would arise, or war would create one.

Other actors that deserve discussion are the Arabs and the Israelis. Both spend exorbitant sums to impact American policy and are, unfortunately, caught up very heavily in our foreign policy for reasons of energy and religion. They will want to maintain the status quo as much as possible and will pay dearly to keep the global order afloat which has made them both rich. They will want us to be their tool to undo Iran before this fight comes to a head and given how much each has invested into domestic politics, nonprofits, and Congress directly through either AIPAC (the Israeli lobby) or CAIR (the Arab lobby), I wouldn't bet against them succeeding.

Under these cultural conditions, sending large portions of our military to the Middle East might prove fatal to our own country, just as was the case in Russia in 1917 and also happened again, though it is not commonly known, in Germany in 1918. But, the gamble will be that just like after 9/11, a common war might be enough to hold the American fabric together based on blood and patriotism a little while longer, and having witnessed it once, with the right provocation, it might work. The Deep State has engineered situations like this many times before, and with Arab and Israeli influence pulling strings, it would not be difficult to find another bogeyman upon which America could waste a few trillion dollars. I don't expect this though, if only because too many good men have bled over there already.

The last countries we need to talk about in terms of foreign influence are Canada and Mexico. If things come to a fight in the United States, or an event happens which destabilizes us to the point we start fighting, there's a good possibility they will get drawn into the fray. Canada, being much more similar to America, and having some of the same underlying tensions, could see separatist tensions rise in places like Alberta and Quebec. I don't foresee them actively threatening America in any scenario but given how aggressively Trudeau has been bringing in foreigners and given the unpredictable actions of the Chinese majority in Vancouver, it's impossible to say what impact a fight down here would have on them.

Mexico is more dangerous. Given the high likelihood that a rebellion in the southwest would have a distinctively Latino flavor, it's almost certain that support will rush to the leftist ranks in California in terms of opportunistic illegals. If there is no functional America to oppose such, Mexico may look more ambitiously about regaining the territories lost back in 1848. How these issues resolve themselves is an open question, especially as there would likely be a divergence between the ideological liberals of San Francisco and the Aztlan types who imagine an indigenous homeland out west for Latinos. The Left will struggle to hold its coalition together, perhaps, considering competing foreign interests, but will have no shortage of partners.

In fairness, if the model of ideological war leading to war on several different fronts is realized, I wouldn't be surprised to see white volunteers who, being culturally suppressed in Europe, decide to cross the Atlantic and take their chances on whatever American state emerges on the Right to fight and find their own freedom. These will be far less organized, but no less present, and could prove the most valuable contribution to come from predominantly western Europe if their access is permitted.

We can't say for certain how foreign actors will engage, but we know they will matter. Without America to guarantee the rules and keep things in line, a position backed by forces for the status quo but which the Left and Right both oppose for differing reasons, shifting alliances may lead to new partnerships, and instability will risk greater likelihood of war not just stateside, but globally, as countries and other actors seek to stake their place in the new emerging order.

Section II: The Players

Group III: Censors and Charlatans

When looking at who controls culture in America today, in terms of shaping political philosophy, the Left has established an effective monopoly through controlling nonprofits, the education system, and the mass media. As applicable to art, culture, and music as to politics and social trends, being able to harness the means of distribution and distinction gives the Left a clear advantage in promoting their position.

Looking more deeply at how this edifice has been constructed, a network of nonprofit organizations who are nominally independent but functionally exist off government largess emerges as the foundation of the effort. Their marching orders come from academics who exist to sustain a message throughout the entire education system, working to marginalize dissent and promulgate to the politically correct orthodoxy which buttresses Marxist thought. Lastly, the media willfully serves their joint purpose by putting out a clearly slanted message through most vehicles available, while working to remove voices who do not conform.

While there are efforts on the Right to build alternatives to this establishment, it is here at the intersection of government and culture where the Left has planted their flag most deeply, with nearly a hundred years effort in being able to shape the minds and hearts of succeeding generations. If not for the radically disruptive effects and low cost of emerging information technologies, this advantage may well have proven unassailable.

Strong, well-funded, and unified, these are the people who are pushing the message leading the Left toward conflict, arguing against compromise and most cynically, painting a deliberately false view of the opposition so they can maintain power and keep the froth high enough to make use of those who listen to their messaging.

Chapter 15: Nonprofits—Doing Good for Good Money

Whereas corporations and financial interests can purchase influence for their agendas, a foray into the contingent public sector begins by looking at those entities which sustain themselves via public support. Whether through direct contributions, or through working the enormous network of foundations, grants, government contracts and charities, the entities in this category are responsible for a great deal of the production and distribution of the Left's cultural agenda.

Starting with the admission that the Left is far better at playing the nonprofit game than the Right, it's important to understand why. People who lean conservative are no less likely to care for causes and, in fact, are often quite generous in their personal contributions to specific causes they value. Most of the causes are not political, but important exceptions are the single-interest groups whose political action committees (PACs) are as much a nonprofit as anything the opposition offers. Yet, due to their belief that existing off government largess represents a form of moral failure, the likelihood of right leaning organizations seeking to survive on government support is much smaller.

The Left has no such objections and they gleefully fund a series of programs, taken in sum, which do much of the work to push the social agenda they want. Even more disturbingly, they manage to do this in a way that seems nonpartisan when nothing could be farther from the truth.

For they understand, as their dialectical reasoning reveals, that the one asking the questions often controls what solutions emerge. If the Left decides to ask which social problems exist, how to solve them, and why these matter, then policy is a mundane issue where the answer has been predetermined by the very inquiry first offered.

In their case, the mantra often ends up being to help the disadvantaged, skipping the debate over why they ended up that way and the moral implications which often apply, and instead just ask how can we help people? Such a question seems to be apolitical, but it implicitly embraces the welfare state and government intervention as solutions, requiring money to achieve a social outcome. It's subtle, but the conditioning which nonprofits rely upon is that government should solve our problems, which the Left promotes as good policy and the Right doesn't oppose because of the taxes paid into the system. Such surrender is a terrible oversight by the Right, but it happens because they don't think to fight at this level.

To demonstrate how far nonprofits can go in shifting policy, look at how the European migrant crisis has been facilitated. Nonprofits, ostensibly looking to rescue people in danger and at sea, functionally are being paid to serve as a ferry service to bring the population marching through Africa across the Mediterranean. It's well understood at this point that George Soros and other wealthy globalists fund these organizations as part of their agenda to remake Europe, and yet, there is no serious legal threat to the legitimacy of these operations or operators who are paid to advance this cause. The wealthy use nonprofits to obscure their operations, choosing who to fund and who to starve, and have no shortage of would be recipients lining up.

The example above is extreme, but I saw how this game worked even more clearly during my tenure as Town Manager. Everyone loves free money. So, towns look for whatever sources of funding may be present besides their tax base, and then they conscientiously sculpt themselves to the expectations that will win them those dollars. Occasionally, whole projects are funded, but often, only a share is given in exchange for enacting a certain agenda. But for a 25% contribution, or sometimes as low as 10%, state and federal governments or foundations can shift how organizations behave. This applies to towns as readily as to nonprofits, which have more similarities than you would expect. When a town government or a non-profit organization brings in tens or hundreds of thousands of dollars, it's presumed to be a great success.

But there are always strings attached. Section 8 Housing is the perfect example of how these play out. Free money is given for low rent housing, and towns take the deal because they often have a collapsed tax base due to other reasons. They get money for a moment but destroy their community because they almost universally imagine the happy outcomes instead of the realistic ones. It's not crazy to say a community without wealth generators is going to languish, yet we see the mistake made again and again, sometimes from naiveté and other times from cynicism, but always for the money.

In seeking funding from foundations and government programs, I've discovered applicants almost always seek out the most anodyne, politically correct solutions, and will embrace as many buzz words as required to be considered eligible. In many ways, the people involved in the process see this as the most civil and inclusive of societies, and it reflects the sort of liberal consensus that underwrites the whole concept of government grants. It works because 95% of the people seeking these funds, which most commonly end up tracing back to tax revenue shared by everyone, share the same slant. There will always be money to encourage and promote diversity, inclusion, and the false ideal of equality.

One might say such actions are healthy, but what they really mean is the subtle propaganda of the Left is everywhere and becomes social policy. What is good for nonprofits becomes good for schools, for social clubs, and even for churches. Isn't it crazy how many congregations put up signs that run counter to the beliefs of their own Bible just to fit into a community non-profit network?

The presumption on the Right has sometimes been that communities of faith tend to lean their way, whereas the Left controls the secular space. While the latter is true, one of the more disappointing and disturbing things observant individuals will discover is just how often the institutional churches work to enact the leftist agenda. While they may not share the same exact morality, the general tendency toward inclusion in churches as well as the desire for resources is why we often see the very people who destabilize our communities being imported, settled, and sustained by entities like Catholic Charities, who has collected more than $1.6 billion for resettling mostly Muslim refugees

The churches bid for this money to help the needy, even though one could argue these people should not have been brought to a place so foreign and would leave if not sustained by government-subsidized nonprofits. The churches then serve, for a share of taxpayer money, to attempt to integrate them into communities. Given the rising civil unrest, we can see how they are not merely failing in that endeavor, but instead they are functionally hastening the ghettoization of America. Such churches seem to believe the central narrative of the Marxists that anyone can be included if they're a nice person.

What makes this particularly strange is one would think churches would understand the importance of adherence to a set of beliefs in making a strong community. Yet, we see them helping Muslims colonize what were once Christian communities, lapsed in many cases because the desire of the church to be all things to all people proved incompatible with the practical moral inclinations of those who stopped going because they wanted fixed principles.

Why this happened has origins back during the LBJ administration where churches started being punished for taking political sides. The tax exemption required for these houses of worship to be able to legally operate came with many new constraints. These impositions on churches by the state should frankly have been challenged as a violation of the First Amendment's free-exercise clause. But unchallenged, these tax requirements caused churches to retreat into safe causes, which were then defined by the government. The churches were dissuaded from speaking whatever truth they would otherwise profess, which frankly often recognized that bringing in groups whose entire history ran counter to those of the flock would lead to crisis.

Absent that message, the Right has stumbled into a cultural environment where they control neither secular nor sacred cultural spaces, and the Christian churches are in decline along with their membership. Without such a moral bulwark, the Right struggles for answers amid secularism, and while there is still a very large contingent of Christians out there who exist apart from the church and in individual congregations, they have never been more apart from politics. And because of their disengagement from politics, they've found their own interests steadily but deliberately attacked. Furthermore, when they tried to play the nonprofit game with the Left, they've faced unequal barriers to entry.

In the context of the larger battle, this shows how the Left has intelligently set up many of the actors needed to logistically sustain their efforts. A bidding system such as nonprofits use ensures there are multiple entities ready to act to enforce policies, and they serve as an amplifier to project cultural norms. When every organization bids for the same contracts, each organization adopts similar policies. Whether they are sincere or not ceases to matter provided their behaviors follow the financial requirements.

The challenge here is for the Right. To compete, it will need to build a civil society, and frankly, it will struggle to work in the nonprofit sphere. Given the pressures of the economy and obligations of family life, Americans generally struggle to devote time as they might wish outside the home. That's yet another reason the nonprofit model is embraced because it absolves people of the personal responsibility, so essential to a society based on care rather than just formalism, of handling issues within their community. But if we accept that our social problems belong to someone else to handle, that someone else will gain legitimacy.

This cessation of accountability is at the heart of why the Left can tell their favorite lie that the Right doesn't care about people. Because even though the Right pays for so much of what is done, they are the perpetual silent partner who has funded, in the largest part, every movement which has worked against their own interest. Mainly due to a genuine belief in the tolerance of allowing people private choices, such magnanimity has been perverted into funding a system that fosters resentment by teaching the corrupt ideology of the Marxist Left instead of just being charitable aid.

It's clever, and it works because the Left understands the power of collective identity. The Right simply refuses to acknowledge the validity of collective identity. This is a strategic oversight that has exacted costs from the entire culture. The Right feels more comfortable speaking in terms of individualism, rather than considering that aggregate

146

effects and probabilities are sufficient basis for formulating public policy. Though they might consider such restraint to be ethical, the social consequences rise to the level of negligence when this means a person must accept detriments from a group as a whole because some members are better behaved. Yet we all do this, accepting groups we don't want, because there might be one good member.

Optimism, idealism, and decency should be assets to a civilization. Yet, if a person or a group extends these courtesies to someone already committed against their interests, does it not end up the worst sort of naive betrayal? That's what the working men and women of America gave to our elites, and as the academics will show, they have been teaching how terrible the traditional people and idea of America have been for a disturbingly long time.

Chapter 16: Academia—Indoctrination from Cradle to Grave

The Left fully owns education. From pre-school to post-graduate and everything in between, there are almost no public schools or universities that don't teach what is essentially Marxism lite, and the publishing houses who offer support materials almost universally offer the same curriculum. From this, generations of young Americans have left college with an idealistic world view that is self-hating of tradition and authority. That we even have a contest in this nation is a sign of how discordant these ideas are with the reality most people live.

How did it happen? As part of their strategy to remake America, forces from the Left worked first to make education compulsory and obligatory as a state offering. The populists who opened the door to public education went a very long way toward destroying the older model where schooling was the responsibility of either the parents or the church. While these both still exist today, more available in some areas than not, most children uncritically receive whatever the state teaches.

The colleges took a little while longer but starting around the same time in the 1910's and 1920's, there was a deliberate effort from people who espoused Marxist ideas to obtain status, tenure, and chairs within prominent universities. A large variety of well-funded members of Jewish and WASP elite families were well-trained. Espousing communist ideals, they took over the Ivies. The early phases of this process can be traced by documenting who started going to which college and when. But the program really accelerated during FDR and by the time the conservative 1950's had come around, the professors in place and new educators coming up were clearly sympathetic to communist   ideals.

This process was also aided immediately after WWII by the GI Bill. Prior to WWII, America did not have many colleges compared to today. School teachers attended two-year Normal school. People going into trades attended schools that specialized in those trades. Many occupations that might require a college education today, did not require one in the past. Colleges were largely reserved for training academic specialists, the cultural training of elites, scientists and   engineers.

But with the advent of the GI Bill, there was a rush as hundreds   of   schools   that   had   previously   trained seamstresses, nurses, welders or livestock breeders hung out their shingles as newly-declared colleges in order to get a share of that money. These newly declared colleges had an urgent need for professors, thus opening the door to uncritically accept untold thousands of instructors and professors with communist sympathies into their midst.

And this is how academia at large supported the cultural nihilism of the 1960's, which was basically an orgy of destruction waged against everything traditional. Civil society was attacked, churches were marginalized, the family was shattered, and what was left by the time all the drugs had been smoked and bras had been burned was empty chaos. From the perspective of those on the Left, this was the perfect opportunity to fill empty heads with their ideology based on envy and grievance, and to stoke the fires of resentment by playing the angry few against the successful many.

Even though their basic ideology is hateful, the logic the Left can use when their better practitioners step forward is often quite convincing because of their command of the dialectic. They're able to push their ideas largely because they ask hard questions that have leading answers. Anyone skilled in forensics knows the key to winning such debates lies in setting the initial frame, and by taking control of the university system, they have ensured they always have at least one leading voice which will be well attended as these conflicts work toward resolution.

What do they teach? Since their universal truth is singular in that state control and absolute equality are needed for a just society, college today has become a search for potential injustices. As they firmly and fully believe man can be perfected—if only we are subjected to the right pressures—they dedicate their efforts to identifying who is responsible for the subversion which has prevented justice from being realized. The knowing professors direct the resultant angst of students toward traditional authority, saying those who built this system of free markets and liberty, and who built this nation with blood and sweat, must surely be the culprits and they disparage and degrade our past and our present.

Political correctness prevents the leftists from attacking one another, even as the contradictions between a feminist, a gay, and a Muslim, three members of the left, are beyond reconcilable. Instead, they are focused upon their common enemy, usually traditional ideals and the people who end up supporting these—who happen to be overwhelmingly White. That's why professors un-ironically refer to whiteness itself as some sort of crime or aggression, assuming there is some relative value that is better than this supposed absolute Utopian value the Left mythologizes.

White privilege is blamed for nearly all suffering in life. They portray the idea of liberty under natural law as a method of systematizing oppression. They declare that America was stolen from the Natives, and built entirely on the back of migrant labor, whether it was Blacks in the cotton fields or Latinos picking produce. They describe marriage as a system used to enslave women to serve as men's sex dolls and breeders. These statements probably sound absurd to most rational people living in America today, but they represent the core curriculum of social injustice believed and taught by prominent academics today. Given such a starkly negative version of the past, one begins to understand why they are so motivated by hatred.

This hatred is useful for the Left because it induces self-hating college graduates to gladly give power and resources over to the state for redistribution over to the less fortunate classes, with the state always taking their cut and assuming authority to make sure the money is spent justly. In addition, having a potential mob of college students who have more energy than experience ready to express their programmed idealism and fervor at a moment's notice is also useful as means of propaganda and activism. With nothing better to do, and a watered-down curriculum, it doesn't take much for professors to send students out to agitate, especially as they now go so far in some places as allowing time off class for these most useful forms of expression.

The worst thing about the whole cynical process is how much good parents pay to send their children to receive these terrible ideas. Where college used to be at least accessible for those who saved and planned just a bit, thanks to government guarantees for student loans, now anyone can go to college. But because these loans artificially raised demand for college faster than supply, the cost of college has become exorbitant. The reason there isn't more complaining about this is because of the ease with which these loans are obtained, but isn't it terrible that students are receiving a lousy education in exchange for loans will take them potentially upwards of twenty years to repay?

I consider this ample proof of what a screw job higher education has become, where instead of knowledge and asking questions being the center of the system, it's a way to create zealots and debtors who will fund the system until it collapses and have every incentive to break the system toward the revolution they imagine just around the corner.

For those pursuing a degree in hard sciences, things are somewhat better, but less so than you might expect. For instance, take climate change as an example of how dogma has infected science. Where traditional science was a process based upon observation and repetition, always willing to reconsider its conclusions considering dissenting evidence, the current methodology states unequivocally that certain things are settled such as global warming and only a liar and cheat could question these ideas. How can one practice science when the conclusions are foreordained?

It's worth noting in this case that climate change serves as a great reason to justify global redistribution of wealth, taking from the evil rich living in White countries, and giving to the worthy poor living everywhere else. So even science, such as it exists in this world, is set to serve the purpose of that larger agenda of remaking the world.

The mindset of the internationalist idealist versus the national particularist is at the heart of the battle emerging in America today. Where people who lived in this country, working hard, who often lacked access to higher education and instead made their earnings through sweat equity, common sense, and real-world experience; these college graduates who are supposed to be their betters lecture them about how they stole what they thought they had earned, and suppose their purchased education gives them license to steal what others took to rectify these wrongs in accordance with what they had been taught. Reconciling these two positions will not happen.

From this position, having secured all the best credentials and plaudits, the Left uses their command of higher education to write the curriculum for lower education as well. Common Core was their idea, a system where anyone could succeed, and even though it frankly plays to the least common denominator, that was fine because there was justice in allowing everyone to win. This rebellion against the natural order is a great way to transfer power to the selectively aware few, but a dangerously naïve way to run society, reducing the very intellectual capacity of our young folk. To what end is this done? Is it power, where those who would otherwise see through these scams are now discouraged to ask questions?

Such an explanation would fit nicely with the insistence we see not just in America, but throughout the West for the forced integration of foreign invaders who are culturally as well as intellectually incompatible with traditional western society. If we become less, we can be the drones that serve the always present but never spoken dictatorship of the proletariat, and the Left loves people who believe the cause and follow orders. It's why they push the plantation mentality on anyone who will receive their message, and frankly, how they control the minds of many poor people who could achieve more, and smart people who think it a virtue to be less than they could.

They will give sanction to any who seek to undo their own achievement in the culture wars and are the progenitors of the propaganda which defames every action of the Right to stand up for our beliefs. They freely and glibly insult traditional people and ideals, calling us any expletive which might stick, equating every move we make with the worst excesses of history while never exploring the far bloodier actions of the Left in places such as the Soviet Union and

China. These people are here for a purpose, which is to set America against itself, and since 1960 at least, they've succeeded admirably.

These Marxist academics having already done their job, I would only ask how long people on the Right will allow such thinking to poison the minds of our young. At the very minimum, parents owe it to themselves to see what their children are taught. With few exceptions, finding a home school, private school, or charter school is a necessary remedy, but these actions will not be nearly enough unless this educational monopoly is broken.

Until the fight begins, look for the academics to recruit people to the leftist side, galvanizing the most radical elements, and to provide an intellectual foundation to justify what is looking more each day like an impending insurrection. Should they win, thought crime against hate speech will rule the day. They will be appointed as censors and re-educators much as was the case in China.

Should they lose, education reform will quickly be on the table. I suspect their tenure will not keep them in the institutions which they have so tarnished.

Chapter 17: Media—Fake News and Worse

Although the Right has recently started referring to the infamous Fourth Estate of the media as fake news, a term now being used ironically by the other side to silence and marginalize non-establishment sources, the reality is the news has been propaganda for an incredibly long time. Going back to the late 1800's, people who had an agenda realized the most effective way to galvanize mass support was with selective reporting, whose tradition goes back in America to Hearst and even before then.

Two facts are particularly interesting about the current media. The first is that they're corporate owned, where over 90% of major television networks and the vast majority of radio stations and newspapers are owned by just a few conglomerates. Look beyond the editorial pages which echo one another more or less perfectly, and you'll see how these all just reprints mostly the same stories from the Associated Press, UPI, or Reuters. The rest is coupons to sell the fish wrap and crosswords to entertain at work.

This has not always been the case. There was once a requirement in the United States that media entities had to be both locally owned and run by Americans, as well as other prohibitions that prevented a single entity from owning multiple outlets within the same broadcast market. With these regulations erased in 1996, the deregulation of the media led to the rise of conglomerates such as the ubiquitous Clear Channel network. What's most interesting, and perhaps telling, is that even though many of these networks lose money, there is never any shortage of buyers who want papers and stations of record.

It's worth considering the Washington Post in this light. Jeff Bezos, who owns Amazon, and whose tastes clearly lean Left considering their whole business model is reliant upon an invisible taxpayer subsidy granted in the form of postage rates literally below cost, purchased this paper to protect his interests. The obvious result is there will never be a story criticizing Amazon for how their work conditions are akin to the Third World with people being written up for having to use the restroom. Less obvious are the editorials which may slant certain directions but will never harm the corporate interests of Bezos' vast and growing holdings. The rich purchase media to shape opinion, not just by lies, but by lies of omission which are far cleverer and more dangerous.

A more troubling fact is that media is now explicitly allowed to propagandize the American people. While media has always been a part of foreign relations, with the Voice of America programming being sent into Warsaw Pact countries during the Cold War with the intent to shape opinions and destabilize that alliance, there had been legal restraints against propagandizing our own people. In 2013, Obama lifted the last of these restraints, and now there is nothing in place to prevent either the government or private press from brazenly manipulating the American people, which perhaps explains in part why the press fawned over him so readily. Not that they ever fail to do so with a leftist, covering up their failures and falsely exaggerating their successes, but with the repeal of restrictions on deliberately manipulating the public in 2013, government was getting into the game as its own propagandist.

Thinking about it more clearly, we've seen a great many more anonymous sources, and the last few years have revealed just how often the Deep State has taken an almost overt interest in shaping the American media narrative. The CIA especially has always made sure to protect itself in the media, but the sorts of operations we've seen under Brennan are much more akin to the color revolutions they launched in other countries than what Americans have traditionally experienced. Judging by how far the Left has radicalized in these last few months, those efforts have borne fruit.

With the current media, we can see clear patterns emerging to promote a leftist position. These are not new, but they are more vigorous than ever before. Any time a Republican comes to power, they are presented uniformly as either evil, stupid, or both. Nixon was calculating, Reagan was an idiot, the Bushes were evil, then stupid, then evil again. And now Trump is a witless moron despite having built a billion-dollar business and having unseated a man whose chief accomplishment was to be a community organizer. Such ideas are clearly absurd to a thinking man, and yet, people fall for them because of the desire of people who wish they were smarter than they really are to believe and parrot what they read.

Consider the case of someone of average to slightly above average intelligence who lives in an intellectual milieu where conveying the impression of smartness matters greatly, like most urban environments at least pretend to be. Being able to recite and agree with the latest story from the New York Times and to adhere to the expected opinions and mores is essential to fitting in and perhaps even impressing those around you. These people do not take the time to understand issues, but rather look for filters they are told they can trust—as evidenced by those around them—and use those as suppliers for their own beliefs. So, our good cosmopolitan listens to NPR, a propaganda outfit, watches MSNBC, and reads the Times. They absorb that information, and from that, deliver a world view. The problem is, at minimum, they miss half the story, and in my opinion, they're now basing their worldview around lies.

They would say the same about the Right, and perhaps there is some truth in that claim. If one watches Fox News, listens to AM talk radio, and reads Info Wars, their opinion of what is happening in America will tend to converge with what information from those sources would predict. My own biases being what they are, I tend to believe these latter sources more, but importantly, it is critical for a person never to love any one source enough to assume they tell complete truth, or even can reach such a pinnacle. It is in receiving a diversity of opinions that we develop a more complete picture of what is happening, and frankly, much of the best coverage of what happens in America comes from foreign news sources, who certainly have their own agendas which tend toward the blatant when it comes to their respective host nations, but whose reserve allows a certain honesty Americans struggle to muster about ourselves especially on sensitive issues.

But the media, especially for those who follow more traditional forms such as television and print media, leans almost 90% toward the progressives, working a network of Deep State sources and biased academics to serve the cause of the Left, working always to attack "injustice." The same social double standards we've talked about elsewhere apply here to the extent that a liberal can lie and sleep around to write stories without anything more than a stern admonition, but someone writing a story which harms the Left will find themselves in need of a new career very quickly. There are some exceptions, but these are rare.

Still, there is an emergent right-wing media as well, as the market opportunity for half the country to be serviced by more than 10% of the programming has drawn some attention. It was no accident that for well over a decade, Fox News was the demographics winner by far, and the careers of talk figures like Rush Limbaugh have been legendary and lengthy. But these footholds have expanded into a new realm of citizen journalism, where people go out with blogs and webcams and record the world as it happens, and they represent a novel and freshly needed take.

It should be a golden age for new media, where we get direct sources and interviews, but this too is in danger. The big corporations who control social media, a distribution network vital to putting out new media content and letting people decide for themselves what is real and what is fake, is seeking every method of censorship available. Whether using third party censors like the SPLC and ADL, notorious left-wing groups, or fact-checkers like Snopes, another biased outfit, they hope to use labels to push people back into their preferred narrative. Where that doesn't work, they use computer algorithms to ensure certain stories and figures don't get as much promotion, even going so far as to selectively demonetize content producers based on ideological position, or to directly ban people for nebulously defined offenses, as has recently become policy on both Twitter and YouTube.

The Left doesn't play fair, but their moves toward censorship are not without cost. While normal Americans are only slightly aware of these battles, these challenges are forcing the Right to become more robust due to at creating truly alternative networks for distribution. In the coming years, you will see a new ecosphere emerge online to cleave the two sides once and for all. The Left will be the respectable legacy media who censors away so-called hate speech, or what a rational person might call dissent. By contrast, the Right will have more freewheeling forums that might offend but will also allow dialogue and dissenting voices to conflict. I suspect people will prefer the liberty of the latter model, and with the cost of information being only a few clicks and keystrokes, the old media apparatus will become increasingly ineffective as it lumbers about in this new world.

Until it does, however, and especially with an eye to older people who tend to get their news less digitally, we can expect the media to push the unrest to a fever pitch as they work in concert with their friends in Langley and elsewhere to destabilize and delegitimize the existing administration. Having lost power unexpectedly in 2016, they will be vicious in seeking to rise to the top again and will not allow the freedom of action we enjoyed just a few short years ago to present our counter narrative. Their so-called resistance shows no scruples about silencing disagreeing voices, first by shutting off the media, but secondly by punching people in the face. Why do you think the media never decries Antifa, even as they show up in thousands, often paid, to attack protesters who go through meticulous procedures to secure permits to be heard in public spaces?

The media has never been a friend to America. It has led us into wars against our interest and has served the interests of those who own it far better than the desires of the American people or anything resembling our traditional system. For those curious about the history of who has controlled the media and why, I strongly encourage readers to start with how the newspapers were bought out by people with a collective pro-Marxist slant around the turn of the last century and see what other commonalities you find. Pattern recognition is a true sign of intelligence, and if you need some hints, start with my previous volume <u>Someone Has to Say It: The Hidden History of How America was Lost.</u> The media was the first piece of the plan to unmake the constitutional republic and remains the heart of that effort today.

Taken in concert with the nonprofits providing boots on the ground, and the academics who rationalize the words of the left, the media completes the triumvirate by which the Left dominates culture in America. They ruthlessly police their prerogative and having little penetration in these areas is why even though the Right dominates elected government, hinting a widely divergent national private opinion, there is a steady drumbeat propagandizing our people leftwards always, making strife much more likely now.

Section II: The Players

Group IV: The Parties

Where both major political parties once worked to reflect a national consensus, driven as much by donors and institutional actors as those of the American people, this arrangement marginalized the seeming balance of the parties against the genuine beliefs of their partisans who are now taking control with highly antagonistic viewpoints.

On the Right, the Republicans struggled for years on a nominal basis of supporting certain social and cultural views but were unwilling to fully engage these battles due to economic contradictions as well as not wanting to face a hostile media. As such, people right of center have watched the GOP spend decades losing a cultural war with the destruction of traditional heritage, ideals, and institutions accelerating. Facing such destruction, the Right backed Trump to preserve their identity, their power, and is now for the first time in recent American history, seeking to use government to enforce their ideals.

The Left had long used government to facilitate a similar purpose, being afforded the luxury of acting at a relaxed pace due to having no functional opposition in the culture war, but recent defeats have heavily radicalized the coalition that made up the Democrat Party. Used to success and fed a steady diet of reinforcement from allies in media and academia, the factions which make up the Democrats, but the Left more generally, are being activated together now in sheer opposition to the desire of traditional Americans to restore their values and identity.

Radicals within the system are becoming more prominent as pressure grows.

At heart of the conflict is the disappearance of a constructed ideal which satisfied partisans of neither faction, and two competing visions of the future. The Republicans serve as surrogates for a particularist or nationalist objective view that has a positive view of history and authority. The Democrats represent the globalist subjective view that is idealistic and sees most history and authority as oppressive. Between two such diametrically opposed views, forced together in the same political and real space, opportunities for convergence dwindle and tensions heighten.

Chapter 18: Republicans—The Stupid Party

There's an old joke that floats around suggesting the Democrats are the evil party and the Republicans are the stupid party. Often shared by conservatives and people to their right, the reason the joke endures is because while the Democrats relentlessly move America to the Left when in power, the Republicans often struggle to effectively harness power when they take office. In this contradiction, we find the reasons why the GOP has struggled to have the impact culturally they could have in the preceding decades and why despite considerable electoral success, the party has been easily occupied by the rising nationalists.

It's worth noting that as late as the 1990's, the two-party system was not reliably an indicator for the affiliations of ideologically partisan. Up until the 1990's, older divisions went back to desegregation and economic policy before LBJ. In these divisions, the Republicans were broadly the party of the Northeast and the West Coast, and the Democrats had the solid South with the Midwest usually serving as the battleground. As regional divisions began to give way to ideological concerns, the map shifted rapidly. The Blue Dog Democrats of representing the South became the Republicans of today, and the old Rockefeller Republicans were no longer the primary adherents of the GOP. Instead the GOP's primary constituency became a combination of conservatives, Christians, and whoever else couldn't support the Democrats.

You could look to people like Lee Atwater, Roger Stone, Paul Manafort, and Ralph Reed as the creators of this new version of the Republican Party, which represented the Bush years coalition of those who wanted small government, theoretically, and to speak for traditional values. As this became the ideological message, and even more in response to the progressive ideas of social justice that infected the Democrat party, the polarization at the heart of the country on culture rather than region became more pronounced.

This model might have proven successful and enduring, except for a bad compromise the GOP made to win their elections. Although the party presented itself as a moral force and was willing to do so on certain social issues like abortion and guns, the free market forces who funded the party undercut its efforts to exist on a cultural basis because of their love of new markets, cheap labor, and job outsourcing. It was those economic realities which were pushed by the elites who donated to both parties which led to agreements like NAFTA, GATT (General Agreement on Trade and Tariffs) and all the other disruptive economic plans that basically shifted economics from a national concern to a global concern.

For instance, having millions of Mexicans move into the United States in successive waves changed the southwest entirely. While these lands were nominally once part of Mexico, they were also chosen for annexation by President Polk because they were the emptiest parts of those holdings, with the quite deliberate idea that two different cultures existed between the U.S. and Mexico. Once NAFTA passed,

Mexicans and other Latinos came flooding into American for two reasons. The first was for the higher paying jobs both at the border and across it, now facilitated by dropping the tariff wall, at the cost of manufacturers all throughout the Midwest. But the second which is not so well understood but perhaps even more important, was the impact dumping our cheap and heavily subsidized corn had on Mexico's traditional agriculture sector. Likewise, NAFTA allowed international agricultural conglomerates into Mexico, where they drilled deep wells that emptied the water table used by the native farmers who could not afford to drill ever-deeper wells. Millions of people lost their jobs in the Mayan regions, and so they were forced to move to survive.

This, as we've now seen demonstrated again and again, is the legacy of free market adventurism which globalists love to support. Borders are treated as arbitrary and people are interchangeable actors who serve only to provide economic stimulus. In fact, many take the radically libertarian position which is culturally amoral, thinking that the homogenization of people is a net good because it increases the wealth of the whole and gives opportunity to the least fortunate to improve their economic status. There is evidence that once a nation survives the exploitation/colony period, they can rise, but all that wealth must come from somewhere, and by and large, it came from depressing much of the United States production economy. The Rust Belt is the most famous example, but it is by no means the only one.

Why this all matters is because the Republicans basically chose to take the campaign money of globalists instead of honestly fighting the culture war, and the Christians have as much a role to play in this as the swindlers. The kindness and generosity of Christians is among their most admirable virtues, but this comes with the remarkable tendency as a global religion (which, as opposed to Islam, generally does not seek to persuade by force) possesses such a degree of hopefulness and optimism that it can border on the suicidal.

Christians look at individuals as people needing to be saved, and as universalists, often, see new people coming to America as a chance to spread the Gospel anew. Believing firmly in their message that the end is nearly upon us, or in the simple righteousness of their mission, American Christians have mostly bought into the idea that America can act internationally for the good of all.

Christians in the Republican base were strongly influenced by these two trends. Meanwhile, the Chamber of Commerce, large corporations, moralists who encouraged a tolerant attitude of indifference toward using government, and opportunistic neoconservative internationalists presented overseas wars at just the right times to distract a grieving nation. This led the Republicans down a most unhelpful path. The cultural battles talked about through all the 80's and 90's were neither fought nor won at home, but instead our wealth, manpower, and even our strongest impulses to share ideas were in many ways sent outside our borders. We were told to be tolerant and accepting again and again, while the Left was telling their cultural forces to take more cultural territory here at home.

A rough equilibrium in the slow building culture war was probably reached sometime in the 1990's, but that only marked a way point in a growing conflict. Why wouldn't it? The Right's desire to avoid conflict and to admit their essential wrongs to seek balance and peace encouraged the Left to further assert dominance. The culture war started purportedly for civil rights and tolerance, which is commonly asserted but not necessarily true. As the current situation illustrates, the culture war instead became a campaign to claim "justice," only able to be satisfied with those who had traditionally enjoyed success in this country surrendering all their power and resources to the newly ascending classes who were motivated by resentment, envy, and hatred.

In a nutshell, this is the crisis of the West. People who are tolerant, who have things and are willing to share them out of a sense of magnanimity, open their doors to less fortunate outsiders with the best of intentions. Their expectation is that their generosity and graciousness will be appreciated, and the invited person will choose to conform to their beliefs to enjoy such blessings. What happens is quite the opposite: People who have been without throughout their lives for various reasons see such wealth and splendor, and instead of receiving the message of how to earn this for themselves, they instead listen to those who tell them how to take what was never theirs, but which they are told was stolen or unjustly appropriated. Whether it is an invasive religion or ideology, it makes no difference, because the Left always knew it was easier to tell people to take what they wanted rather than earn it as part of a common culture or nation. This has always been their strategy for taking power, and it has frequently succeeded.

By contrast, the forces of the Right never understood this, because they didn't want to see that their culture was fading. The signs were everywhere to be seen, in how the media always pushed the envelope, how the scholars always leaned left, in popular music and how popular culture erased higher aspirations. The new migrants who arrived by the millions were bringing new ways of life, often diametrically opposed to our own. And the radicalized poor, many of whose sub-optimal conditions were exacerbated by the globalized free market actions for which the Right was more than equally responsible, joined together in common cause against a wealthy elite they now saw as having exploited them. As these ideas slid into place right under the noses of an inattentive Right, they were irrevocably labeled as an enemy by many people, and we see today the bitter fruit of the Left's resentment, not just in the angry minorities and out-groups, but generations of young entitled white people who bought into the Left's narrative sufficiently to work against their own interest.

The Republican Party reflected these efforts to respond to a changing world in a very principled way in terms of what happened policy wise. What this led to were wars to kindle patriotism, but which were only of dubious benefit, if any, to the average American. In truth, our many interventions probably only exacerbate global migration patterns, increased terrorism, and further depleted our Treasury.   But from the cultural side, the position the Republicans took of being the party that would try to educate people about the issues was catastrophic compared to the Democrats who instead motivated people through envy, fear and hatred.

The Right had messaged inner cities for decades that opportunity could be theirs, and the messages seemed true because they were coupled with race-based policies that basically offered bribes to create pre-ordained outcomes. These policies requiring hard work proved unappealing save to a select few, forever held up as shining examples. But 90% of the people chose instead to align themselves with the Leftist opposition that promised easy solutions.   By the 1990's it had been obvious to people willing to make sincere observations about politics that most immigrants were not assimilating.   In addition, home grown minorities and discontents, were radicalizing.   Pat Buchanan loudly rang the alarm in 1992, with Ross Perot and others to follow, but the GOP did not want to have to say anything to offend any group they hoped to eventually win, and so they relented to what would become the politically correct language that has become so widespread today.

Giving the other side the ability to control language was a monumental mistake, because when they allowed the Left to be the singular arbiter of justice, decency, and even certain aspects of legality, they moved with admirable decisiveness to enforce their dogma.   White privilege, microaggressions, safe spaces, and non-binary gender all are examples of ideas that come from a much simpler theory: Deprive your opponent of legitimacy and space to operate and you win.

This explains how the Republicans behaved under Obama. Despite clear and repeating waves of the American majority rising like the Tea Party to shout that they did not want socialism, that they did not want a fundamental transformation of America, all the Republican Party could do with control of successive Congresses was nothing. Their campaign donors wouldn't let them escape the global free markets that kept bringing in new Democrats, and their own greed played no small part in their willingness to ignore the very people who sent them to Congress. As a result, the energy of the Republican base dissipated, Obama got re-elected, and while baseline Republicans and fleeting demographic advantages permitted retention of the House, the GOP essentially failed as a national party.

Interestingly and perhaps usefully, because the top-level players in the Republican Party were either too compromised, corrupt, or just ineffectual, state and local efforts improved. Unable to make things work at the higher level, some of the most effective activists worked to take over State Houses and Governorships, and here, there were the glimmers of a more vital defense. There were still holes in their intellectual arguments, but at least the energy found some expression to stand, in contrast to the media messaging that Leftist change is good and anything old is automatically bad.

America had been ready for something different for a long time. But no one ever expected that Donald Trump would be the harbinger of the culture war that had been brewing for decades. A New York moderate on many social issues, Trump understood something far more fundamental that allowed him to shoot past established politicians like trained ponies. Americans were sick of an unfair system where good people were being told they were the problem, where all they once believed was good and just was said to oppressive, and of smarmy elites telling them what was best. The system was ripe for a turn around after decades of seeing hostile Democrats and useless Republicans, and so the silent majority roared to a huge upset victory and with it. And that victory came with certain expectations.

America First means a lot to the Right. It starts with the understanding that for America to remain a successful country, we need a single culture. We do not have that, and despite efforts by civic nationalists to substitute symbols for common ideas, we will have to fight to impose that or divide along cultural lines to some unforeseen end. America First means keeping jobs at home and only making international agreements to the benefit Americans, not as part of some global project. Most people on the Right spent the last thirty years trying to engage the world, and we've realized they aren't like us, don't like us, and don't belong with us. Other than their willingness to take what we are foolish enough to offer, I think that even many immigrants would admit the same.

The Republican Party, most crucially, is now becoming a particularist party. Instead of the old game of trying to be all things to all people, it has admitted the essential reality in government that if you're not winning, you're often losing. It will no longer compromise indefinitely to enable what the Left has been pushing, but instead will increasingly articulate a vision for this nation as unique and exceptional, rooted in our past, and seeking guidance from our traditions even though they have lapsed in many respects.

This transformation is by no means complete, but as politicians observe the success Trump is having, as they see people embrace the strength and clarity of always putting the country first instead of trying to compromise to fit a predesignated ideology, the Republican Party is quickly shifting to match suit, with old politicians finding retirement the best option, and new energy rising through the ranks. As they meet greater success, what will inevitably develop is the same as any other sane party: a group that represents the interests of its constituent members, which for the GOP are basically those who want America to be the way they perceive it used to be.

Look for such understanding as the least common denominator to push the culture war to new heights. Now that Republicans are playing for keeps by the same zero sum rules the Democrats adopted decades ago, when they take power, their ideas will be pressed into law. Abortion will be made illegal, marriage will be between a man and a woman once more, Christianity will no longer be discarded, and gun rights will be protected. All the energy that has been repressed for thirty years will be expressed through Congress, the Supreme Court, and State Houses, and will, as is already happening, utterly infuriate the Left.

Because these leftists live in their own cloisters, they don't understand that the project they pushed to remake the American people was never a popular effort. It had areas where it was widely accepted, like the college towns and big cities where government always set the rules out of necessity, but the vast stretches of the heartland and anyplace more than 50 miles from a major city never went for any of these ideas. They just didn't have anyone to fight for them. Now, they do, and having had that taste of victory, the Right isn't about to relent.

The Republican Party will be forced to work in this direction. If they refuse to do so, they will be replaced. The other thing any long time GOP voter will commonly say is they're conservative, rather than Republican, because they don't trust their party. To the Right, ideals have always mattered, and that remains true today. That's why it took so long to organize and will take longer still, but the one and perhaps only thing that could make this happen has come to pass: The fear of what the Left intends.

Chapter 19: Democrats—The Evil Party

The institutional Democrat Party, in many ways, is struggling with the same forces pushing power out to the more radical positions, because of their current and sudden inability to deliver electoral results. As a centralizing party, their practice over the last few decades has been to work hand in hand with the massive bureaucracy and the friendly bastions of academia and the media to promote a gradual transition toward the society the Left prefers. A less kindly but more apt description might be to call what they pushed as the sterilization of the Right, with strategies designed to change the voting demographics to their permanent favor and minimize the influence of the Right through social mechanisms designed to compel silence.

The system was working like a charm, to be honest, so long as the message delivered was about hope and change and never too explicit about at whose expense this new society would be created. With telegenic speakers like Bill Clinton and Barack Obama asking for nothing, promising everything, and eschewing radicalism for a deliberately constructed idealistic version of what was possible, this brand of hope sold far more effectively than the self-defeating globalist free market ideology crippling the cultural Right. And the Democrats were rewarded with successive Presidencies as well as success in controlling the Congress as often as not until at least 2010.

As with the Republicans, the current Democrat coalition grew out of strange circumstances and was a radical transformation from what we saw around 1960. Before Kennedy, the primary political conflict in the nation in many ways remained between the North and the South, with divisions dating back to at least the Civil War never having been fully resolved. As Lincoln had been a Republican, the South had remained solidly Democrat in solidarity against the hated Yankees, and that generational hate lasted more than a century, which kept the South in the Democrat camp far longer than ideology would have predicted.

It was only when Presidents like Kennedy and Johnson followed up Eisenhower's efforts toward desegregation that the Southern Democrats began to disassemble. The orderly way of life in the South had been thoroughly upset. The Democrats, in their decision starting with LBJ to embrace race as social justice more so than economics, choosing the facile but reliable resentments of cultural Marxism upon which to build their party rather than the old economic model of FDR, left the Southerners as men without a party, and as nature abhors a vacuum, the Republicans figured out a way to flip the South.

As this happened, the Democrats went further along the trail to the left, seeing the old centrist model as being less effective, and instead mapping out a path to ultimate victory. As had begun in 1965 with the passage of the Hart-Celler Act, millions of foreigners were being admitted legally through Third World countries. Even more were able to get in through chain migration, whereby having one family member as an American citizen can be used to expedite others into the nation.

As many people were able to come in this way, the Democrats found even more support could be had by embracing illegal immigrants, seeking amnesty for farm workers in wave after wave, so many that California turned from a once solid Republican state to a Democrat stronghold by the 1990's. Seeing these trends and being race realists themselves, the Democrats made the decision at some point around 1992 to fully embrace the international flavor, and they would become the party of the outsider.

Betraying their longstanding union base throughout the Midwest, their desire for new voters to push their core ideology of centralizing power and forced redistribution, Clinton created all those broken factories in hopes that a generation later, a changed America might usher in a permanent Democrat majority. Racial grievances by minorities and immigrants against a common culture were permitted and even stoked as time went by, and the united nation was sacrificed for political gain and for ideology.

It's worth noting a major difference between the Left and Right politically here, which is that collectivism lends itself very easily to universalism. If your understanding of politics is as a process to transform men into a certain desired outcome, then it matters far less what a man believes coming into your party than your ability to push them into believing what you want them to take away. Whereas the Right is always trying to defend particular ideas, and often fights with itself regarding the best way to accomplish an end, the Left seems more capable of working in unity toward a common trajectory, even if there are disagreements, and with contradictory factions united in common cause.

The rhetoric of the Left and Democrats is usually toward the amorphous phrase social justice. The reality usually equates to taking power or wealth from the dominant social group and giving it to people who are on the outside. Their definition of justice is such that power itself is the primary concern, and without the sort of questions the Right would obsess over about who deserves power or who would most wisely exercise control, the Left instead uses a strategy of equalizing power to those who are the most despondent or disaffected in society, believing this redress will lead to better outcomes.

Within this ideological framework, it would be considered inappropriate, ignorant, or supremacist to ask why certain groups or ideas are more successful than others. Taken to an illogical extreme, this leads nature, truth and reason themselves to be called hate speech, and hints at how you can have studies published that put forth a gender studies interpretation of Antarctic Ice Melt. Such research exists, and it shows how far gone the extreme Left is in their thinking, but more importantly, it reveals another of the divisions we can't bridge.

Although the Left is universalist, they're subjectivists. They are willing to concede whatever version of reality you desire to you, so long as you allow others to exist at an equal level. I have no doubt most people on the Left understand the concept that any numbered genders beyond two are silly, but if allowing someone their charade for a little while makes them happy and gets an ally, it is a small price to pay. Besides, they dislike, perhaps as their heritage of the nihilism of the Baby Boomer generation in serving as the ultimate iconoclasts, being told what they are supposed to believe. Such permissiveness has allowed them to bring together many competing groups, but to keep them motivated, they needed a common threat and enemy.

Believers in objective reality lean Right far more often than not and make the perfect foil. As the Right tends to believe that there is one reality and one set of rules that should apply to everyone, this comes out support of law and order. The Left, seeing authority as valuable to social construction, perpetually stokes resentment against these rules. The presumption that there is a singular experience of reality irritates the Left to no end, and it is how they keep their culture warriors ready to fight. They must be ready to oppose the assumptions placed upon them, and with a lifetime of angst and anxiety girding their discontents, these people are primed for battle.

For many years, the Democrats have been able to keep them under relative control by pushing a more measured agenda by constantly moving in one direction. As America embraced political correctness, they felt they were taking charge of the country. Within the urban enclaves and college campuses, the Left surely has already succeeded, making policies to protect any group they so choose and removing all traces of the patriarchy, including so many of the statues that serve as flash points as they did in

Charlottesville. They assumed the future was theirs and saw the race blind, need conscious, government run gentle future as desirable and inevitable.

Then, it wasn't. While the Democrats knew the Republicans would occasionally gain power, they trusted the courts to legislate victories for them, and did not anticipate any major reversals to the cultural gains being made. They watched the Republican party fritter away majority after majority, accomplishing little save wars which built up a police state and an ever-larger Federal bureaucracy which the Democrats could use to their own ends even more easily, and assumed that was all they could do. But on the way to a new world order, the nationalists revolted and those who were said to be disappearing quietly into history suddenly came back with a vengeance.

It turns out the penetration by the Left was as wide as a veneer, but only deep in a few places. Many Americans still believed in the Constitution, and merit instead of resentment. A few had even gone so far as to look at the same obvious facts upon which the Democrats had been quite obviously acting for many years, and started pointing out the reason they supported bringing in people from outside might not be because immigrants were great, and more diversity means more viewpoints to share, but because people who were going to be at the lower end of the economic status and were minority overwhelmingly vote Democrat.

Sane people said these things. Pissed off young people who weren't as constrained also said the same things, often with dark humor and angst about a future where they saw the likelihood they would be the second-class citizens under the Democrats' scheme. Once libertarians and optimists, this was the impetus behind the rise of the far right, people who realized they were always being set up to be the fall guy as the counter culture shifted strangely toward traditionalism and prudence. Through biting sarcasm, now not permitted to the Left which once owned humor, it was the Right that began to be able to poke fun at the other side and offered a threatening appeal to the young.

Such resistance could only be explained by the Left as the worst forces of racism, bigotry, and the greatest of all evils: Nazism. So, they upped their pogrom against those on the Right, painting with a broad brush, and described all who opposed their efforts to remake America as basically evil. They started with a few extreme targets, but with their anger stoked and their fury rising, accelerated by this unknown sensation that policies could move against their wishes, their tantrums have gone in many different directions of activism and calumny.

Even before Trump got elected, we saw the model of using activism and mass mobilization to intimidate society into compliance taking root. Think of the Black Lives Matter marches and how cops ended up shot. I wonder who paid for those, for the millions of activists, and how they had such time to gather. Or think of the Million Woman March to protest supposed constraints against feminism, in which women wore hats supposed to represent pussies on their heads. A strange fetish if you ask me, but an indisputable move toward thinking direct action was the way to seize power.

With the loss of Hillary Clinton, who the Left was promised would win by their allies in the media, they felt the country has been stolen. Today's perpetual news cycle that whips up resentment on every action taken by Trump, where the popular vote is always listed, and where no good news is ever reported, only further encourages their anger to manifest into something more dangerous.

This is no accident, and it's worth noting, that in many ways, the Democrats may be losing control of their party. While the Left is winning the culture war, the Democrat Party whipped up resentment to maintain a governing majority, but they did not govern as extremely as their partisans would like. So long as they delivered success, such arrangements were tolerable. But now, we see the splintering of the progressive faction, who wants the express lane to communism, beginning to take control.

I firmly believe Hillary would have won if she wasn't white. I say this because in the modern-day Democrat party, they have become a coalition of identity groups, and after Obama, blacks who vote 90% for Democrats, were not going to be content with not being at the top of the ticket. They still voted overwhelmingly for Hillary versus Trump, but did you notice how many fewer turned out—in places like Flint, MI and Milwaukee, WI? And therein lies the problem for the Left: their constituent groups are in danger of radicalizing to the point where the Democrat big tent falls apart.

The only way they can solve this problem and refocus as a party is to give more say to the minority groups in running the party and focus on the three areas on which all members of their coalition can agree. These are that big government is good, the Right is bad, and fighting them is the most important thing they can do. Since their intransigence has painted them into being the resistance party now against resurgent nationalism, we already see the hints of how they've romanticized their struggle into a war for justice.

This would be bad enough, but thanks to their allies in the media and many local governments, violent actions they have taken directly have gone unchecked, and this is unlikely to change. In addition, the Democrat Party, not wanting to alienate their most vigorous activists, has never criticized their left flank, even when it engages in illegal acts and violence. By contrast, the GOP delights in passing judgment against those on the far right they deem too extreme, even if only in terms of rhetoric, and this difference matters because the Left will follow the path of whomever delivers results. Even symbolic victories in the streets, such as a group like Antifa claims, will be praised if the Republicans can't do anything with their majority.

The longer this situation persists, the more the Democrats will pull hard left. And given how such radicalization forces a binary choice, it's likely we will see a stable Republican governing majority emerge for at least a few years. Current demographics and regional affiliations will lead to a more radicalized Left that exists partly outside the Democrat Party while taking over substantial parts of it. Given their dissatisfaction with a near-term Republican majority, this will manifest in separatist impulses.

From my perspective as someone knee deep in these conflicts, millions of people are expressing separatist views already. This happens more openly on the Left than the Right, for several reasons. But it is quite certain these contradictory visions of America cannot coexist under the current system. How we resolve those differences is an awful question that must soon be answered, for if no consensus emerges, how long can it be before someone decides to try to force their own solution?

Given their tendency toward universal solutions, the radicalism rising on the Left, the fact that the Right is currently in power, and the nonstop media shilling toward anger and resentment, there's reason to expect the Left might decide to strike the first blows. With their cultural monopoly potentially at risk through either regulation or a successful form of civic nationalism, and their many allies in the Deep State steadfastly opposed to backing away from globalist competition to a position of nationalist protectionism, the stage is set.

The Democrats will do what they can to keep control, giving away power to their own radicals to hold their party together. In so doing, they will alienate the center of their own party like the #WalkAway movement has begun to reveal. But meanwhile this circumstance will push their most passionate believers who dominate primaries into offering more radical selections of candidate. Just as with

Tea Party candidates in 2010, these people will lose as the apolitical mass in the center are frightened away, but I suspect strongly the lesson they'll take is that the voting system cannot deliver justice, so they will seek another method to impose their will.

Such would be a huge strategic blunder since through sheer demography the Left is on the precipice of the unbeatable majority which they have been striving to achieve, but the Right is starting to realize this, and it is no accident you see not just Trump, but many on the Right inviting such overreach by the Left. Why we would go so far is simple: We don't want the same America anymore. That's true for partisans on both sides.

While the squish, which is what I call the 60-80% of Americans who are mostly apolitical, who think this process is just voting in elections, probably don't want these fights, they will not be able to avoid the coming maelstrom. With millions of angry partisans on both sides and a system which has been transformed into essentially winner-takes-all where views are imposed upon the losing faction, America has too many divisions to hold together through the sorts of conflicts already beginning.

Democrats and Republicans alike choose to pretend this isn't happening, but the Left certainly knows better and they're already organizing in groups for dark days ahead.

Section III: Divisions

Introduction

To imagine how civil conflict might proceed—whether through political combat, low scale intermittent political violence, or a full breakdown scenario—the hardest thing to assess would be the opponents. At the very minimum, this book assumes people will be motivated to seek security, to meet their basic material needs, and are most likely to do so with people with whom they share common purpose or identity. While scenarios exist where the breakdown is so granular that control devolves to individual towns and neighborhoods, this book assumes there will be broader groupings that form either upwards from this, or which hold together from the onset based upon certain key shared characteristics.

For ease of reference, these are called the Color Wars in this book, where each potential side of the major conflicts in America is assigned a color, and the two or more sides mobilized on that basis are considered. Four major divisions are profiled in depth with other peripheral divisions also being profiled as less probable fault lines. The four this book highlights as primary are: Ideology, Residency, Race, and Culture. Each side has factions who line up along Right and Left lines, and the basic theory here is that once one conflict is engaged, the overlaps in identity and affiliation will pull people into one camp or another. Included in this section will be maps that show the considerable geographic overlap of many of these. Consult the following chart to identify faction by color and/or side.

Chart 1

	Left	Attribute	Right	
BLUE	Democrat	**Ideology**	Republican	RED
GRAY	Urban	**Residency**	Rural	GREEN
BLACK	Black	**Race**	White	WHITE
BROWN	Latino	**Race**		
YELLOW	Asian	**Race**		
PURPLE	Progressive	**Culture**	Traditional	PINK
	International/ Globalist	**Nationalism**	Nationalist	
	Atheist/Islam /Jewish	**Religiosity**	Christian/ Pagan	
	Artificial/ Embracing	**Technology**	Naturalist/ Skeptic	

Worth noting is that these categories are not absolutes, but rather the expression of tendencies based upon voting habits, lifestyle choices, migration patterns, and aspects of shared identity that transcend these categories. Some groups affiliate more strongly than others, and there are groups, such as suburbanites which I profile who are sufficiently divided that they could conceivably go either way, depending upon circumstances, which will be discussed herein.

Section III: Divisions

Group I: Ideology

The first division in America to be profiled is the split between the Left and the Right, represented sometimes by partisan affiliation between Democrats and Republicans as a means of showing a broader trend. Forces of the Left are those who broadly believe in larger and more involved government, progressive ideology, subjective morality, and who tend to be more forward looking. Forces of the Right, by contrast, tend to favor smaller and less involved government, conservative ideology, objective morality, and care more for history and heritage.

We see this argument act out and accelerate through our political process, and the hyper partisan identification of each party as evidence of the irreconcilable split. Here in 2018, multiple polling agencies report for the first time in their recording history which stretches back about twenty years, majorities in both parties report they feel unsafe when the opposition is in power. While there has always been mistrust of the other side, these surveys offer one more hint to substantiate the theory that this anger is not just hot, but increasingly deep.

Since politics is arguably doing more than any other endeavor to heighten the anger, tension, and growing hatred between the two sides, this is where we start. Ideology represents what might be the most likely battle lines as conflict accelerates. The inability of the two sides to find a workable consensus given their diametrically opposed view points and relative parity in numbers ensures these conflicts will not soon be resolved and are most likely to flare further.

190

To give context to these discussions in a geographical and historical basis, two maps are included below.   The first is of the 2016 Presidential Election results by county, which shows that America leans Republican geographically, and the densest populated areas are heavily Democrat.   The second is a map from 1996 showing the results from that year, highlighting who has been changing their voting habits, which will also substantiate the connections between these categories as theorized in the sectional introduction.

Since these maps will print in black and white in the print edition,   I   will   host   original   copies   of   these   at http://www.nationalright.us/demographics for your reference to see them in full color for additional clarity.   These maps are sourced from Wikipedia.com.

Map 1

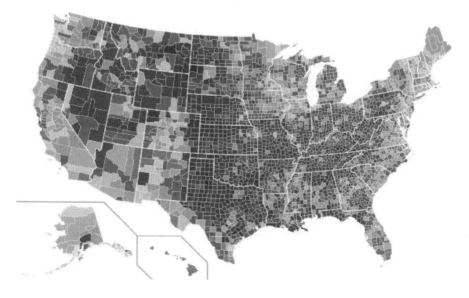

Map 1, representing the results of the 2016 election shows broad swaths of red from Appalachia to the Rocky Mountains, only periodically interrupted by blue havens in major cities. The bluest places on the map include the corridor between Boston and Richmond, California and the Pacific Coast, and growing chunks along the border between San Diego and Brownsville as well as areas where Black voters represent Democratic holdouts in the South and Midwest.

Map 2

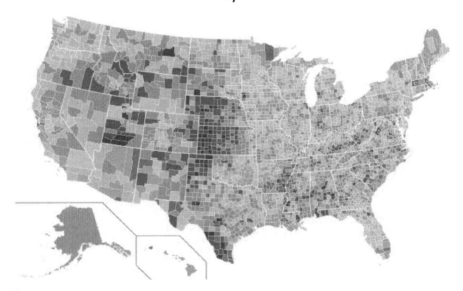

Map 2 displays the results from the 1996 Presidential Election between Bill Clinton and Bob Dole. Note how much lighter the map appears in general as the country then enjoyed partisan splits which were far less pronounced or geographic. The Democrats then possessed much of the Midwest excepting Indiana and the South was a competitive region for both parties.

Chapter 20: Team Blue—Democrats and the Left

The only constant in American politics today is that the party out of power at the Federal level feels like the country is irredeemably screwed. Such is the state of the Democrat Party and the Left generally in the 2018, where they prefer to find refuge in Harry Potter books and Star Wars references that encourage them to believe their resistance against the Republican Revolt is a grand struggle against an evil foe.

The truth is uglier. After more than fifty years of dominating the cultural landscape in what has been largely a one-sided struggle, ever moving the country more toward leftist ideals, the Right has finally shown up to the fight. Where those on the Left felt little restraint in using their time in government to impose their values across America over the objections of thoughtful people who were willing to settle for tolerance, they now are experiencing what Republicans and conservatives have had to swallow for at least the last thirty years, and it seems to have left them a sickening taste.

Those on the Left tend to be more idealistic and Utopian in how they see society. They imagine the perfect system can work away all the differences between us and people can coexist in peace, harmony, and mutual respect. Even writing such ideas sounds dangerously optimistic to my jaded ears, but it is a philosophy of youth, hope, and renewal that is not without place in society especially when balanced with wisdom of years' experience. We need people who are dreamers who imagine the world can be a better place and put energy into action.

The problem is the Left long ago stopped trying to persuade people to follow their visions and decided it would be easier to compel their support. Rather than building upon the impulses that in many ways launched their efforts toward free speech and expression, they've succumbed to a stultifying culture of political correctness that is as off-putting as it is socially destructive. They have become the censors, retreating to their ivory towers and secure enclaves, and they use their social power to destroy those who oppose them rather than persuade those who disagree.

This has been a recurring problem for the Left in seeking power as they fall so in love with their dreams of the future that they come to value their system, usually Marxism as it is now, above the desires and interests of the people. As a result, they try to use the education system to re-educate people, media to indoctrinate people, and the Courts to force people into compliance. Sometimes with well-intended idealism and other times with more practiced arrogance, the Left generally assumes they know best, and feel little hesitation about imposing their ideology for the good of the little people.

Think of how they refer to much of America as "flyover country" where "deplorable" people hold outmoded ideals. Theirs is a cult of youth, always seeking out what is new, fresh, and trying to take comfort in their universalism. However, such unanimity is only ever surface deep with the Left, because while they are willing to work

194

with many different groups in accordance with their uncritical love of diversity and inclusion, they tend not to look as closely at those coming in as they examined those who were already here.

For that reason, the Left today consists of a collection of groups who share surprisingly little in common if you look at the surface. Muslims, feminists, gay advocates, bankers, welfare recipients, internationalists, institutional unions, and undocumented people (or as the Right calls them, illegals) have little in common. In fact, they have many competing interests: Try reconciling Islam and feminism or explaining how poor Blacks in the South will have better job opportunities by granting amnesty to millions of illegals. It would seem this collection should not work, but it does because they are united by fantasy rather than reality, and the Left is smart enough to paint a picture where these dreams are realized because they identify a common enemy.

That enemy, as you might have guessed, is the Right. By the Right, I mean anyone who has power, be it economic, cultural, political, or even historical, and they are targeted for destruction because their possession of resources stands in the way of realizing the dream. It's weird how this motor of perpetual angst proves so powerful. The cultural Marxists who dreamed up the politics of power and resentment may not have understood economics, but they did have a keen insight into human nature.

Everyone says they want equality. It's a basic human proposition to want to be beneath no other, and that's why even when it isn't fair, people default to an even split as the least controversial settlement in many arguments. Yet, look a little deeper beneath the hood of how issues are settled, and what you discover is the equality people seek nearly always involves a person who does not have something wanting half of what another already has. Few seek equality with the poor and destitute, or those who suffer or choose a less comfortable or lucrative path. We only seek equality with those of higher status, and for the Left, that means the enemy is anyone who has status or assets.

In America, that means if you were part of the historic majority, you're the bad guy. Conservatives are bigots, Whites stole the country, marriage oppressed women, and straight men are evil. I could add other groups, but you get the basic picture, and this pantomime is how the Left keeps their carnival of discontent rolling from town to town, by painting a very bleak picture of those who made America. In their ideology, America could not have been built and won through hard effort and labor, but instead was stolen from their constituents, even if those constituents weren't even here at the time. There can never be anything good said about our nation, and we all saw this in how Obama's favorite pastime was to apologize and show deference to any foreigner.

Empires have risen and fallen on guilt and retribution, so it's obviously a powerful enough tool to reshape entire societies and civilizations. We are witnessing in real-time how guilt has persuaded much of the West to give away their countries and surrender all that their ancestors earned, to offer redress to an aggrieved mass, rather than to the children they were persuaded through policy and propaganda to never have. Most generously, one could argue it shows just how ethical and thoughtful the majority has been in sharing their wealth, but the problem is that the Left will never be satisfied with mere sharing: anything short of everything will never be enough.

Historically, when the Left gains complete power in a country, the nation tends to go bankrupt and hungry rather quickly. This is because they focus so much on redistribution that no one wants to work anymore. The formerly productive class goes into political exile, the gulag, or sullen compliance. The ascending recipient class, who came to power by taking what others had built, continues their expectation of receiving special status, yet there is now no one from whom they can receive their pay. So, they liquidate all the assets and use force to make the people who once were productive provide again, becoming tyrants in their own right. Eventually, a dull sense of living resumes until some point when the black market rises enough to fund an alternative or a mass insurrection, at which point a country becomes immunized from the dangers of such romantic idealism for a few generations.

Another sad joke commonly heard is that communism has only failed in the past because it wasn't tried properly. Tell that to the millions of dead throughout Europe, Asia, Latin America, and Africa who were sacrificed to try to prove this system, which is totally disconnected from how people behave. Such idealism is helpful in small doses, and useful when applied voluntarily, but too many years of success coupled with too deep of resentments in many of their constituent members have caused the Left to believe so much in the righteousness of their cause that they will fight to enact these beliefs without any regard to historical outcomes.

It helps neither side that we now live in echo chambers. Compare the two maps at the beginning of this chapter as evidence of an increasingly accelerating trend where people choose to live in places with people who think like they do. In the last twenty years, it's clear that people who think Left have left the country and the heartland, with it losing connection to both those values and those people and have come together mostly in just a few cities and their surrounding areas. They have built the version of America they want in those places, and glorifying such progress as beautiful, they want to share it with everyone. When everyone around you thinks like you, it's easy to forget that isn't really the case.

Since 1996, technology and communications have also played an incredibly disruptive role in the widening polarization of America. Whereas cable news was relatively new back then and network news and newspapers were still considered a consensus publication, media has now become its own form of entertainment, where the sides are weaponized against one another, taking partisan snipes constantly. The Left enjoys the conceit of imagining their media is more legitimate mainly because it has been owned longer to their side, hinting at how deep the propagandizing has gone. But the NY Times is just as biased as the NY Post, and MSNBC is no more honest than Fox News.

It's completely understandable why someone on either side would choose to watch things that reinforced their worldview, but the price of such voluntary isolation is that people taking in such divergent information and narratives will have radically different views on what is happening in the world, and from that draw opposite conclusions about what is necessary.

I'm an unapologetic rightist, but I force myself to watch what the Left says to understand their mindset, and they live in a world that seems like complete fantasy to me. They imagine the federal police are being turned into a modern-day Gestapo to separate families arbitrarily and that we're five minutes from a second Kristallnacht. It is incredibly irresponsible reporting from a publishing industry which surely knows better but has decided it is in their interest to agitate the Left to the point that they are on the verge of revolt. There are certainly sources on the Right that do the same, but never with such intensity and resources devoted to radicalizing.

The Left is being made to feel they're facing an existential crisis where all they have seized politically in the intervening decades may be erased. Their constituent groups are all being motivated by whatever means necessary, and they're being told government's unwillingness to impose certain of their social views represents some great tyranny. The truth is, the farthest the Right can get absent conflict is to remove government mandates that compel people to act against their interests, but such logic falls on deaf ears because the Left has been trained not to listen, discuss, or work with those who disagree.

An America with "safe spaces" that exclude frank discussion is one where guns will eventually do the talking, and unless we engage in a major way soon, that will be the only way left to resolve these differences. To be completely frank, the America the Left envisions is built on a repudiation of what was built before. It imagines a place disconnected from our history and our past, and for those on the Right who try to ground themselves in reality, how much fantasy can be indulged before there is a breaking point?

I sometimes wonder if the shrewder hands directing the Left, who realize the contradictions between the rising and radicalizing subgroups are becoming more difficult to manage as they succeed in growing their numbers, know that if a revolution doesn't happen soon, their effort will collapse. Their actual end goals diverge even within the Left, so much so that if any subgroup reached their complete victory, they would then have to immediately label their former allies as guilty of subversion. Just as the Bolsheviks did with the more numerous Mensheviks, leftist revolution tends to be the triumph of the most radical and violent over the idealists in the moment of doubt.

If history serves as a guide, and I believe we do better in trusting fact than theory, such will happen with the Left. We see this already in progress in the Democrat Party where

Pelosi and Schumer are fading from influence, and an ideologue like Maxine Waters now gets heard promising punishment without warrant and strength for their cause. For idealists, reason was only ever seen as a hindrance to their passions, and now that the adults in the room couldn't deliver, look for the Left to find more socialists who make Bernie look positively restrained, and even for communism to be revitalized.

Why? Because they believe the hype about the Right, and that the civic nationalism being offered is really the rebirth of fascism. Any honest historian could point out the myriad reasons that isn't happening, but ironically, it is their very incapacity to engage in dialogue with those who disagree which enables the far right to rise in response to their provocation. So, if they keep at it long enough, their prophecy might prove self-fulfilling.

Geographically speaking, these people are condensed overwhelmingly in the major cities, with strongholds in California, the West Coast, and in the so-called ACELA Corridor between DC and Boston. Most of the population of America is concentrated in these bubbles, and look for these areas, especially out west, to serve as hot spots as these conflicts accelerate.

Chapter 21: Team Red: Republicans and the Right

This is no longer your daddy's Republican Party and right-wing movement. While there are plenty of people who still read National Review and remember Bill Buckley fondly, years of cultural backpedaling and the clear results they've had in unmaking the fabric of the society which once was a shared vision for America has transformed the Right into a movement more willing than ever before to fight to restrain their opposition, reclaim their status, and restore the culture to what it was.

Whether they act explicitly on their impulses, one clear distinction that defines the Right is their belief there is a better way to do things. Moral impulses matter, and good policies stem from good beliefs. This ideology invests much more into building up the individual through a set of instructions and practices, trusting for people acting independently to create the best outcomes. Such liberty has proven less than resilient against people promised the easier path of others assuming their responsibilities, but for those who strive and devote effort, the path and opportunity for success remains open, perhaps more so than ever before.

The problem with such thinking is that even though it creates individuals who are far more empowered from a political perspective, and whose ideology is usually backed with many more facts and examples than the prepackaged conclusions of Marxism, the Right loves to indulge in their own fantasies of seeking the most ideal yet imperfect conclusions, a deliberately contradictory phrase rooted in the commonly held dictum that man cannot be fully perfected, at least not by the state, and so government exists not to empower people, but to restrain our worst tendencies from emerging.

This fear has ever been the root of the Right's obsession with smaller government and can be traced back directly to the Founders, to the passionate debates by Patrick Henry against James Madison in Virginia, arguing the Bill of Rights would be necessary to ensure government did not unduly tread upon the prerogatives of the free man. Madison thought it superfluous, which perhaps it was in his time, but imagining a Constitution today where Freedoms of Speech, Association, to Bear Arms, and against Self-Incrimination were not explicitly reserved, there are few states that hesitate to trample those freedoms many Americans hold sacrosanct.

Because of these fears and trying to prevent government from transgressing upon the individual unduly, the Right has the problem of dividing itself into ever smaller fragments based upon their ideals of the perfect society. Although the Republican Party holds their own tent aloft, the debates between libertarians, conservatives, constitutionalists, traditionalists, and others are interesting, but consume valuable energy which the Left, by contrast, would use toward activism. Even now, these debates usually end up, whether in Congress or in a beer hall, with the resolve to do nothing and to hope instead for external actors in civil society to fill in the gaps.

Obama changed that for many Americans. It's not fair to just blame Obama because the Left had been sliding America leftward for many decades before he arrived on the scene, especially in the cultural aspects, but I think he was the first avowedly socialist president. Take Bill Clinton as counter-point. Although one could reasonably argue his embrace of NAFTA did far more damage to America than anything Obama passed, he mouthed platitudes about traditional culture and touched on the fringes of reforming welfare, perhaps a necessity given how Republican the Congress became, and therefore did not set off alarm bells on the Right. The Left, when cautious, has always been able to count on the restraint of their opposition, using tolerance as a mask through which they could establish their radicals for later actions.

Obama was different. He spoke of radical transformation and referred to normal Americans as people who bitterly clung to guns and religion. Upon taking office, he forced through a health care system wherein people who did not want to participate were compelled to pay for the privilege of non-involvement. This was something different—an intrusion that awakened a sleeping giant, where government shifted from protecting the outcasts to imposing fines and levies on the majority, and the Tea Party movement which dominated 2010 was the first sign of what a raw nerve had been struck.

The problem from the perspective of the Right is that while new blood came into the system, there was no national or notional apparatus to utilize this energy. So, despite electoral success, the restoration impulse behind those Gadsden snake flags fizzled as the institutional Republican Party, driven as ever by commitment to their donors and in fear of hostile media, retreated to the bland positions of supporting free markets and opportunity. They spoke about stopping what the President was doing, and voted that way when in opposition, but their enduring inability to repeal the Affordable Care Act, more commonly called Obamacare, even once they became the majority in both houses of Congress, shows the lack of spine to which they still regress.

The base realized that, and Trump seized his opening. The fortuitous combination of having enough money to buy his way above the system, and a sharply divided primary between establishment candidates created a unique opportunity. More than anything else, I believe Trump's insistence on being politically incorrect and pathologically unapologetic riled up the heart of America in the conservative base. Like a beaten wife who had turned the other cheek one too many times, the base finally slapped back with a vengeance and put up Trump in frustration against a party that had been on the defensive for far too long. Walls needed to be built, pride restored, and people start speaking the truth instead of being stuck within the constraining paradigm of political correctness, itself a clear construct designed by the Left to create certain outcomes.

It turns out that the anger in America wasn't just constrained to the Republican base, but also included wide areas of the nation, especially among those places which were deemed losers and had been punished by the Left for the preceding 8 years. Rural folks who they tried to push into the cities fought back. The Rust Belt, told their jobs were never coming home and that things could only be built elsewhere, came home to vote. Christians were promised Christmas would return once more, and the war against morality would no longer just be an endless retreat. Trump has honored his word, reminded the nation that had fallen asleep here in America what we once were proudly about, and I do not believe the giant will sleep once more now that it has been roused from its previously undisturbed slumber.

Nationalism was a dirty word for both parties. Such derision was naturally embraced by the Left as their universalist ideals for government lend toward greater centralization and internationalism. But globalism was a foreign concept implanted into the Right during the Sixties. The traditional isolationist impulse that had followed through most of American history was temporarily forgotten after World War II with the Soviet threat, as that specter held the country together on both sides. But as soon as the Cold War was won, the Cold Civil War began, as the lone remaining superpower was freed from the military obligations of the Cold War and could chart an independent path. Only now have we paused to ask the question of what our independent path should be, as I don't think anyone bothered to ask because it was just assumed America as victor would press our system around the world, and the Cold War consensus would hold. Clearly, it has not.

Today, the Right is ready to come back home from all the wars abroad. We watched as a generation of men went and bravely served in Iraq, Afghanistan, and elsewhere, and saw the ingratitude of the world, the damage to our psyche, and the tremendous cost. We have learned that cultural conflicts cannot simply be resolved by democracy and throwing money at them. A heightened realism pervades the new nationalism which recognizes cultures just aren't interchangeable, and people carry with them the baggage of their past, culturally and personally, wherever they go.

One thing people don't recognize, and is far more important than commonly reported, is that idealism in many ways motivated public support for the ill-considered American interventions abroad. While I sincerely doubt the officials and talking heads pushing for these wars believed such claptrap, and instead were manipulating the American people into allowing them to play hardcore geopolitics, the reason so many of our citizens backed the wars was first from fear, but then later in hope that a better future could be had, believing women could vote and democracy might work. After the Berlin Wall fell, it seemed as though a universal moment for getting past the old conflicts was possible, and even though it is just as impossible to make peace with Islam today as it has been since its inception, we believed the lie.

Now, increasing numbers of Americans don't believe that lie. A lie that was at least plausible in the wake of the ending of the Cold War has become unbelievable after numerous terrorist attacks and cultural destruction. We know the world is a place not like our own, and for those on the Right at least, it is better left outside our gates. Or, rather, it should be kept outside the gates we want to build. We want to build very big walls to keep people away and leave them to their own problems rather than have them bring their problems into our towns and homes. America gave up trillions of dollars and thousands of lives to try to make the world better, and the response of those upon whose behalf we acted was to yell at us, lecture us, and sometimes shoot at us. I don't blame the world in the least. People have the right to defend their own lands, traditions, and cultures, but we're rediscovering on the Right that we can do the same here at home.

Looking closer to home and with wiser eyes at America, we see that our own culture is in decay. The Constitution has been ignored for years. The millions of people coming here, many of whom are very good hard-working people, nonetheless have their own ideas about what makes a country successful, and they think differently than the old consensus of do-it-yourself that built the country. They want to impose views inherited from their home cultures, and the Left enables this to seek power for themselves.

The failure of the Right was to allow the Left to build the government to such power that it could impose views. Just as nature abhors a vacuum, such power cannot go without someone attempting to use it. The Left did so for eight years. And now, even though it didn't want to, the Right has become in some ways intoxicated by the same formula. In truth, the Right has accomplished more in the past two years than the preceding twenty, but the cost of using government as a tool to have one side dominate the other is the conflict which invariably ensues if common goals are not shared. Which, quite obviously, they are not.

As a reactionary, I think I'm ahead of the curve in admitting we can't go back from this point because we know beyond any shadow of doubt that the Left will only use government to continue remaking America in their image, which we've been told quite explicitly does not include us or look like us unless we submit fully to their every demand, no matter how farcical. Compromise has been off the table for many years, but the Right is only now realizing that was the case, seeing how poorly our time in power is being received.

From such a foundation, the Right is embracing nationalism, vigor, and an all-out war against political correctness that at heart asks the question: "what is America?" Trump's form of civic nationalism is where this conversation starts, but the dialogue on this side has shifted to who can be a good American, what ideas must they hold, and how do we deal with those who do not belong. Views widely diverge here ranging from those who think all are still welcome versus people who prefer exclusion, but it seems likely that this is where the polarization will reveal itself, and the central thesis of this book.

As the ideological divides harden, and we see different groups adhering to one side or the other, driven as often by fear of the other as hope for their own nominal faction, identity politics which have long been the realm of the Left will become common practice on the Right. In truth,

209

voting habits already reflect this with most Republicans being White, rural, traditionalist, and Christian. But the Right has always presented a degree of inclusion in the moral path it favored, which is why the open borders policy endured, and how the Left was able to use tolerance to work toward supremacy. Now, those doors are closing, especially as changing demography has made it clear that the new Americans are not becoming the next generation of Americans who will subscribe to the old dream. That dream no longer exists save as an aspiration, because it was killed long ago by the Marxists who took over this culture and decided dividing us into several tribes was a better idea.

As Lincoln shrewdly opined, a house divided against itself cannot stand, and multicultural America is no nation at all, but just a set of laws and symbols with resources being fought over by different groups. Ideology reveals this, but by no means represents the only way to view this conflict as we're going to discuss in more detail. But it is the most useful heading to gather the two factions.

So, who is the Right? They're the people who believe in America as it was, who live usually in either the suburbs or rural areas, and who trend older, paler, and in the upper middle strata of society. From the Appalachian Mountains to the Rockies, they occupy the center of America, and they are in many cases the people who do any of the work that exists outside the cities like farming, mining, logging, and drilling.

Within this blend of ideas is emerging an idea of restoring the American nation and to form the identity anew, building a culture based upon the ideals we once held, updated for the new age, and driven by people instead of a hard and fast ideology. It's messier but cares more for morality, and their revolt is now being represented by the President.

The questions are: "will they use their power," and "how quickly can they learn?"

Section III: Groups

Division II: Residency

As ideology has divided the country as never before, it becomes apparent that people who lean Left have overwhelmingly gathered to enjoy the comforts of the cities, leaving a much more ideologically homogeneous population in their wake in the rural areas they abandoned. Right leaning ideas have proven attractive to people who tend toward conservative views, so people with those ideas and the means to leave the cities have either migrated to small towns and the country where possible, or states with lesser population density. For those whose economic status requires them to remain closer to the city, we see suburbs in many places being ringed now by exurbs where people will drive upwards of an hour to go to work to insulate their family from city life.

Chart 1

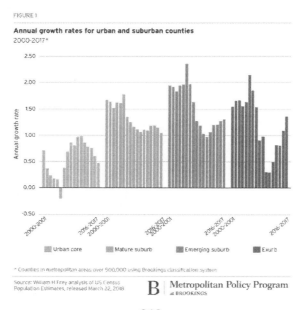

FIGURE 1

Annual growth rates for urban and suburban counties
2000-2017*

* Counties in metropolitan areas over 500,000 using Brookings classification system

Source: William H Frey analysis of US Census Population Estimates, released March 22, 2018

B | Metropolitan Policy Program
at BROOKINGS

As **Chart 1,** *provided by research by the Brookings Institution makes clear, the growth pattern of people moving further out nationally to get away from the cities is accelerating. While growth is happening in all areas, what these statistics suggest is the cites are retrenching, but people who do not want to be near cities are finding ways to leave with increasing urgency. Such information correlates with* **Maps 1** *and* **2** *from the preceding chapter where the partisan affiliations are grouped in similar fashion with increasing divergence between those factions.*

These divisions have major consequences in the electoral game where the Republicans now have geography working for them as our system, in seeking to value states equally rather than voters, favors low density states relative to high density cities for representation purposes. A necessity of uniting disparate subcultures at the onset of the republic, such consideration probably remains important to protect regional distinction today, but this division will only further agitate the Left who will see the diminution of their influence due to long-standing structural factors as a form of intentional subversion to be targeted for reform. A hint of this can be seen in the pending referendum to split California into three separate States, which while reasonable for administration reasons, will never be accepted by Right leaning states because it would create four more Left-leaning Senators.

Although **Map 3**, *courtesy of Business Insider with US Census statistics, only shows most major densely populated areas, it's worth showing how many people are bunched in such small geographic centers in America, seeing these as primarily leftist strongholds.*

Map 3

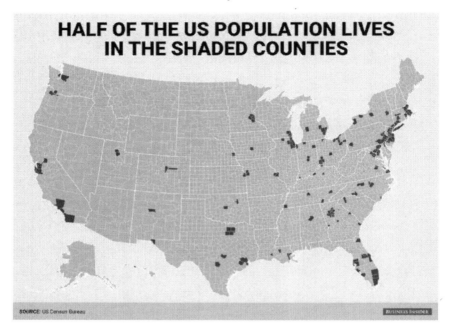

HALF OF THE US POPULATION LIVES IN THE SHADED COUNTIES

SOURCE: US Census Bureau

BUSINESS INSIDER

When two different groups of people with different ideas live in different settings, the opportunities for divergence quickly widen. Country life, without the dangers and interactions which are routine for those who dwell in the city, tends to prefer a hands-off approach. By contrast, due to the many issues which arise by having such masses of humanity in close proximity, city life becomes unmanageable without substantial accommodation, usually solved through regulations.

Conflict arises when these two contrasting world views are forced to compete for control of a singular Federal system that has moved from allowing states and localities to choose their own solutions toward a single centralized one size fits all approach. Every time America has tried to force this single vision, conflict has resulted, most spectacularly during the original Civil War.

We tread the same path today, and when people are forced to share a single commanding state with divergent visions, the potential at least exists for a recurrence of such violence should a cultural consensus remain absent or authority be satisfactorily devolved.

High level analysis aside, if you get in your car and drive between where you live and where the other side lives, note how different these Americas look, and remember this is happening in places throughout our country. The urban/rural split has never been wider with the suburbs being the compromise ground in between being pulled either way.

Chapter 22: Team Gray: The Urban Dwellers

America is primarily an urban country at this point when looking at where our people choose to live. Statistics reported by the US Census in 2015 assert that 62.7% of Americans live in cities, which are metropolitan areas with greater than 100,000 people, but these people interestingly only occupy 3.5% of the total land area of our country. The number rises to about 80% of the total population in the West where there are far fewer towns between cities, unlike the East where the many small towns and earlier settlements keep the total closer to 50% once you get away from densely populated coast. Without question, most of the wealth and GDP of the United States comes from the cities, where financial and manufacturing facilities are primarily located, and where the largest investment in infrastructure is made.

Cities currently dominate the political discourse, with most major universities being nearby and almost all major media outlets being stationed in one of the largest and most densely concentrated areas of people. Most prominent are the Northeastern Corridor with Boston, New York, Philadelphia, and Washington, followed closely by the Los Angeles and San Francisco surroundings, and Chicago in the Midwest. News comes from these places, and because of that fact, tends to consciously or unconsciously reflect the view points of urban dwellers.

As would make sense since the major cultural institutions overwhelmingly tend to stay close to cities to reach both the widest audience and receive the most generous support, the cities lean overwhelmingly Left. Nearly every major city in the United States is run by Democrats and has been so more or less consistently for at least the last fifty years. A few exceptions exist, especially in the more pragmatic parts of the Midwest, but the reality is that the Left has run politics like a machine in many of these cities for generations, with Chicago perhaps being the most infamous example.

Life in cities is inherently different than country living. In cities, necessity dictates a set of ever-changing compromises that are necessary for people to get along. These compromises would be less pronounced in a society where a common culture existed, but within the social reality of our current age, that means government has become much larger to deal with a myriad of different issues. Having people who speak different languages and come from different backgrounds, while allowing for an exchange of ideas that can be productive in encouraging creativity and novel forms of expression also comes with considerable social cost as those dissimilarities also create more tension and potential misunderstandings. To mitigate these risks, cities are compelled to create a great many more laws than country folk require, to have many more assets to ensure clear communication and access to services lest the misunderstandings evolve into something more sinister, and generally be more intrusive into the lives and rights of their citizens.

As can be observed just as easily at the Federal level, as government gets larger and has access to a larger percentage of resources, the desire to have access to those funds similarly increases, with opportunities for corruption growing. Certain major American cities have been aware of this relationship for well over a century, and what tends to happen is the creation of a political machine to satisfy these needs. Prominent citizens or corporations give generously both to projects in the city as well as compliant officials in exchange for favorable policy concessions or increased access to government planning. The cynical could call it corruption, or the pragmatic might call it patronage, but whatever you call it, cities have long been a bought operation in America.

This matters especially for our current situation because in many ways, these individual governments exist almost independent of State and Federal governments. Even though the superior legal entities often attempt to compel cities to respond to their policy through control of the streams of revenue that facilitate certain programs, especially those from the Federal level, cities are often tasked with administering those same programs, and so they have functional control of how moneys are spent and who runs the endeavors. This means that as the Left runs local government, even as regimes shift in Washington or whatever state capital, their people will be responsible for how the dollars get put into practice and whether or not policies are implemented.

From this, it's easy to see why a policy like sanctuary cities, which explicitly and illegally contradicts the Constitutional instruction delegating authority over immigration to the Legislative Branch of the Federal Government, is easy for towns to implement. If they don't do their job as required, or even go further to warn illegal occupants of Federal action, the higher level of government is substantially handicapped by such intransigence. In practice, most cities tend to be very nonchalant about following Republican efforts to restrain their policy, and supportive of Democrats who eagerly funnel money and resources to their friends and allies.

It's easy to lose sight of just how many resources are at the command of cities, but as an illustrative example, let's consider the New York Police Department. Their budget alone in 2018 was $5.6 billion dollars, larger than all but the largest corporations and representing a huge outlay of funds, influence, and capacity. They have their own counter terrorism division that rivals the FBI for scope and ability. Considering their duties to protect a multicultural haven with over seven million residents and many more visitors at any given time, they have a huge responsibility. This example, though particularly grand, shows that if cities were to forge an independent path, they would have substantial capacity to do so.

What is worrisome is that cities, in fact, are starting to do just that. Just as states have done for a very long time, cities actively get involved with Courts and go shopping for friendly judges to either expedite or retard policy mandates from State and Federal governments. Such lawfare is an increasingly common practice used to force the Federal government to enact policy against itself, to be entirely fair, both sides engage in this behavior regularly. From the perspective of a taxpayer wanting efficient governance, it's a bit insane that money is given to two entities to fight one another with a third being paid by your levies to arbitrate. Considering such suits often take years to reach conclusion, if that even happens, one begins to understand just how broken government has become, a further reflection of the ideological and cultural divides crossing our society.

The problem for cities, however, is all the compromises they make create an environment which is difficult for people who seek a more unified purpose. Put differently, if one wants to expose their family to certain common ideals, it's hard to find that within the diverse multicultural consensus that is almost inescapable as a means of keeping peace between the disparate groups in an urban environment. Therefore, you see two different strategies families with means employ to escape these challenges and attempt to seclude themselves to a safer and less divided culture.

The first strategy commonly used is gentrification. It would be considered impolitic to exclude people from lower socioeconomic strata for blatantly stated political reasons, so city folk with means will often create or utilize structures where a high financial cost of entry serves as a barrier to less well-heeled residents. A subtler form of redlining, (the practice whereby certain areas have properties not sold to people who don't fit a predesignated characteristic) using cost to deprive access is a favorite trick of urban liberals and whites especially. Whether it is the costly neighborhood, the private school, or whatever other unique opportunity, they have learned to insulate themselves from the consequences of their own publicly advocated policies, ensuring the advantages they want for their children and families in terms of safety and social progress are retained.

Sometimes, I have thought one reason we see so much White guilt emanate from the cities is because the people who live there know the programs they so vigorously support from the public sector to care for their fellow cohabitants are inferior. They know this implicitly, as evidenced by their non-participation, which people on the Right rightly cite as hypocritical. Yet, they offer up platitudes and other people's money to assuage their consciences, of which cities never seem to lack because they gather so much.

The second option we see is people who commute into cities who do not necessarily want to necessarily, but who make an economic decision that the additional resources they can gather from such employment are worth the inconveniences. Usually, as people move out to further suburbs or the exurbs we will cover in two chapters, they're doing so out of a desire to not be involved with the city any more than necessary, and to effectuate an even more meaningful separation from the culture and often the ideals of the city.

Given the opportunity, it is likely many Americans who live in cities or live near them would prefer to live elsewhere, but as we shifted from an agrarian economy to a manufacturing and then service based economy last century, without some form of deliberate planning, it was inevitable centralization of people would grow. To make clear just how densely packed cities are, the American average according to the US census is 1,594 people per square mile as opposed to a rural figure of 35 people per square mile. There are 46 times as many people in the cities, all being pushed together because of not just the economy, but also government policy which being driven by a centralizing entity, encourages people to live closer together to realize cost benefit in transmission of services.

In short, while many love the city, others are stuck there because they spent their earlier lives developing the sort of specialized career sets which would have no market in rural areas, and where their very value is contingent upon being part of larger corporate or other efforts that require many people working in conjunction. In a very real way, we have become servants to our own technology, automation, and organization, and this too reflects one of the key elements of the urban dweller. While they may be better educated, they tend to be imbalanced in what they can do.

In the city, if you need help with a given service or task, it is not difficult to find and locate help. Whether from an existing social network or as a purchased service, help is at the ready. In fact, owing to the many compromises city dwellers make with traveling more and working long hours at a place of employment, standard practice is to use some of those additional funds to outsource responsibilities to other actors. Cities mandate many of these by taking tax revenues to provide sanitation and what not, but a number of these are privately selected as well. The value of the urbanite is in their specialized knowledge, and so anything which can be done to allow them to perform the skill which is most economically valuable is prioritized over routine grunt work.

When everything functions well, this means the cities run as smoothly as can be expected and represent achievements that can explore larger questions harnessing the talents of many different people and creating economic opportunity. But it is a fragile system in many ways, and despite having some redundancy by the sheer quantity of people and available resources, when things go wrong in the urban environment, a calamity can quickly ensue.

Take food as the most basic example. As I learned during years as a courier, 95% of the food in the average American supermarket comes from at least 150 miles away and has a shelf life of 72 hours. Cities, other than an occasional public display, do not grow their own food and do not grow nearly enough to feed their own people. Instead, they rely on country people to pick the food and to deliver it via truck for consumption. If that food didn't come, the response of the urbanite would be to seek food elsewhere, from perhaps a food bank, or to seek to escape outward to where food is more readily available. Which is what all the millions of them would do at once, flooding into areas where there are no houses, and supplies are not robust enough to support them.

Resource dependency is the Achilles Heel of the city. Whether food, energy, or any of a host of other items, city folk primarily do not know how to sustain themselves outside of their environment. As someone who has lived both ways, I can attest country life forces one to become much more aware of different responsibilities and many people, though not all, become more self-sufficient in having at least the knowledge and some capacity to produce or gather food or fuel for their family or homestead.

It is indisputable that cities have more power when things go right, and as their own experience attests, they use such power to curry political influence not just locally, but nationally, and perhaps with the best of intentions, seek to expand their accommodations into national policy. They believe, sincerely, that government is needed to take care of problems because their cities would fail without such interventions. Yet, this way of living is antithetical to many who live outside their midst, including to some extent those who commute into cities, who prefer instead not to be pushed into conformity, but are happy to enjoy the greater liberty as well as the greater responsibility they must assume for self-reliance elsewhere.

This was less of a problem when Federal and, depending upon the specific location, State policies were less comprehensive. But now that government has grown to regulate every aspect of our lives, driven as much by the needs of bureaucrats and the fields which sustain themselves off such regulatory needs to be active, our government has become a tug-of-war between sides seeking to force their ideas on the others. What started as largess by the cities, with more idealistic forces pushing these ideas for their own motivations perhaps, has become a sort of zero sum game.

What does this mean for the city? As Federal policy moves to the right as it probably will for the next few years, resistance within the city will encourage further radicalism, especially on the Left. The density of cities makes it much easier for them to organize and act than their counterparts. Given the city's current dominance, their superior population, better funding, and clear cultural support from the Establishment, they may push as far as permitted. The Federal government will struggle with this, and depending upon how angry they get, at least some cities may try to enact functional autonomy.

If this becomes the case, we could see Federal forces put into cities to quell riots as well as National Guard forces put in place by governors. Such animus is very probable should Trump win re-election and the current trajectory of rising polarization continues.

Although they lean Left, the cities have the ongoing problem of needing to hold together culturally disparate populations with divergent interests who live in economic inequality, tacitly supported by their own elite class. They only can be held together by creating a common external enemy, who though identified as traditional sources of authority leaning rightward, just happen to live primarily outside the cities in the rural areas of America.

Should the Left come back to power, the policies they enacted during Obama which were frankly designed to discourage people from living outside the cities, seeing rural life as a waste of energy and as backwards and provincial, will be enacted with gleeful fervor, punishment to be enacted against a revolt the cities know was primarily against them, their culture, and the future they desire.

Chapter 23: Team Green: The Country Folk

I never really appreciated just how different country life is until I came to live out here. Just for context, the town where I presently live has under 1,000 people, and I doubt there are 5,000 people within a fifty-mile radius of me. There's a lot of open space where one can breathe, and it is utterly beautiful. But for all those wonderful things, there are many trade-offs. A trip for anything beyond the basics at the local market means an hour drive to another supermarket, or two hours to one where the prices are fair. Doctors are just as far, and when technology goes out, the service call doesn't happen quickly.

For those who are committed to the fast pace of city life and come here for vacation, they take the slower pace of life in the country as a welcome respite, for about a week, and then they go back to the mania. But once you live here, time transforms, and you realize it matters far less how quickly you move than what you do with the time. Having such time to think and to plan, details come into focus and a person finds ways to make their life better, or at least to better fit their current needs.

Not everyone lives in as removed a place as I've chosen, but an important difference that seems common to all country folk because there are so many fewer of us is that we have to learn to solve our own problems. Growing some extra food is a major convenience, and everyone knows the local farmer, rancher, or where fresh milk or eggs can be had. The trade-off here is fewer choices are available, but the ones out here seem better because you can trust their origins. The time gives one perspective on making choices, and in so doing, one becomes accustomed to deciding for oneself what to choose.

There is much truth in the stereotypes that everyone living in a small town or in the country gets to know everyone else. Truer for those born in a place than those from away, it still is more common than not to get to know a much larger percentage of the people out in the hinterlands. There's something essential to knowing one's neighbors rather than living in a sea of humanity. A person can build trust with a person they know by name as opposed to people they will never see other than to know they inhabit close space. The expansiveness of this attitude once marked all of America.

There was a time not so long ago, when we were largely an open continent with possibility and hope as the message. And though the risks were great, and calamities were many, we were an intrepid people willing to challenge ourselves to live on the land and forge our own paths. We did not ask for government to do anything other than to not restrain us from finding our own story, and that was freedom for America. That was the country that immigrants braved, not one where they would receive cradle to grave support, but merely an opportunity for something more. It's a spirit that has dimmed in the lights of industrialization and urbanization but continues more in the country than it could in the city. In the countryside, memories are passed along more directly, and people recall their ancestors who built this country with pride and longing.

While people who live in the city see such notions as hopelessly outdated and irrelevant to their daily experience of life, the opposite is true in the country. But more than that, people who live in the country have been watching for decades as city growth has not only siphoned people and resources away, but also imposed new mandates and restrictions upon them to reflect the urban consensus. Issues that are abstract and involve good feelings in the city often threaten the very way of life for those who live out in the country.

Some of the best examples involve the overreach of the environmental protection agencies, both at the Federal and State levels. Whether it is loggers who harvest timber to provide for their families, fisheries who draw out salmon, miners who extract minerals from the ground, or drillers across the great plains, there are hardworking people across America who make their living from the land beyond the farmers. Yet, so often, these people are not permitted to do what they have always done because the prerogative of the urban majority would prefer to treat those areas outside the city as essentially parks. While such impulses may be well-intended, they represent an attack on the lifestyle of many people who live in less populated areas, seen as the latest attempt to compel people to return to the city.

An example I can share of how this works is the logging industry I understand well from living up here in Maine. People in cities think cutting down trees means the death of a forest, but the reality is that a working forest is much more "sustainable" – to use the popular buzz word – because people care for the resource and have cycles of harvesting and replanting that sustain a far healthier ecosystem than the strip logging urbanites imagine or by turning the land into a park as they often suggest, which results only in neglect. Not only does working the forest create jobs, it encourages usage of a renewable resource and decreases foreign dependency and overall cost. But the propaganda of environmentalism often exists outside of economics, an issue where the learned ignorance of the urban crowd can prove quite painful.

Every Left-leaning leaning regime since at least FDR has tried to pull people from the country, so their myriad programs created job opportunities designed to transfer poor rural populations into urban centers. For those who live in the country without means, it's a common occurrence to be advised that to receive benefits, relocation to a more centralized location is required. While this makes sense economically, and rural folk try to resist seeking direct government assistance more-so than urban dwellers, such impositions only increase cultural tension.

A central theme of this book is that culture matters a great deal, more even than economics, even as those pressures work against reconciliation. In the country, Obama's snide remark about how people love their guns, God, and religion was actually spot on, and people wear that as a badge of honor. Because they know their neighbors well, they share greater concord with their neighbors and seek to live a moral life with instruction not from the state, but through a voluntary effort. To preserve such blessings and liberty, they purchase guns and are not afraid to use them.

While it is undoubtedly a rite of passage in many areas for young men and increasingly young women to learn to hunt, fish and many other useful skills, the national mythology that was once presented that the reason people had guns was to hunt was just that: a myth. The Founders who launched their revolution against the English Crown understood full well that a well-armed militia meant citizens who would enjoy sufficient power to dissuade the state from infringing too far upon their liberties. The reason we have the Second Amendment is so our government cannot compel us to do other than what we want, which is why people in the country lead the chorus of the Right against any restrictions whatsoever, and this will never change. It cannot change, because we see both from foreign example and from their own encroachment, how the cities will try to regulate away our prerogative to not just self-defense, but self-determination.

With this understanding, it's very important to consider the country, despite its thinly populated areas, as the heart of the Right and the area from which any decisive action from that faction in a civil conflict as likely to emerge. The best trained, most capable, and most self-sufficient people live in these areas, often with ample access to energy, food, and other basic supplies needed for an engagement. Such facts are not lost on the people who live in these parts as well, and they have been preparing in some cases for decades against the very possibility of the radicalism now manifesting on the Left.

There are many people ready for such a fight. In being an activist, I travel frequently but I tend not to go to big cities, but more into small towns most will never have heard about. I talk to people who have gone back to the land, who are homesteaders and preppers, people who have chosen to live at the fringes of society. While some are generationally tied to the land, a surprising number are people who have deliberately chosen to downshift their life because they wanted to regain control. They were tired of working a job just to get paid and wanted something more.

I think of some friends of mine who used to be heavily involved in the DC military establishment. Now, they run a small homestead which is somewhat between a farm and an overgrown garden, and these city folks can butcher a rabbit, pluck a chicken, and grow whatever they want. They work long days, sometimes upwards of twelve hours, but they also love their lives because their happiness and survival are contingent upon only their own efforts. They don't have a lot, but they value what they do possess, and celebrate the fruits of their own labor. Most importantly to them, they are no longer obliged to count on anyone or listen to anyone.

Liberty is hard today. Liberty requires a degree of personal independence that is only theoretical in most people's lives because of either the specialization of their work, or alternatively, because of a lack of personal skills needed to survive. This is a new situation in America, relatively speaking, where we as people are not able to sustain ourselves. And it is probably the heart of how the Left keeps most people compliant, because to challenge their dogma is to risk your own employment or status and be trapped at the lowest periphery of society.

It has sometimes been said the only free people are those who are very poor and very rich, and what you discover in the country is the two easily and readily overlap. People who own vast mills and sprawling farms live and interact with people who just produce enough to get by down the street. Each left the city to have a different lifestyle, and while there are obvious differences, the overlaps pull together in that both have a degree of autonomy the city would not allow.

With such freedom comes a rebellious streak and considering how often it has been tried by not just Democrats, but Republicans, the rural areas were hot for a revolt against politically correct speech, better known as BS in these parts, and we saw that play out in 2016. Trump won because the rural areas turned out in utterly enormous numbers to offset the more populated cities, not because he exemplified their views, but because had the good sense to leave them alone and to call a spade a spade.

Common core is the perfect example of this. People who have been educated for generations using basic arithmetic and being taught that America is a good and just place have zero patience for a story which presents us as the evil oppressors and uses a system of estimation so complicated engineers struggle to make sense of it. It strikes rural people as propaganda, a trick designed to change our children from who we are, a conviction I personally share and the reason why it is universally hated, a feeling which transcends rural areas to many other parents throughout the land who bother to research this plot.

To offer useful predictions and analysis, I make certain generalizations that have obvious exceptions, but one crucial difference I have often observed between the small towns and the cities might be that city folk are often clever but not always so wise. Urbanites are better adjusted to the trends being pushed for adoption in society and more able to exercise the double think that requires from time to time, called more plainly "do as I say, not as I do." But country people don't see the point in making such rationalizations, or deceits to get along, because they don't have to live with such unhappy compromises. They have less, therefore they want less.

Which way is better is a matter of opinion, and so long as both camps were able to go their own way with minimal distraction, it worked. The country folk are like their city brethren in ignoring laws they don't want to enforce, though the agencies seen as most intrusive up here aren't related to immigration, but rather pertain things like land and resource usage. A common trick is to stay so small there aren't enough resources to enforce unwanted laws, and to keep things in house as much as possible.

Small towns and rural living are much more a feature of the East than the West and looking at the maps of where

Trump was most successful, one cannot help but notice his support throughout Appalachia and the Heartland where many small towns with few people were able to pool their might to win an election. Take Pennsylvania, where much of the population lives in small to medium sized towns between Pittsburgh and Philadelphia which are Democrat anchors, and how vigorously they turned out.

You don't see that out West as everyone lives in cities, at least to a much greater extent than east of the Rocky Mountains. The number rises to nearly double the amount of urban population for many areas according to the census which might offer an additional insight as to why the West is getting bluer as the East is getting redder. While people look often at partisanship, residency deserves much more attention, as the lifestyle people live directly impacts not just how they look at government, but their ability to functionally assert their independence.

The challenge for the open spaces and the small towns that dot the landscape is twofold. How to survive in a world where everything is built in the city is a major obstacle that is asked every day. In some ways, a world where Amazon can deliver nearly all you need to your door is easier, and yet, how does the mom and pop store which keeps the town alive continue? For towns with a successful anchor like a college or a natural attraction, tourism does much of the work, but such jobs are mostly low paying and have no future. Agribusiness has had some success, especially with organic products fetching a deserved premium, but centralization is again a problem here as well.

Assuming a town finds its way past these economic challenges of day to day survival, the other issue which is perhaps more pressing for this narrative is people who are used to doing things their own ways tend to be very particular. Rugged individualists enjoy a degree of trust, but also a degree of freedom of action that makes political organization very difficult. The trend on the Right of being very particular about one's beliefs transcends towns, and the parochial nature of conflicts between even small communities is sometimes amazing.

To be honest, sometimes it is self-defeating, and too often it has proven exactly this way. All the weapons in the world have proven thin defense against a government empowered by a left-leaning populist majority to constrain how they live, if such actors are smart enough to move patiently. Such is how liberty was lost, and while there are certain red lines like a gun grab, it turns out getting people motivated to act in concert is difficult. Less so now perhaps than it has been for many years, but even still, the Right will not want to make the first move in any fight, even if such reluctance will lead to the slow destruction of the towns and values they love.

Such restraint might be overcome with sufficient provocation, and people are thinking and talking about how to make this happen, but that's one other thing about country life. There's a lot of chatter, but decent folk who live on their own tend to live and let live, and that very decency is often what makes them most vulnerable.

Chapter 24: Team Peach—Suburbia

The suburbs are a uniquely American invention, created after the highway boom of the 1950's, of neighborhoods that are not quite towns, but rather a collection of houses, stores, and businesses in the orbit of a city. Lacking either the intimacy of the long-established urban neighborhood or the quaint comfort of a small town, these areas simply exist. The new trend is to make them feel more like home through evocative architecture, but the tell is usually in how many box stores are there, and the same name brands permeate these dense clusters of people who mostly commute.

Without intending offense, suburbs are weird. I grew up in one in the northern part of Phoenix so I'm speaking from experience. Suburbs are places where people live, but where identity gets shunted into other outlets. These days, video games and social media are probably the most common choices as so many people retreat into technology. Between the combination of policy and pragmatism, what the suburbs mainly represent is an attempt, for those whose life choices make the city obligatory, to exert some degree of autonomy. Suburbs are places that exist primarily as what they are not, a way station between two worlds that has become a novel third entity.

Most of the color names in this book are deliberately obvious, but it's worth mentioning why Peach is the color for suburbia. More than any other area, the suburbs will be where the people who are apolitical and think everything will be just fine will reside. They don't live a bad life by standard American reckoning. Their schools are usually better, the paychecks are fatter, and as much as anywhere in this country, those areas ringing the city show the most ideological diversity. Although trending slightly Republican compared to traditional norms, the split is still mostly equal, accounting for local trends. Perhaps because of this, suburbanites will likely want to go along to get along.

Throughout this book, the primary frame of reference has been the rising battle between Left and Right, expressed through different aspects of conflict which line up along other axes of identity nearly as easily, but there truly has also been a third faction: Those who support the status quo. The moderate consensus which the media promoted until relatively recently in many ways reflected the suburban position which is tranquility through avoiding contentious social issues and focusing instead on economic benefit.

Although it is true suburbia tends to have permissive social views which differ greatly from the impulses of radical transformation expressed by the urban discontents, but which also lacks the moral rectitude of the country people who often still attend church and worship regularly, a less generous interpretation of suburbia is the faith of the suburbanite is strongly placed in pure and simple materialism. Their cathedrals are the strip malls and box stores where one measures progress by the aesthetics of their appliances or how lovely their next new car will be. Living well means having much, and this definition of successful life has consequences.

When we look at the economy before Trump, there was a bipartisan consensus behind free markets that seemed blithely oblivious to the reality that our trade and tariff policies have been sending our jobs abroad for decades. Cities and towns alike throughout much of this country, especially in the earlier developed Northeast and Midwest were hollowed out with nothing but miles of empty carcasses of mill buildings and decaying factories left to remind us that these were once great production sites. This is not just true of major cities, the old company town which had been a viable model for the medium sized city was just as devastated, and what rose in their place? Suburbs.

As the definition of economic growth shifted from production to consumption, so too did the ideas of what constituted wealth from something publicly visible to corporate balance sheets and shrewd financial maneuvers. Whereas at one time shipping American jobs overseas would have been considered economic treason, by the 1980's, people looked at using cheap labor overseas as a benefit, and even managed to present such actions as moral. This was an earlier wave of globalism that made all which followed possible, emphasizing national disconnect for individual benefit, and could only work in a world where people were atomized from one another and removed from the consequences of their actions.

A city would have protested. A small town would have fallen apart. But the suburbs were uniquely indifferent, a place where interactions tend toward the superficial, and so the growth of an America that looked right but felt empty was perfect for an economy based upon building wealth without substance to follow. As long as those managers making the tough decisions to save money could continue padding their retirement accounts and take nice vacations with the family, it seemed like no one cared that America was no longer able to produce what was required to meet its own needs. Other parts of the world could handle the dirty parts of life.

This compromise between the institutional forces of the Left and Right was held in equilibrium in this status quo because each side got something. The Left got to bring in new people, their shock troops of the future in a host of legal and illegal immigrants to do the difficult work of farm labor and service employees since they kept costs lower for the upwardly mobile. Of course, we've seen the consequences of that, and give credit to the Left for playing the long game. For the Right, since they submitted in the culture war, they could instead speak the language of free markets, and with hopeless idealism think that capitalism alone would convert people to the American culture. It succeeded for many, but not nearly enough, especially given who was admitted. But having a hefty bank account eases a wounded conscience, and so this balance endured for some time until the consequences of these decisions overwhelmed the moderates.

I cannot say with certainty that the moderate apolitical types are outnumbered by those who are more devoutly partisan. majority, but their casual indifference to the broader cultural patterns affecting the country is a big part of why America has these conflicts today. They were responsible for the American sell-out, a fact realized with equal intensity by those on the far right and the far left, and the sole thing upon which both sides might agree is that continuing along the status quo path represents nothing but draining the vitality of America.

This being the case, if you have the opportunity to talk with anyone who is passionate about their beliefs, you will often find the group they like least are these people in the center, who comfortably reside in the suburbs, whose American dream they want to see disappear. This being the case, one might question why I don't present them as a third faction capable of self-defense for the status quo, but the reason that isn't suggested is because they're not political. Or rather, the way they express their political influence is through the corporations who hire and sustained them buying office holders on both sides to maintain control.

It was a remarkably resilient system which might yet restore itself, but I think that is now unlikely because of how widespread the anger throughout the nation has become. The Right under Trump has embarked on a nationalist path that will open doors at home by closing the doors abroad that allowed sending jobs overseas for a quick buck. And the Left, while much more internationalist in focus, is not going to rebuild their philosophy after these defeats around the banker plan to slowly develop the world; their changing demographics demand more direct action and government intervention.

The post-Cold War consensus is collapsing, and we see the consequences of this worldwide. One could argue the European model is much like how we're describing the American suburbs: happiness is secular materialism with a dash of social conscience. And we can easily see how ineffective that has proven to the challenges of mass migration. Soon, Europe won't be populated by Europeans. And to be indecently honest, America was sliding down that same path. Too many people have spoken against that now for this to be resolved without some sort of action, but a day is coming where the question of nations versus global actors will require resolution. This American conflict, as huge as it may become, is but one theater in this global campaign that will consume much of the western world, and potentially other areas as well.

Is it fair to put all this on suburbanites who were just working their jobs and following the American Dream available to them? Of course not. Most people in any situation are only vaguely aware of the full depths of political maneuvering affecting them. But a more balanced criticism might suggest their opportunism was a bit cynical and their specialization as purely most-efficient economic actors, should things come to a head, will offer little protection.

From the perspective of civil conflict, the suburbs truly are a no-man's land. Offering neither the protection of the city nor the resources of the country, they feel like a place where one gets stuck while heading somewhere else. As battle lines harden, it seems likely that the people in the suburbs will be drawn to one side or the other, with the primary factor deciding which way people travel being where greater safety can be ensured. Because once the shelves are empty at the big stores and Prime isn't making home deliveries, the beautifully manicured lawns are not going to feed anyone.

Writing about this area is difficult because the non-ideological suburbanites are going to have little agency, as a class, in battles fought by people with stronger and opposing beliefs. Individuals will gravitate to either side, and we see hints that at least a big portion of suburbanites are leaning toward the rural Right leaning faction in just how far the exurbs have spread. Consider those the people that realize the old consensus is breaking apart, but there are people pushing back into the city as well, and between them lies a battleground.

In politics, we decide elections now by who wins the suburban vote, and it will be interesting to see how quickly, and if they radicalize in support of either the now nationalist Right or the soon-to-be fully socialist Left, or if someone with lots of money will jump in to offer a third way to keep the current consensus. But for all their import politically, it's funny how they shift from being a power source to a large group of people who have the least to offer if things go hot.

The longer this conflict is delayed, the more people will leave this comfy center to seek protection for their families pro-actively. But for the moment, they retain considerable power in deciding who will control government, an utterly crucial starting point for any potential outbreak, and potentially in preventing a fight from happening. We'll discuss this in far greater depth as we hit the scenarios and see the suburbs try to play peacemaker.

Section III: The Groups

Group III: Race

Much like a pendulum, race went from meaning everything back in the 1960's to meaning little in the 1990's, and now is swinging back into vogue as having great import. Before the passage of the Civil Rights Act, the White majority enforced its control through legal structures. To remedy these concerns for greater peace, most structural impediments were removed to try to realize equality between races. The Right agreed to this based upon the mistaken belief that a common culture could be maintained, but the Left then began their process of radicalizing minorities through Marxist activism designed to foster a permanent majority through resentment and identity politics.

These actions were concealed for many decades because of the relative disparity of the numbers of people in the different racial groups. And that the point of equilibrium where race had become a less prominent source of public discord was reached around 1990. Yet, upon achieving relative equality, the Left continued their efforts to further stoke resentment through race baiting, and the Right obliviously followed along thinking that the equilibrium represented the new norm rather than the midpoint of a shifting pendulum moving toward what is now termed the "coalition of the ascendant," a group aspiring to seize power from the traditional White majority rather than sharing such status.

That many Whites are involved with these actions are a sign of just how confused ideology and race have become. To explain this, we have to look more closely at how subgroups within the larger White community are behaving, and as controversial as

245

this might be, what seems to best explain these contradictions is that while most self-identifying Whites are moving Right, Jews are uniquely moving Left and should therefore represent a different group altogether, in much the same way as Latinos are treated as a distinctive ethnicity.

One thing that is clear is that as culture has devolved along racial lines, the lack of common vision of the future is pushing the races toward greater political polarization. Blacks have been voting overwhelmingly for Democrats for many decades now, but Whites are increasingly self-identifying as Republicans. Latinos are more complicated but are trending Democrat with increasing speed. Asians are more varied, but the initial indications are they too trend leftward. There is every reason to believe these trends will only accelerate, and as the maps below will reveal, the relationship between which groups live where geographically and the emergent voting patterns is highly suggestive.

Map 4

Map 4 displays where White, non-Latino populations live in the United States. The figures in this and each of the succeeding maps in this section are based upon the 2010 US Census and were compiled by Randy Olson. Note the clustering from the Mountain West across the northern tier, through the Great Plains and throughout Appalachia and then New England. Excepting the Deep South, this reflects the Republican results in 2016 with high fidelity.

Map 5

Map 5 demonstrates how Black populations are most densely scattered throughout the Deep South and then within cities along the Atlantic seaboard and in clusters throughout the Midwest like Chicago, Detroit, and Cleveland. Although (and perhaps because) Black populations vote overwhelmingly for Democrats, Whites who occupy those same spaces now tend to vote overwhelmingly Republican as in Mississippi and Alabama

foreshadowing the emergent national pattern of identity-based voting habits.

Map 6

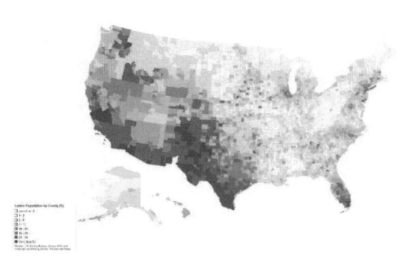

Latino Population by County (%)

© 2014 Dietrich Jells

Map 6 shows where the largest clusters of Latino populations are found. As one would expect, they are most commonly found near the Mexican border, along the Pacific Coast, in the Miami area, and around New York. Latino immigration has had one of the largest impacts on changing voting patterns, as their tendency to break nearly 2:1 for Democrats has helped turn the West Coast into a Democratic stronghold and has converted Nevada, Colorado, and New Mexico to the Left. Given this map, it suggests the next states to turn might be Arizona, Idaho, and Texas should more Latino immigrants arrive, or identity politics based patterns harden.

248

Map 7

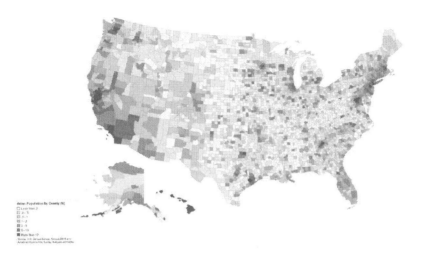

Asian Population by County [%]

Map 7 shows where Asians are settling in America. With the biggest clusters in California and Seattle, they also have a presence in many American cities including around DC and New York in larger numbers. Asians tend to vote much like Latinos, with different subgroups showing different characteristics. Indians tend considerably more Republican than east Asians.

These maps suggest that identity politics are playing an ever-increasing role in how people associate and vote, and parallel both the residency and ideological patterns from preceding chapters. The very success of the Left in radicalizing minorities to enact their vision is causing an active reaction from the Right to become not just implicit representatives of White culture, but to engage more explicitly in identity politics. As the racial and cultural lines commingle, look for racial conflict to increase and become, whether publicly mentioned or not, a main dividing line in the rising tensions throughout the country.

Chapter 25: Team White—Whites and Europeans

For clarity, we will define White people as people who are primarily of European extraction and who self-identify as such. Race being such a sensitive issue, as acceptance into certain identity groups carries either explicit or implicit benefit, these chapters will assume a simpler test than genetics: If a person acts in a way which culturally passes for a race and can visibly pass for that group, they're assumed to be a part of the tribe. Such is how we live our lives and manage our own preconceptions, so it works here as well.

White people remain the majority of the people in the United States. According to the 2017 census estimate, whites make up 60.7% of the current American population, although it's worth noting that the past few years have seen minorities, driven more by Latino births than any other subgroup, reach parity with White people in the terms of new births. Even though the White majority remains dominant, demographics absent any new immigration which is not accounted for in these statistics, the future along the current trajectory will see a further diminution of white influence with White people becoming a minority by 2043 at the latest.

The heaviest concentration of White people is in the north as opposed to the south, and in the east more than the west. Rural areas in America are overwhelmingly White compared to cities, and states which voted Republican in the preceding election are Whiter than most of those who voted

Democrat, with the New England corridor being the most prominent exception.

Given their historical dominance, White people tend to collectively possess the most wealth in the country, although this so-called White privilege is somewhat misleading. There are also many Whites who live in abject poverty or who have a modest middle-class existence, given the large quantity of people involved.

White identity itself is a very strange thing that requires much discussion. Before the 1960's, most Americans who were White had no problem identifying with this label and took it as a source of pride. Because most of the country was almost completely White so there was little need for that distinction, it wasn't used as much as other divisions. It was far more common to adopt distinctions between Catholics and Protestants or between immigrants who were of WASPish (White Anglo-Saxon Protestant) extraction as compared to later Catholic immigrants from places in eastern and southern Europe, as well as Ireland. But as these successive waves of immigrants settled into America and the relatively slight differences between their cultures and versions of Christianity were reconciled in a broadly compatible social matrix, America began to define itself as something of a White Christian nation. Although there were always a few minorities descended from the days of slavery, with their own unique claims, they were a very small number and not widespread. In many parts of America, a person could grow up and live his entire life, never having seen a person who was not White other than in magazine photos.

So, 1950's America remains probably the pinnacle of White America where a common culture existing upon the nuclear family, something of a unique American digression from the extended families more common elsewhere around the world, the Christian faith, and a work ethic based upon personal responsibility and diligence endured. The United States was a happy and productive country, having emerged in global dominance from the Second World War, and in relative social equilibrium.

It's an oversimplification to say this was all destroyed in the 1960's, as the Fifties themselves hinted at the communist subversion which was well underway in terms of getting people into the media and universities who had a different view, more akin to the Soviet model. They were able to get McCarthy tossed and the examinations from Congress removed, but the passage of time has made those like the Senator who spoke out against the rise of Marxist influence in America look eerily prescient.

The communists took over the schools, the publishing of textbooks at all levels, the control of many newspapers. First radio and then television invited anchors paid by those same people into our homes to reach a generation who listened with awe to these new technologies. Americans heard a message of free love and a world where borders didn't matter, and that all people were inherently good and equivalent. Old ideas which had built the country were put into disrepute, and idea after idea was torn down.

From a cultural perspective, the pillars of White civil society, which were the church, the community, and the family, were obliterated. America worked because morality was always a social obligation, but one that existed outside the government's authority. This changed as the Marxists pushed hard, especially under LBJ. Churches were silenced by threats from the IRS, judges converted the courts from an institution that protected families into forums that set women against men, and new programs emanating from and accountable only to Washington centralized power in a place most people could not reach or influence.

From the racial perspective, a country which had integrated well and was happily overwhelmingly White, with a vital and ongoing effort to lift the Black minority, was transformed deliberately into a different demographic blend. Whereas immigration before 1965 explicitly advantaged those seeking entry from Europe on the theory that people who shared common ancestry, faith, and traditions would best mesh together, the logic of the Cold War putting ideology ahead of identity was used to pass the infamous Hart-Celler Act of 1965. Thereafter, America would be a country receiving most of its immigrants from the Third World, where one family member could bring in an entire clan, and where a lottery to redress historical imbalances would replace a more thoughtful merit system.

It's no accident this passed under Lyndon Johnson, who more so than any other American President, bears blame and responsibility for setting us on the path to civil conflict we tread today. His policy programs which explicitly shifted the idea of the Left from economic development to cultural warfare created an environment that shattered the once dominant cultural paradigm of "one America" into a culture divided by race based upon who could best use government to their advantage. The cultural Marxists supporting him knew this was their intent from the very beginning, but it took the forces of the Right at least thirty years to begin seeing how insidious this plan was, and sadly, another thirty more to begin acting with forceful certitude in opposition to these actions.

It's worth asking why did White people do this to themselves? There is not a singular answer, but there are a few thoughts. First, from a positive way of looking at things, the desire to realize equality and humane treatment to all races was a real and shared impulse of many during the 1960's. While many of the organizers were far more radical than their followers, probably a general tendency of most political movements at the time, recognizing the legal equality of Black Americans as well as Natives and other groups was something most Americans supported in accordance with the ideas of liberty. There were holdouts, but the White majority, and I would venture to say the Right generally, have always, rooted in their own Christian background, wanted to find an equilibrium where people are respected as individuals rather than as part of a group.

But the second answer, which will probably get me into some trouble, is that there are subgroups within the White group who don't act very White. By this, I mean Jews, who while lumped in with other Whites, tend to behave very differently. Because of the excesses of the Nazi regime in Germany, Jews have been able to escape critical inquiry for over seventy years for their actions in America and the West, which conceals a trend whereby they have been the single largest force behind the hard shift leftward in America.

Strong claims require strong evidence. We often talk about who controls academia, the media, and entertainment. Jews graduate from Harvard Law at a percentage today more than 46 times what their percentage of the population would suggest. 93% of the media is owned by Jews, and they have been deliberately buying papers and networks since their big migration wave at the turn of the last century. And most tellingly, if one goes back to the 1950's, the last time America could consider such things before the media blockade was complete, well over half the publicly shared membership of the American Communist Party was Jewish even though Jews were less than 2% of the population. The same pattern recurs in the Socialist Party chaired by Eugene Debs.

Researching such claims will get you blacklisted from universities and banned from public media, but it is the reason why there is a rising undercurrent against Jewish influence. Such angst is driven by the punishment regime the ADL along with their allies in the SPLC enforces on those who report these inconvenient patterns. Not content to compete in a free marketplace of ideas to discuss evidence and find truth, the ADL and SPLC destroy the jobs and families of those who notice inconvenient patterns, and systematically deny any access to public discourse. It is wholly un-American to embrace such censorship, or to levy such penalties on free discourse, but as these people are now being given the right to choose not just what goes in print or on the air, but also to control social media like Facebook and YouTube, books like mine are some of the last to point out the trend before us.

I do not believe that all Jews are communists, or that they are bad people, or deserve specific sanctions for these trends. But I think we need to talk about why they act this way, what in their culture makes them act so differently, and to understand just how monumental a role they have played and continue to have in pushing the Left forward. Because when you look at who pushed most strongly to change America from the country it was to the country it has become today, they were the key influence. The same is true in Europe as well, and for those seeking greater understanding, please study the Frankfurt School Institute for Social Research for further insight.

This trend continues today, and I'll offer one last fact about why we should potentially consider treating Jews as deliberately separate from other White people before getting back to the broader White majority. As the Left has embraced identity politics, in many ways radicalizing minorities against the majority through doctrines of racial resentment and White privilege, Whites vote more Republican and we see identity politics beginning on the Right, as expressed (albeit inarticulately) by the Alt-Right

256

movement, but as likely to manifest in coming cycles as better-established identity organizations.

With 58% of White people voting for Trump in the previous election, he was able to flip states throughout the Rust Belt to break the so-called blue wall and achieve victory. He made gains with every group in the White categories ranging from educated to uneducated, men and women alike, and across most ethnic subdivisions from different countries and religious affiliations within Christianity. The only group of White people who didn't support Trump were Jews, who voted 70% for Hillary, a divergence of 28% from the norm which doesn't even consider the fact that 58% is inclusive of the Jewish vote.

Race is a funny construct. One's racial background is partly genetic. But it is also partly cultural in the form of a set of beliefs that one affixes to their heritage and future. But it is also part choice, in that for race to have meaning, people have to embrace it as a form of identity. In America, as much as in response to the other where every other race is encouraged pride and positive identity, White identity is emerging. It is increasingly unified geographically, culturally, and politically, except for one major group: Jews. Take them out of the equation, and weird quirks about the Northeast and urban areas make better sense, the White liberals in the city shrink considerably into the Jewish subset, and the White voices supporting the Left are massive reduced.

I firmly believe, in America, it is the right of any group to speak their mind and take positions which they believe. I also believe, for the benefit of us all, people should speak honestly about their intentions as I have done in my books. So, I submit to you that Jews, through their own actions and culture, have set themselves as a unique ethnicity apart, and for analytical purposes, need to be treated as separate and distinct from any other White group. As one does this, what becomes clear is that the opinions of White people are far less conflicted than the media presents, and an emergent political consensus is forming to reclaim a culture much more like the 1950's than today.

This latent energy has been building for a while but has failed to rise to the level of public expression due to several factors. First, the desire of the mainstream media to delegitimize white identity as a means of political expression has been ongoing and enforced through social and financial sanction. I lived it; I know. Second, political actors on the Right were unwilling to positively embrace White identity because of a desire to avoid the condemnation of media (which could be fatal in an electoral system) as well as the hopes of reaching minority groups with a message of opportunity and self-development, as opposed to the redistribution policies featured by the Left. We will discuss those more in succeeding chapters, but apart from some success with Asians, Latinos vote 2:1 and Blacks vote 10:1 for Democrats, which suggests such strategies have had limited efficacy. Third, the donors who have historically written the checks for the GOP don't like the controversy inherent in race-based politics, and served as a final barrier to entry, keeping people like Pat Buchanan who foresaw these trends decades ago from crashing the party.

Trump changed everything. If you honestly look at the crowd at one of the massive rallies Trump holds regularly throughout the heartland, you'll notice immediately, as the Left does, that his support is overwhelmingly White. There will be a few prominently placed minorities directly behind the President, people who rightly have determined they will get a bigger taste of a growing pie by following his path to cultural renewal, but these are exceptions who prove the larger case. Consider their placement a political reflex from years of trying to represent all Americans, but the difference now is the Right is moving forward with the agenda they believe, regardless of whether everyone is aboard or not.

Trump is White America in revolt, where people who represented a moral majority defending a shrinking culture have been pushed into fighting back for the country they once had. After years of trying to share America and meet the Left halfway, after sacrificing much to meet minorities half way, and even be welcoming to all these newcomers in the hope that American ideas would prove bigger than identity, Trump's election signified the end of trying to do things the nice way.

It's no accident that the biggest issues for Trump's administration have been political correctness and immigration. For years, things people have said in private conversation have been repressed publicly out of a desire to encourage those at the bottom to avail themselves of

259

opportunities. Although programs like affirmative action have long been loathed by many Whites, recognized as they are as unmerited subsidies to create a ladder for those of lesser qualifications, they were tolerated in the hope they would be used to ensure peace. But these overtures were rejected by the minorities who chose to throw in with a Left who promised to give them what others had earned. And seeing this trend, the Left has just continued to import people from a Third World rife with corruption where the redistribution policies they love so much are normal.

As we bring in people from these foreign cultures, we lose the old America. Look how Mexicans turned California blue, but further still, into a socialist haven where there are a few rich people and people now live in campers and homeless camps. I wish I was making this up, but the facts are there to be found, though the media never reports them. They are flipping the entire southwest, and as they seed cities, immigrants from places like Somalia, a country which has no connection to America whatsoever, are planted in places like Maine or Minnesota to turn us also. Following their cultural and sometimes religious imperatives, they come here, and are subsidized to breed new Democrats while the rest of us work to figure out to pay for our own kids.

There are many polite White people who look the other way. But the number shrinks each day, and with the incessant political and cultural conflicts, and the clear and raw hypocrisy of how the media treats Whites as opposed to all others, things are changing quickly. Had things proceeded more slowly, and had the Left been gentler than Obama was, perhaps Whites would have remained asleep. But now that so many are awake, regardless of what they say to pollsters and polite society, things cannot go back to the way they were.

Whites can see what will happen should they lose their majority, and those who look honestly at the demographics know the tipping point comes around 2040. This date might arrive far sooner if Democrats who will open the borders and legalize millions of illegal immigrants, as they are unabashedly signaling, regain control. Racially aware people pushed Trump through the GOP primary process and into the Oval Office to prevent this, not out of hatred of the other, but out of mere self-preservation. Because when the Left has organized minorities to hate the outgoing majority, there is an example today to show what happens.

Look at South Africa, at the brutal murders of White people who gave away their once First World country to have peace. They gave their homeland to Blacks for racial peace, either not realizing or perhaps, not caring enough that these people were communists in waiting. Now they are being butchered, murdered, stripped of their rights, and not even being permitted to leave because they are to be used. The ideology being employed against Whites here with the doctrines stating we are to be held accountable for all history's wrongs is no different, so why would any sane person expect the outcomes to differ then either?

Such thinking is very sad and depressing, but one more reason why Whites as the bedrock of the Right coalition, are moving toward the idea that conflict is preferable to submission. This trend is hidden a bit by the fact many older people seem to just want to comfortably run out the clock on their lives, but if you want an honest accounting of how people think when they're not being threatened, with a mind to how the younger people who will shape the future see things, spend a few hours reading /pol/ over at 4chan and you might walk away with a new appreciation.

The last point which needs to be made about White identity is this: There remain many White people who are resistant to embracing who they are, wanting to either remain idealistic about race relations in America, or seeing such action as exacerbating these tensions. The latter criticism is especially valid, which is one reason you will see the Right talk in terms of culture, ideology, and residency before race, but considering how broad these all overlap, what will end up happening, whether it is explicitly voiced or not, is people will make judgments where race serves as the assumption for all these other values. In less heated times, such presumptions might be overcome, but should conflict grow as this volume predicts, there will not be time to make more than these snap judgments, which is why, should a civil war arise over race or ideology, the odds it will take on racial characteristics as well are extremely high.

Chapter 26: Team Black—Blacks and Africans

One of the very few areas where I agree with the Left is that a White man can't understand what it is like to be Black. Or any other race for that matter, because we live such different lives. And unlike the traditional view of the Right where we have pretended race doesn't matter, I think such an oversimplification is both naïve and unhelpful. Of course, race matters, and while opportunity transcends race, certain doors open and certain doors close depending upon these forms of identity.

Firmly believing it is important to be aware of one's own biases lest one succumb to that worst tendency of the journalist hacks with their pretensions of objectivity, I can only offer that I will try to do justice to how I observe other races behaving, and to envision things from their perspective to offer the fullest account possible. As my account will certainly fall short of the fullest expression in these areas specifically, I encourage others to look at what Blacks and all other races say for themselves, so then you don't have to rely simply on yours truly as intermediary. Those caveats clearly and honestly made, here's what I see:

Before going into deeper detail, let's look at Blacks demographically. Blacks are primarily of African origin. 13.4% of Americans identify as Black which has been a relatively stable percentage of the population for a few decades now. Overwhelmingly concentrated in the Deep South, there are also pockets of Black people in many major cities, who tend to live near one another. While rural Blacks are common in the South, they stick to cities almost exclusively elsewhere. Blacks vote overwhelmingly for Democrats with 89% of those surveyed having been reported as voting for Hillary, with their support consistently remaining around 90% across election cycles.

Blacks in America should be divided into at least two groups who have very different claims in this country. The first group are those who are directly descended from slaves, largely of West African origin, whose families predate the Civil War, and whose history in America goes back two centuries or longer and who have their own distinctive American culture. The second group are those who came in successive waves after 1965 including recent immigrants, and whose culture, often coming from Muslim nations, is radically different and more aggressive. Realizing that the joining of families over times makes it impossible to fully separate one group from the other, just as with Whites, I'll try to distinguish between the two more based on behavior than strict affiliations where relevant.

It's also important to realize that within Black America, there are differences between those who are darker and lighter in status. The reality is after centuries of cohabitation in a White country, there are many people of mixed race who fit uncomfortably into the categories this section has drawn. For those of mixed ancestry who are very light, it is possible to gain entrance into some sectors of White society. For those who are darkest, usually the opposite is true, with people in between having mixed experiences.

American society is ill-equipped to talk about these differences, so I'll use the example of how Mexico, which like many Latin American countries with a small White over-class but many people of mixed heritage, deals with these questions, because it seems like the Black community itself behaves much like they do. Greater status and desirability are attached to lighter skin color because of the social benefits conveyed, but resentment flows most strongly from those who are darkest because of their perceived or actual social disenfranchisement.

Such conclusions might seem controversial, but as Blacks across all shades and variations are actively encouraged to express positive racial identity, most likely to be harnessed in support of the Leftist agenda the Marxists who make these rules support, one can look across social media and get a quick flavor of this phenomenon. Should a darker skin man of prominence go out with a lighter skinned woman like a mulatto, criticism is quick about abandoning his race as if they weren't good enough. Should a Black man date a White woman, such angst rises to a roar, especially for prominent people, as being a race traitor is considered particularly egregious.

It's worth noting the discrepancy in how these behaviors are treated publicly for Whites as opposed to Blacks. As an experiment, go onto Twitter and look if Black people making racially insensitive comments about other Blacks, Whites, or any other race are censored for offending community standards. With few exceptions, you will find they are not, and people making these comments will often be verified, monetized, and allowed to post without any constraint. By contrast, should a White person make any comment deemed even slightly unseemly, it's amazing how quickly the bans come out. Such actions illustrate how race is used to forward a larger agenda.

My own belief and that of most on the Right is that the Left uses Blacks, encouraging their anger and resentment, to ensure their votes are perpetually secured. They do this by encouraging a plantation mentality where Blacks are offered a certain small guaranteed fixed subsidy, such as welfare, affirmative action government jobs and other programs, and certain legal privileges and considerations, in exchange for the certainty they will vote to sustain their subsistence. As long the money keeps flowing, the votes keep coming, but the tradeoff for Black America is they are held hostage to the deal from the Left.

Whole books have been written which intelligently describe how when populations trade in their prerogatives for action in exchange for government support, they lose agency and succumb to political indifference. The combination of such idleness with the surety of economic maintenance encourages behaviors of irresponsibility, and we see hints this impacted Black America in the elevated crime rate, drug usage, and breakdown of the family compared to any other racial group.

Statistics bear out the assertion. If we assume that having two parent families is beneficial for children, as bringing more authority and resources to child rearing, Blacks have an enormous disadvantage today. The Annie E.

Casey Foundation reports that for 2016, single mothers constituted 66% of the households in which Black children were being raised. It's remarkable to imagine 2 in 3 Black children growing up without a father, but this fact goes ignored as it fits the larger leftist agenda of reducing authority outside the state. By comparison, 42% of Latino, 24% of White, and only 16% of Asian children are being raised by a single mother.

From this breakdown in the family, other disadvantageous trends predictably result. Less access to higher education, greater likelihood of committing crime or having crimes committed against them, lower economic earnings, and a tendency toward government dependency all follow for the Black community. This was the deal they were given by the Left after LBJ shifted the promising efforts to integrate the then small Black population into the larger White majority toward politics which deliberately endeavored to use the Black population as a splinter faction in both politics and what evolved into the larger culture war.

As race splintered politically, culture followed. While there had always been Black culture in America, with features like gospel, jazz, barbecue, and rhythm and blues being unique contributions that became part of a larger American cultural scene, driven by people largely descended from the antebellum populations of America, there was a radical shift as races approached legal and political equity sometime around the end of the Cold War. Whereas Black culture had largely been part of a shared American tradition, it was now encouraged to diverge toward an angrier and edgier view, with hip hop and gangsta culture prominently pushed by the media. One might conclude the reason this happened is that as the reasons for political resentment fell away from the Left, opening the door to the Right to reach out to minorities, it became necessary to begin anew the cycle of isolating Blacks from Whites to grow government authority.

Crack was a part of this. What was done to the Black community to tear apart their families happened with government acquiescence from our Deep State friends in the intelligence agencies whose hands appear dirty, is happening today with meth and heroin throughout White populations in Appalachia. These drugs play a huge role in destroying families, and our utterly inadequate response to either of these crises is disheartening. But it fed the resentment that built the hostile culture whereby it was seen that Whites used drugs to keep Blacks down, and a new generation of radicals ensued.

Since I find the basic leftist theory of empowerment by taking on terms meant as derogatory like nigger in the case of Blacks and shouting them out as absurd, I can't pretend I see where hip hop, Ebonics, and various other measures as anything except a clever way to trick self-righteous people who were hurt into facilitating their own marginalization. They were deliberately isolated from other opportunities through these forms of expression, but such separation does serve a higher purpose: It ensures cultural division is at the heart of America, moves along racial lines, and as such, is nearly impossible to reconcile. Using the same pattern with Latinos, as well as certain groups with strong non-racial identity, the New Left was forged.

This is a coalition of pissed off people who feel they are "different" and deserve equal status to the culture they were tricked into avoiding. From such a starting point, it's easy to see why the majority often lacks empathy, but that's long been the problem for the Black community, where they have been susceptible to listening to those who present a momentary solution that creates a worse long-term issue or dependency.

While the trends described above apply primarily to those of African origin whose lineage stretches back before the post-1965 immigration act, the inclusion of many new Africans into the mix who shared little in common culturally but were racially related to the existing populations served to facilitate the desired radicalization by the Left. Somalis and immigrants coming from East Africa are the perfect example, who come from Muslim countries long troubled by violence.

Black nationalism had a long and storied history in America going back to the Black Panther movement of the 1960's, which endured beyond the passage of the Civil Rights Act, and then found new means of expression. Just as many people listened to Malcolm X's message of self-determination as listened to Martin Luther King's message of inclusion, and the division between inclusion and self-sovereignty has never been fully settled within the Black community. It continues today in more radical forms like the Nation of Islam, a group driven more by race than religion, and Black Lives Matter, a radical group who expresses the separatist instinct.

We must talk about Obama in some depth because his election represents a seminal event in race relations, although it perhaps did not accomplish the goals intended. In electing a Black President, many Americans across both sides of the political aisle probably hoped this would serve to salve long simmering racial resentments and prove, beyond any shadow of a doubt, that America had moved beyond racial conflict. Such hopes, though nobly expressed, ran against nature and reality, and therefore idealism gave way to the more bitter resentment we see manifested today.

When you look at the actions of someone like Eric Holder who handcuffed police nationwide to enforce the laws while the Justice Department actively funded organizations who supported mass Black rallies, it was hard for any person looking at these facts to conclude anything other than a separate set of rules was being created to place Blacks above the law. Such inequity had been hinted at for years, going back to the Civil Rights Act itself which basically gerrymandered Black congressional districts, but after years of special consideration for Blacks, the idea that a Black administration would so blatantly favor Blacks above others was more than the race blind Right could swallow.

One could argue, as the Left does, that Obama was simply doing what White Presidents had done before him in looking out for the interests of their own people. Such criticism strikes me as entirely valid, and from the perspective of race realism which is growing in America, it's

270

easy to see the American consensus which endured culturally as being contingent on an ethnic super-majority which could certainly be inclusive, but only inasmuch as population didn't create a scenario where a coalition threatened to displace the majority. As this has changed, so has the attitude on the Right.

What this means is despite the efforts by President Trump to reunite the country on a cultural basis, these will likely fail due to the reality that race-based cultures have already diverged. While there are Black people who identify with White culture, and even more White people who identify with Black culture, these fragments are not going to prevent the larger trend of accelerating racial resentment, with fears of rising identity politics on the Right serving to stoke minorities into fears of what an unapologetic White majority might attempt. In taking the most extreme and marginal voices from the Internet as examples of what is being planned, the media stokes these fears.

Under these circumstances, while opportunities will remain open for Black people to jump across racial lines to become part of the broader culture, I suspect we will see a closing of the ranks become more common as the political discourse forces people to commit to one of these opposing sides. Given their current affiliation and given also the reality that those areas where Black people most commonly reside outside the cities are the same where the most conservative of Republicans and Whites live, it's almost impossible to imagine Blacks abandoning the leftist coalition. While there will be a radical fringe, the problems in their own community are such that organization will likely remain limited to a racial basis and any threat of violence will stay mostly inwardly focused save for individual actors driven more by criminal acts than political ones.

Blacks will vote for Democrats and by extension support radical solutions for government, but aside from those in the cities as part of larger ideological coalitions, they probably will not launch any sort of direct racial conflict. The many years of suppression in the South will repress any stronger impulses, and Black America remains in the position they were driven into taking a half century ago of being dependent upon others and having their group fortunes determined as such. Therefore, the South, despite having so many Blacks, remains solidly Republican, but areas where Latinos are ascendant, are behaving quite differently and much more aggressively.

Chapter 27: Team Brown—Latinos East and West

Considered an ethnicity rather than a race, Latinos represent a combination of White, Black, and Native influences and are people who derive from areas of the Caribbean and Latin America. There are considerable differences between people from the various parts of this broad region, and even within those who originate there based on the specific country of origin and genetic makeup. Because of these gradations, a survey of the Latino population will have to consider specific cases, but the primary point of emphasis will be the broad wave of immigration that has come predominantly from southern Mexico and down through Central America to Columbia.

When looking at the map of America as shown in **Map 6**, it's clear that the largest portion of the Latino population is in the west, and heaviest in proximity to the Mexican border with rising populations all along the Pacific Coast. Defined as Hispanics by the US Census, these people represent 18.7% of the total population according to the most current estimate. With a 2% growth rate, Latinos are now responsible for half the population growth in the United States. It's also worth noting that Latinos lead the way in new births, as every group in America is having more births than deaths except for one: White people. Such information may slightly obscure how births are happening given the rise in interracial relationships which also report a growing birth rate, but these figures show how the browning of America is a clear and unmistakable demographic trend.

To add further detail to the geographic picture, Latinos out west tend to be of either Mexican origin or from countries in a belt from Venezuela through Panama and the other countries of Central America up to Guatemala. Conversely, the other major concentrations of Latinos are in south Florida, home to the Cuban exiles who behave much more like Whites demographically and politically, and to Puerto Ricans who reside both there and in New York, who are much more liberal in their voting habits. Before covering Latinos out west, a brief discussion of those in the East who have a considerably smaller impact will be helpful.

Cubans, along with people from the Dominican Republic and other islands, have long been in Florida, with ties going back as far as when Florida was still a Spanish possession. But the largest growth in their community was when the many exiles came in the 1960's after Castro led his revolution to turn Cuba into a communist country. This seminal event defined the Cuban exile community of Miami in such a way that their primary issue for decades was opposition to communism, and so they behaved in many ways like other White voters, and for the purposes of our survey, if not the direct classifications used by the government, functionally have tended to behave just like them, preferring Republicans to Democrats and integrating as effectively as any subgroup from Europe ever did.

Puerto Rico is a different case. America owns and administers Puerto Rico as a possession, won after the Spanish-American War of 1898. Currently populated by over 3.3 million people, the island speaks Spanish as the primary language, but also has the unique ability conveyed by U.S. citizenship to enter the rest of the United States at will. Various governmental and economic pressures have pushed people off the island, and those leaving Puerto Rico came to settle primarily in Florida, New York, and a few other places in the east. Historically, they've trended leftward, and given their small numbers and early entry, their politics tended to get caught up with Blacks in terms of alliances in the East, and so their voting habits reflect a similar tendency. Their culture has remained more distinct, due both to the language barriers and racial difference.

As for Puerto Rico itself, it continues as a commonwealth of the United States, enjoying certain tax privileges, but lacking representation. There has been some activism in the past decade toward seeking statehood in what has been a contentious and confusing process, but there has also been considerable resistance to that idea as well, as Republicans generally who have no desire to create more Democrat seats. It seems unlikely these issues will resolve any time soon under the current cultural environment, exacerbated by a major debt crisis and hurricane damage on the island. Given these factors, Puerto Ricans will play a minor role, but for the purposes of larger consideration, serve as an extension of the Black community rather than that of the continental Latinos.

Having covered those exceptions, the primary thrust of Latino immigration has long been North through Mexico. The history of conflict between the United States and Mexico has been well-documented and serves as an important backdrop to the issues which have emerged. As America expanded westward after the Louisiana Purchase, Mexico began moving northward as they won separation from Spain. Texas was once their most Northeastern province, as they owned much of what is now the American Southwest ranging all the way west to California. Such areas were thinly populated by Mexicans who overwhelmingly remained in the Aztec heartland, and frankly had more Native Americans than people of either American or Mexican extraction, but lines on the map were drawn that way.

American expansion westward took on new speed after the War of 1812 which essentially confined British influence to Canada, and President Jackson enacted policies to encourage a land rush westward. As new settlements were claimed, and lands East of the Mississippi River began to fill, settlers invariably spilled over in Texas. At first invited by Mexico to settle the empty lands primarily of Northeastern Texas, Mexicans grew concerned that the new settlers held loyalties to the American civilization from which most originated rather than Mexico. A series of measures designed to constrain the Americans backfired, leading to a revolt by Texas, and the revolution for which the Alamo remains famous today as a last stand where many famous American patriots died in service to the eventual cause of Texas freedom.

In time, Texas would be annexed into the United States, and as President Polk came into office in 1848, the doctrine of Manifest Destiny was in full effect with the goal for the United States to reach the Pacific Ocean. Potential conflicts were considered with Great Britain over the Oregon Territory, then claimed by Britain, America, and a weaker claim by Russia, and Mexico to add California. With a settlement reached to divide Oregon along the 49th Parallel, which serves as our current border with Canada, American forces penetrated California and sought to encourage a revolt for annexation. Predictably, battles arose, and the Mexican-American War was begun, culminating in an American invasion of the Mexican heartland from Veracruz, and the treaty of Guadalupe Hidalgo whereby California, Arizona, Nevada, Utah, Colorado, New Mexico, and disputed parts of Texas were ceded to the United States in exchange for a severance. The later addition of the Gadsden Purchase, a small thinly populated area of southern Arizona, set the current border as exists today.

From the American perspective, these lands have now been part of the United States for over a century and a half. But from the Mexican perspective, these lands were stolen and should rightly be part of Mexico. The lines drawn were contentious, because even as Polk had instructed his emissary to seek more lands, racial considerations frankly drew the line as far north as it was taken because the idea at the time was adding Mexicans to America would represent a poor decision, so the treaty tried to carve out valuable regions without many people. Nonetheless, resentment simmered for many years, and border raids such as those of Pancho Villa became the stuff of legend in Mexico, and America always kept a close eye on Mexican resentments, using fear of such as part of the reasoning for entering World War I.

After that time, relations normalized, and the rapid growth of California brought in the first waves of Mexican immigrants who largely came north to work in agriculture where they settled in California and Texas. This established the basic pattern whereby farm labor would be seasonal and bring people north for the extra money. Some would return home and others would stay but send a substantial portion of their earnings home. This pattern continues today as many millions of dollars, earned both by legal and illegal immigrants, is sent primarily by wire back home to Mexico. Although the economic pressures remained constant, there were times when America was more welcoming to such labor as during FDR, and times where it was decided too many Latinos had come, as during Eisenhower where the infamous Operation Wetback deported large numbers of people.

After 1965, in parallel to the pattern observed with other populations, Latino immigration surged, bringing people from points further south than Mexico in substantial numbers for the first time. More than that, with increasing clarity for who was legally and illegally entering, we saw the migration patterns bring massive numbers of people. Where there were slightly under 10 million Latinos in America in 1970, this number has increased nearly six-fold since then to 57.5 million today according to Pew Research.

When breaking down how such growth happened, two factors played a huge role in supplementing the traditional migration patterns. The first was NAFTA. Passed into law in 1993, the North American Free Trade Agreement basically encouraged American firms to build factories, called maquiladoras, directly adjacent to the American border to take advantage of Mexico's less well-developed labor and environmental protections including much lower wage requirements. Such factories, though paying poorly by American standards, were considerably more generous than other native Mexican opportunities and they drew many people to the border.

It's worth noting that many of the people who came to work there were just as drawn by the fact that their traditional employment had been destroyed. Southern Mexico had long been the staple of their agriculture producing corn for the tortillas ubiquitous in Mexican diets, but with the passage of NAFTA, the heavily subsidized American corn industry dumped so much cheap corn into Mexico that it collapsed that sector of the economy. American agricultural concerns likewise moved into Mexico, sinking deep wells into aquifers that were quickly depleted sufficiently that the shallower wells of the native farmers went dry. This put even more Mexican farmers out of work. Effecting countries throughout Latin America, the free trade pressure pushed people north to the border, where some chose to work, and others chose to enter illegally into the United States seeking even better wages as well as generous public benefits.

The Republican Party, seeing the growth rates of the Latino population in western states where they had traditionally been either competitive or even had a majority, like California was not so long ago, in accordance with their free market policies, served the interests of business over culture and despite resistance, offered a mass amnesty under Reagan to millions of illegal Latinos in the United States. This granted them legal status in the United States and the voting privileges either they or their children would take.

The Democrats happily agreed to these new entrants, and it was in the 1990's that Democrats platform shifted from supporting union labor who had been the key to their dominance of the Midwest, to supporting low wage work in an international fashion as a means to invite the Latinos into their new coalition based on color. Whether it was opportunism or intent, the outcome was the same: The Democrats bought into the same free trade agenda they had opposed for many years. In this way the new post-Cold War consensus became two free market internationalist parties whose disagreements on economics and culture were constrained to arguing about social issues and wage laws, while what became the Rust Belt was sucked dry.

The Republicans offered opportunity. The Democrats offered subsidy. The Democrats won, and their willingness to serve as highest bidder has helped to radicalize Latinos leftward in America with voting patterns favoring the Left nearly two to one. Just as importantly, these demographic changes have made the entire Pacific Coast an impermeable stronghold for Democrats for Federal Elections. Having such dominance, the Left is enacting the same sort of plantation policies used to radicalize the Black population into generational cycles of dependency, and we've seen the same rise in drug usage, crime, and other social indicators.

It's interesting to see the difference in how Latinos have behaved politically in California versus Texas. When settled in areas that predominantly lean Right, where Republicans dominate, and where Latinos are a smaller percentage of the population, they seem to integrate better into what we could call the White electorate. Such has held true in Texas, settled earlier, and having taken in less percentage population increase than California. But even there, those numbers are growing, and the Tejano culture of the Mexican and other Latinos comes into contrast with the existing American country culture. Such division tends to encourage separation and Latino growth leads to political divergence. In other words, the more Latinos you add, the more leftist they behave.

Why that should be the case perhaps has to do with their Catholic roots and emphasis on strong and extended family structures. Far more than other groups in America, those who express strong religious values have children, and Mexicans practice this far more commonly than White America. They tend to band together, and as they do tend to have less wealth, the message of resentment has found fertile ground, ironically not so much with first generation immigrants who experienced failed leftist policies in many of their home countries, as we see most spectacularly in Venezuela today, but rather in second generation and later activists who believe they should have greater status in America.

These are the kids of the laborers who go to college, subsidized by programs that express racial preference for all minorities save Asians, and who go there to learn ideologies of racial resentment, White privilege, and for the Latinos specifically, of how these lands were stolen. Different movements exist, but Aztlan is a perfect example, where the argument is taught that the southwest was stolen, and Latinos are encouraged to work toward reclaiming what was lost for either Mexico or as a new land.

A culturally homogeneous America which spoke a single language for public discourse could contest these claims and potentially integrate people. But as we no longer have a common culture, and those entities that run culture today preach division and discord, efforts toward integration are woefully inadequate. So, we have a foreign culture now settling in territories America won through conquest, using a foreign language as the primary means of communication and open to a counter ideology of reconquest. Set this amid the backdrop of a drug war that is incredibly violent between not just gangs, but between communities and law enforcement, and it becomes clear that a powder keg could be brewing out west.

I grew up in Arizona. It was once a state settled primarily by mid-western pragmatists who settled there for warm weather. Phoenix had 100,000 people and the state was reliably red. Now, Phoenix has millions of people, Spanish is spoken as much as English, and the Latino population has exploded. The state, though still Republican, is closely following Nevada, Colorado, and New Mexico to the Left. And if we have seen only one thing demographically, once a state becomes a leftist stronghold based on minority rule, those states have never gone back to supporting the Right or voting Republican. It's hard to imagine they would do otherwise given how the Democrats promise them all everyone else has to offer, but such aggressive envy is impossible to counter and once stoked, seems hard to satiate.

Absent some major change, the Latinos will prove the decisive bloc in determining America's future. As they expand to consolidate control of the southwest, they are already coming into the South, into cities like Chicago, and because of their very fecundity, already represent half the future population coming into existence today. This was why the Right tried to win them over. Even though it is possible that new wealth and status may moderate their positions, both history and voting suggest it more likely we see them follow the leftist path of revolution and control so common throughout Latino dominated countries in both Central and South America. What is clear is the America they will create will likely look very different than the one which we have traditionally known and recognized.

Chapter 28: Team Yellow—Asian and Natives

In some ways, lumping Asians into one category when they obviously have different and distinctive cultures is not fair but given that Asians represent the smallest racial demographic in America, it makes some sense, because they have tended to blend into other existing communities from a political perspective. Culturally, however, Asians work very hard to keep their own communities intact, and in this, they are much like some of the earlier European waves of immigration where they integrate more successfully but go through an isolation process to inclusion.

For historical reasons that make a great deal of sense, ethnicity and country of origin matters far more sense to Asians which makes splitting them into categories more contentious than usual. With the recognition that many of these individual ethnicities don't like one another, we're going to consider four different groups briefly: These are East Asians, to include people of Japanese, Chinese, and Korean extraction, Southeast Asians from Vietnam, Thailand, Malaysia, and the Philippines, South Asia, to include Indians and secular types from Pakistan and India, and lastly, people from the Middle East who will be mostly Arabic. Obviously, these groups are very different, and while this volume believes those from the eastern regions of Asia will have the greater influence for reasons to follow, I will try to touch on each if only to acknowledge their prerogatives. Lastly, I will include a brief snippet about Native Americans in this chapter who are the original Asian immigrants, and who while a very small number of the

American population, deserve acknowledgment of their history.

The most recent Census statistics claim Asians make up 5.8% of the population, and across groups have the highest growth rate at 3%. They are overwhelmingly clustered on the Pacific Coast although they are growing in major urban centers like DC, New York, and Boston. Gathered statistics do not differentiate which groups are settling where, but what evidence exists suggests people from East Asia are more in the West, people from South Asia in the Midwest and Northeast slightly more than others, and Arabs have long gone into Michigan specifically.

Since voting isn't broken down by subgroup, we'll have to use the estimate of Asians in general to draw certain broad conclusions. Exit polling reported Asians voted around 65% for Clinton in 2016, reflecting a pattern which appears similar to Latinos where there is some integration into the Right, especially for those who have been here longer. This seems consistent with how areas with high Asian density lean quite leftward. As far as how subgroups voted, it seems likely based on policy preferences, Indians were the most rightward leaning group, with Arabs driven by concerns over policies about Muslims favoring the Left, and east Asians leaning generally leftward.

It bears observation that if the Left tries to amend their racial policies to offer Asians advantages, this would create problems with their Black and Latino voters, because Asians, due to certain cultural and intellectual reasons, don't require the same preferential considerations to compete. In fact, were they given preferential consideration for colleges, as just one example, based on test scores alone, they would likely dominate every university. Their stronger cultural cohesion and increased agency make Asians a very different minority group to consider, less dependent in many ways and more like the emplacement of a rival civilization.

East Asians include Japanese, who are a small percentage of the total, but primarily Koreans and Chinese. Koreans are most numerous in California and tend to blend into lower income communities with upward aspirations. All these communities, as well as the Chinese, tend to remain closely knit and in near proximity to one another, purchasing from the same neighborhoods and building distinct clusters in cities.

As an incredibly populous nation, China has sent the most immigrants here of any of the different countries under consideration, and as they have their own history of colonization throughout both Asia and in America, they demonstrate a unique strategy. Starting with immigrants arriving into San Francisco after the gold rush of 1848, Chinese people have come into America seeking work and opportunity. They worked to build the railroads and settled in major cities, many of which have a unique Chinatown district that has resisted integration and maintained a unique cultural identity.

The largest of these is in San Francisco, but Los Angeles, New York, and other major cities have similar places, and we see Chinese residency is heaviest along the West Coast and specifically in the Bay Area. It's also worth noting the heavy penetration of Chinese immigrants into Vancouver, British Columbia, as this fits a larger pattern of Chinese ringing the Pacific Ocean, potentially sending their own colonists to the West Coast in the same fashion Europeans once populated the American East.

Although earlier waves of Chinese immigration came without heavy resources, people arriving from China today often have considerable resources and move for political reasons or to shuffle money away from the communist regime to America where it can be used with less restraint. Chinese investment come through both immigrating citizens, and connections to the government of mainland China, suggesting the immigrants of Chinese extraction may, in some cases, have government support.

The western conception of citizenship is largely rooted in legal identity and location whereby moving to a new land conveys a new identity. But for many Asians, and for Chinese specifically, the Han Chinese are notorious for defining belonging on strictly racial terms, as minorities are actively discriminated against in China. We have also seen examples of Chinese expansionism ranging from centuries of Han mercantilism into Malaysia or even Singapore, or the annexation and population replacement of Tibet, an issue which once featured prominently in global activism but no longer draws such attention.

China has a long history of sending colonists elsewhere and then using those people as justification to stand up in defense of their people, defining citizenship ethnically rather than legally, a trend we see other countries such as Israel use in determining not just right of return, but foreign intervention. So, keeping this model in mind, as we see more Chinese influence grow in California, a state whose leftist tendencies have wandered into socialism and which has many people who would support communism, it's a valid to question the effects of Chinese influence. It is a challenging question but considering the way the media keeps silent about Chinese violence and totalitarianism, many on the Right wonder.

When you couple this with the foreign relations reality that America loses over 500 billion dollars per year in trade to the Chinese, that they represent our single largest foreign debt holder, and that their economy is largely driven by exports of manufactured goods to the United States, the tensions between the two countries in what is a productive but strained relationship cause concern. As American nationalism rises on the Right and we see these disparities called out for redress, it's likely these arguments will push those Chinese in America more toward the Left, in reflexive defense of their ancestry and relations.

Other Asian groups do not have such strength and influence and instead have a pattern more common to other minority groups who have come after 1965. They gather in urban areas, work for common benefit, and their slight leftward tilt becomes more pronounced in succeeding generations. With respect to the most common sources of immigration from Southeast Asia, we have Filipinos who came from the once American colony released after World War II and a tumultuous occupation, refugees from the

Vietnam War, and then a smattering of people from Thailand, Malaysia, and other countries. These smaller populations feature most heavily in cities and tend to live in the west.

South Asians are different. India, along with Pakistan and Bangladesh, which represent three nations carved out of the same civilization due to religious conflicts between Hinduism and Islam, has an increasing impact upon America because of their long colonization by the British and command of the English language, as well as enormous potential as both a labor and consumer market bringing them into American influence. We see Indians in every major city but given their specific antipathy toward Islam based upon centuries of conflict, their integration is somewhat reminiscent of the Cuban scenario where they have been much more hostile to the Left specifically because of how friendly the Left has generally been toward Muslims. Predictably, as the old-world conflicts color the first impressions of new immigrants, Pakistanis lean leftward.

There are larger clusters of Indians in the east compared to other Asians, having had a considerable presence in upstate New York, which can be explained in part by the many people from South Asia who migrated into the Canadian province of Ontario in the last forty years with their more generous immigration policies. From there, we see them spreading throughout other cities, but Indians seem to integrate most seamlessly into White communities and have used their education and talents which they bring with them to occupy places more in the middle class and professional tiers in America.

Tensions exist because American companies, seeing India as an opportunity, have been regularly outsourcing jobs to India. Nearly everyone in America has probably had the experience of dealing with an Indian call center, but less well known is how much of the software engineering and information-based industries also choose to operate in India but sell in the United States. While these relationships remain relatively cordial, with India and America being driven together by their mutual concerns about Chinese expansionism, challenges with Islam, shared language, and democratic norms, the Indo-American relationship has struggled at times as well. But for the most part, Indians are sliding into the White orbit as well as any group can.

I neglected to cover the Pakistanis in detail because in many ways, they fit better with the Arab immigrants. While not a huge number numerically, people coming from the Middle East obviously draw specific scrutiny because of the wars that have been fought over there since World War II and the different groups they've sent. Talking about immigration from the Middle East must be separated into two waves, and then it gets more complicated, as successive generations from settled immigrants have sometimes radicalized with support from new people coming over today.

Before the First Gulf War in 1991, many of the immigrants who came from the Middle East were legitimate refugees fleeing from Islam. Examples include Lebanese after the storming of the barracks and Persians who fled the Iranian revolution. Largely moderate and secular, these people sought their own communities in peace, and integrated quickly into American society in their small numbers and as people who often possessed education and useful skills. Persians are a good example of another group that was able to integrate well toward the White conception of unity around the cultural norms of traditional America.

After our invasion of Iraq, things changed. The radicalization of Islam and proliferation of terrorism is an incredibly complex topic worthy of its own volume, and much of that book could be dedicated to America's confused role in such actions. It must be noted that America's many mistakes in this area played a substantial role in creating these problems, and in the flood gate of immigration they have opened throughout the West. But our geopolitical strategies driven by energy, monetary, and other issues served to facilitate the spread of jihadist ideology, and it's fair to conclude our gas dollars helped fund many of the imams and mullahs who spread Wahhabism.

While the media defines such ideology as radical Islam, I dissent and instead say that Wahhabism is the most historically accurate version of what Muhammad did, spreading Islam through conquest and force. This ideology which combines religion in service to the state remains a major threat to the American and western ideal of separating faith and reason, which might be perhaps why the Left has paradoxically embraced Islam despite it standing in clear and unambiguous doctrinal opposition to so many of their inclusive and tolerant beliefs. Consolidation of power finds no more perfect vehicle than Islam, which is why you see governments throughout the entire West, and frankly far worse in Europe, simply cede authority to Muslims and how they run things, as perhaps a test run to implement such measures of their own.

Whatever the case, immigrants from the Middle East after 1991, and even more after the great tragedy in 2001, were likely to be ripe for radicalization and bring such ideology to the United States. While the Republican administration under Bush covered for their Saudi allies, America has awakened to the severity of this threat, and with the nationalists having pushed aside the neoconservatives, the Right is finally beginning to speak with greater clarity and honesty about Islam and the dangers it brings. With such division, those who are Muslims are voting overwhelmingly for the Left.

Finally, we conclude with Native Americans who are descended from the various tribes who occupied different areas of America before White expansion across the continent. Representing just 1.3% of the American population, much of their population was either long since integrated into the White majority or exists in small numbers on reservations. Those who remain largely either reside or were settled in the mountainous regions of the west and extremely rural areas. For certain thinly populated states, this vote can make a difference, and such surveys as exist report that Native Americans generally tend to vote Democrat at a rate similar to other Asians.

The history of conflict between the Native Americans and Whites is a sad and sordid affair, but also might serve as a cautionary note for what happens when an existing majority encounters an aggressive and expanding minority. Our own history shows how even though kind words are exchanged, cultural differences lead to conflict, and desire for control over one's own destiny takes what might start as a war of words into force of arms. The winner sets the path forward, and the losers take what they can get, marginalized until they cease to matter as political actors, living their lives in memory if they are permitted that outcome.

It's a sobering thought. We like to imagine our technology and learning has brought us past such zero-sum solutions where there must be a winner and a loser, but why would we reach that conclusion? Just because the scale of our weapons has narrowly restrained our most violent impulses, our technology allows us to see in real time how conflict burns constantly, hot or cold, throughout the world with human suffering as the result. Yet, so long as people have love for one another, for identities they cherish, and have the faculties to think and agree, they must also be able to disagree and use their courage to stand in opposition to that which threatens such love or idealism. Whether we fight for our identity or our ideas, we fight because we care, and if there is one thing of which I'm certain, it is that so long as we remain creatures who use reason to achieve our passions, there will always be another fight to be had.

Such is our nature. That is why people fight to take control over one another, and upon winning that fight, move on to the next battle. We define ourselves by what we are as much as by what we are not. And in a world where culture has broken apart, this explains why race is regaining prominence. In a world where all is disruption, we seek to belong, and what could be more basic than seeking out those who look and act like we do? As things gets worse, this is precisely why race will matter more. As we transition from the conflicts of race to the cultures they are spawning, it takes an incredible and almost unrealistic amount of optimism to imagine anything but trouble ahead.

Section III: The Groups

Group IV: Culture

The final groups in our survey focus on the divergent cultures being promoted by the Left and the Right, identifying their most prominent supporters and their most fervent disagreements. A special emphasis is given here to identity groups which are based on lifestyle and non-political beliefs which are equally important to understanding the widening division between these opposing forces.

The Left is portrayed first as an assembly of groups seeking to remake society where they most often had traditionally not enjoyed the same access or prestige. Suspicious of traditional authority outside the state, they embrace alternative family structures, novel gender identifications, and basically have a permissive attitude toward any non-traditional belief. Feminism is lauded.

In contrast, the Right represents the customary way of viewing things that was more prominent in the past, defending longstanding practices as both natural and reasonable. Much more prone to religion than secularism, the basic belief in objective right and wrong puts the Right at odds with the more idealistic and subjective views of the Left. Femininity is preferred.

While these values were once seen as being on sliding scale that allowed for compromise, years of cultural warfare which have essentially consisted of a slow motion surrender by the Right has created the expectation from the Left of full acceptance of their culturally transformative views at the same time a reactionary impulse has been mobilized in opposition.

A final chapter is added here for conflicts which also will matter significantly, such as nationalism versus globalism, Islam versus Christianity, and the divergent roles of technology in life. At present, these conflicts are rated as less essential to the civil conflict than the four areas profiled in greater depth, but any of these could expand very quickly, with the role of technology particularly likely to become a new dividing line in society as automation transforms into the newly beginning world of artificial intelligence.

Chapter 29: Team Purple—The Progressive Way

In the leftist worldview of culture, the basic rule of thumb is that the old ways were bad and only existed as means for those in authority to control and repress those groups they sought to deny from the power structure. Normalcy is a deliberate social construction used to isolate, shame, and encourage conformity from alternative visions and lifestyles, and the best way to liberate these practices is to remove barriers.

One might conclude the Left believes in nothing based upon such a reductionist approach, but they would make the argument they believe in everything. As stated elsewhere, the unique appeal of the Left is in their contention that as power is increasingly centralized to the state, individuals will be freed from all other concerns to pursue life upon their own terms, defining reality to match their ideas so long as they don't threaten the power relationship whereby economic control is centralized. This facet of cultural Marxism has proven remarkably resilient and has been able to unite many disparate cultural partners in intersectional activism who, theoretically, should not be able to work together.

An alliance of gays, lesbians, transgenders, feminists, Muslims, and atheists would seem at first glance to be unsustainable. Their social beliefs are self-evidently incredibly contradictory, yet they, along with other niche groups who almost universally gravitate to the Left, manage to work together because they target a common enemy relentlessly and deliberately: The Right. Their goal is to unmake what exists, and such nihilism, though incredibly destructive to society over the long term, tends to endure longer than one would expect because of how well the Left farms out resources to believers through government and nonprofits, and because the Right's basic theory of non-involvement with government allows such activity to go not just unopposed, but often with funding from traditionalists.

In this volume, I talk often about cultural Marxism as the primary means by which the Left operates, a contention which some might oppose by saying such a definition is too extreme. Whether it is or not, the differences in left-wing thinking are not in principle, but only in scale and scope. The shared principles of leftist beliefs seem pervasive enough to gain control over culture, and trust that politics will follow as out-groups are organized against the threats represented by tradition, patriarchy, or whatever words are most effective. All prove equally valid as targets.

In some ways, it would have been easier to start by writing about the Right before covering the Left for the culture war, because the positions of the Left are mainly a repudiation of what was previously held to be true. But my unspoken formula for ordering these chapters is to usually feature the side or institution with greatest prominence first, which in the case of cultural conflict, is undeniably the Left. As earlier chapters discussed in depth, the triumvirate of controlling education, media, and nonprofits to promote and most importantly, fund their social ideals, has no equivalent on the Right, and therefore as the Left has consolidated their position, we've seen them move from what was once an insurgent strategy to one of maintaining social dominance.

Check out my earlier book if you want more depth on how it happened, but for our purposes here, we can simply assert the free speech movements of the 1960's and the dissident intellectuals who brought feminism and then gay rights to the fore were able to conquer the elite institutions, ensuring the voice of expertise was handed over to the radicals. What began with demands to open debate and consider new possibilities, goals driven by the desire to unmake the cultural consensus which the West had largely held for decades if not centuries before, quickly expanded to occupy most of the idea space in the West, eased along the way by incredibly generous contributions by those who saw control of culture as assurance of their dominance of the state.

In their social engineering, the Left was incredibly thorough as they concocted a project of Orwellian scope to rework language itself. They understood that to voice an idea required a certain basic understanding, and so they exploded language into expressing new power relationships that followed their basic belief that authority is unwelcome. What started out simply has evolved into the politically correct doublespeak of today where pronouns are interchangeable, relationships are defined as aggression, and most importantly, censorship is internalized.

If so many concepts put in the public marketplace of ideas from the Left seem absurd and unintelligible, it might be because such jargon is designed to confuse the uninitiated and keep them from the corridors of power, excluding those who aren't in their club from the conversation. For the same reason lawyers still use Latin, barriers to entry are a way to limit the free speech of those who oppose them, and the Left takes every opportunity to discourage debate over their core principles.

Instead, they have opted for a strategy much like the Catholic Church employed successfully for centuries in Europe. They control the great cathedrals, broadcast the self-appointed experts, and encourage the belief their knowledge is above the laity. Those who question the regime are rebuked, first privately and then publicly. Those who threaten the regime are targeted for destruction, and like any heretic from medieval times, they are stripped of rank and status as examples.

Even though it may sound crazy to say we have such a regime existing in America today where we supposedly applaud free speech, you won't have to look very hard to find someone who has lost their job for saying something impolitic. Sometimes, it is an unpopular opinion. More disturbingly, sharing facts which don't fit the prevailing narrative, or an alternate view of the past will get you sidelined. Anyone right of center has probably experienced mild versions of this rebuke on social media, but as one rises in prominence in expressing these threatening ideas, usually most angering because of their conventionality and potential for mass appeal, the penalties grow in strength.

The Left controls culture in the same way it controls politics. Those admitted to the inside are permitted status, wealth, and privilege. But those who oppose them are treated as enemies to be destroyed. Such a system employed from the very beginning of a person's life when they see images on television that fit the narrative, and those are reinforced after years of indoctrination in public schools has become so all-encompassing that people sometimes don't see that it has been deliberately fabricated. Think of it like the Matrix, where a story is told so often and so regularly, people legitimately imagine that is all there is. That's what the Left tries to make you believe, hoping you censor yourself internally, counting on the basic human psychology that most people ache to belong.

With that considered, let's talk about some of the constituent groups of the Left, and we will start with feminism. For those who are interested in the details of this ideology, there are different identified waves which go further into the minutiae of how women should liberate themselves from men, and generally seem to increase in militancy as has been the case generally. But the basic idea is that women, in the traditional family structure, were historically oppressed and kept from opportunity. As legal rights accrued to women, social conventions were then targeted, and even the family itself was finally attacked as the obligation women were assumed to have to care for children was presented as some sort of imposition.

I find it very difficult to escape my own strongly held conviction, coming from the Right, that such thinking was driven largely by women disillusioned by their inability to find placement in the traditional system whereby husbands and wives found one another as a rather happy conjunction to have children and carry life to the next generation. But one thing about the Left is that they hyper focus on the feelings of the individual. Such emphasis works very well because feelings cannot be rationally assessed but only validated, which allows the Left to embrace anyone who feels they do not belong, satisfying the deep desire for those who are outside to come in from the cold.

We see the results of feminism in that women's discontent is greater than ever before, as expressed by one public survey after another. At this point, gender relations in many ways have reached such a nadir that many men are choosing to avoid interacting with women at all. The contradictions between what liberal society expects them to do are irreconcilable with the natural impulses between men and women, where women are still attracted to strong and dominant men and men still desire women in a traditionally feminine mold. And the price of taking either path can be too high within the hostile legal climate feminism created. Maybe that is why so many feminists now wear burkas, because as a protected class in the leftist hierarchy, Muslim men are permitted masculinity.

Feminism does more than just offer women options and opportunities for a career-driven life but exerts pressures on women not to assume a maternal role. Less explicit than implicit, I've heard so many stories from women who want a more traditional life but were pressured by peers into remaining in unsatisfying jobs because to do otherwise would be to betray the sisterhood. Like any other gang, feminism encourages loyalty and conformity, emphasizing the importance of the ideal at the expense of the individual. Whatever good it may have accomplished in opening doors for women which were once closed, one wonders if this outmoded ideology isn't closing many doors today which women will have many later years to regret.

But the consolation for not having the traditional family is sex. The Left encourages lots of sex, in lots of ways-- each of which is called healthy. The gay agenda that began with the stated desire to merely be permitted a degree of tolerance has evolved into deviancy whereby nearly everything is permissible. A person is encouraged to explore their desires, to engage with different partners, and to even arbitrarily select new identities as it fits them. Transgenderism is but the most recent expression of this belief where we see an explosion of new genders and behaviors being encouraged.

A more wholesome time might just label this whole effort as fetishism, but lest we dismiss what is happening as simple debauchery, there is a major cultural element here dedicated to destroying the idea of normalcy and health. As we stray further from that which sustains families, the historical source of authority that counterbalanced the state and held people together, the atomization of individuals increases and their ability to effectuate change, let alone promote ideas across generations vanishes. Morality itself begins to seem outmoded and there is always a new delight to distract.

While I understand, as most people from the Right do, that homosexuality has existed as long as history itself and will likely continue to do so, the tolerance granted was intended to serve the purpose of allowing people to quietly live their lives and contain their sexual preferences to their bedrooms, an aspiration most on the Right share for heterosexuality as well. Unfortunately, in a clearly recurring pattern, any offer to tolerate even a little of what the Left wants is inevitably exploited to seek dominance. This is why you see rainbow flags everywhere, and people taken to jail as deliberate targets for seeking to exercise their conscience in opposition. "Support us or you will be targeted," and as that push accelerates, the silent majority has fumed.

More disturbing personally, however, is just how far the fringes of this experimental attitude have gone. We now see parents sexualizing their children, attempting to alter their genders, and the media and most shamefully, even medical professionals, promoting this as normal. There was a time when such thinking was called pedophilia and considering how rumor after rumor leaks about how such wickedness is at the heart of the system whereby people are held together by blackmail, one wonders if there is any sexual activity the Left will ultimately determine to be inappropriate.

Perhaps their secularism is why they cannot. With all due respect to those secular humanists who live ethical lives, there is something in our social framework where absent a higher authority, it seems humanity succumbs to its most base animal instincts to feel good and take whatever we want, no matter how wrong. As we see barriers removed and the ideas of right and wrong made arbitrary, we've instead replaced wisdom with a form of self-perpetuating cleverness. It keeps everyone happy by ensuring no one cares for one another so deeply they might seek to limit the other.

Tolerance sounds great, but if we call it indifference, does it retain the same luster? And more importantly, how do you hold people together people who simply tolerate one another and have no common cause greater than that to unite them? You can give them things to keep them mollified, which the Left does in spades. But if you lost control of the government and could only hand out smaller goodies at the local level, what would be left but to blame the evil people who sought to constrain you?

This is how the Left feels today, where they own a culture which is being questioned and at risk of being unfunded and confronted. Years of deliberately planned and reinforced indoctrination are being activated to warn of the return of the bad people who want to bring back morality, authority, and discipline. And they don't want that, so the collective tantrum you see wherein women embarrass themselves by wearing vaginas on their heads will continue. Perhaps their own very inefficacy will ensure they remain harmless and ludicrous, but it is just as likely that their gullibility might push some radical elements into taking far more dangerous and aggressive actions.

What we do know is those guardians of culture will be relentless in protecting their prerogative, and their agitations will be a steady drum beat pushing their adherents toward this fight so long as the Right retains or expands its beachhead recently won in government. They are in this for total victory and will not relent voluntarily.

Chapter 30: Team Pink—The Traditional Way

It's not quite as simple as saying the Right wants things to be precisely as they used to be, but it's closer to the truth than not. Nostalgia is rampant on the Right both for those who lived during the past and remember simpler times, and people my age who look back to how America seemed before all these cultural conflicts and imagine it was so much happier. The realist in me knows the 1950's weren't that perfect, and yet, there is still much to admire in a country where social roles were better defined.

Tradition and authority go hand in hand. Every society, even our own confused America, believes there is a right and wrong way to do things. Our current paradigm is to accept everything, tolerate all, and not ask too many questions. But this leftist construct is an inversion of the western ideals which built America and upon which our prosperity was founded. We were once taught to question everything, to exercise judgment, and to accept only that which we thought was good. It was a judgmental society, no doubt, but also a society where judgments were balanced with reason, nature, and clemency.

We knew who we were. America had a culture based upon individual enterprise, hard work, social responsibility, and support for our families as the best part of our people. It was universal in the sense that anyone who shared these values could become a part of what we were doing, but our values had strong foundations in traditions of using reason guided by our Christian faith and virtue to better the world.

We were still connected to each other, and even though there were undoubtedly those who felt outside the system, the idea was to embrace the majority without persecuting the minority, living the liberty enshrined in our Constitution.

I can fully understand how the Left whose impulse is to destroy that which came before in pursuit of a perfect, but ever unachievable ideal, could see such conventions as a straitjacket. But for others of us, they feel more like a snug blanket keeping one warm from the cold wind blowing outside. There is a longing for rules to give order to life, perhaps even more so today than ever before. Technology changes life daily, society seems so disordered, and we see all manner of cultures overlapping but only interacting superficially. It didn't have to be this way, and people on the Right want things to become simpler.

Though some would argue that we can just turn back the clock by undoing all that has been done, it won't be that easy. There are many people here who won't fit in that world, so as the Right moves to remake things that were lost, they will inherently create enemies among the many people who've been taught and trained to act differently. Such is inevitable, but what exacerbates this conflict further is that even as traditionalists move as gingerly as possible to reinstate not even institutions, but basic ideals like the existence of only two genders, the institutional Right has spent decades skirting this culture war.

Such a statement might sound ironic given how so much of our political discourse in the 1990's was obsessed with social issues, but did you ever see the Right use government successfully to defend their beliefs? The courts ruled time and time again to expand definitions of marriage, to expand access to services, and to constrain traditional modes of religious or family expression. Courts overwhelmingly have ruled against men, straight people, Whites, and traditionalists, and have constrained states and other actors who try to secure traditional values through law. Congressmen, though they spoke often of shared values, did nothing to protect those values, even as the Left continued pushing through their agenda to unmake traditional culture.

To be fair, the Right was always going to have this problem because it fundamentally hates the idea of using government to adapt culture. There was a time when this was not the case, but one must go back to the days when monarchy and aristocracy were defenders of the realm, and where parliaments were understood as strictly monetary affairs apart from culture. These ideas pre-date the American experiment. Our own creation was built on the idea the state would protect civil society from undue interference through explicitly protected liberties and severely restricted and enumerated powers, and we would trust our civil society to provide for morality without the compulsory power of the State.

In credit to the Founders, such a system worked very well for a long time and built this republic from proverbial sea to shining sea, but what it could not anticipate was just how many powers would accrue to government, and how those, coupled with the trends of industrialization and urbanization, would cause people to embrace a far larger government to meet their needs. Whether or not such growth was necessary is central to this dispute, but as it happened, the Left learned to use the state to finance their culture as the Right steadfastly refused to do the same.

Through carrots and sticks, the Right was beaten into a state of submission where it could exist culturally but had ceded any pretense of dominance. It would just become another subculture, as it largely has today, most prevalent in rural areas and places of low population density. Any evidence that this culture was once more than a relic has been targeted for destruction, and when you see the removal of statues and verse pushed forward, it's because our past is being erased so that the future to be written can paint the traditionalists however it chooses.

Whereas our Founders were once celebrated in schools for their wisdom and courage, they're now deliberately tarnished and accused of failing to meet modern codes of ethics. Where our past once conveyed a shared sense of pride, our last President opined only now that a minority had come to power were we deserving of such joy. We are told again and again how awful we were, and that all we accomplished was not truly of our own efforts, but stolen and misappropriated. We are told to shut up or get fired, and to quietly go away and fade into the past.

Sadly, for a host of different reasons we've discussed some in this book, the Republicans elected to defend tradition offered only token resistance, and America has long been on the road to being just like everyone else.

Everything is allowed, nothing is special, and we are no longer the indispensable nation, but instead the exemplar of all that was wrong. While the cities nodded along dimly in their international world of materials and wealth, there was enough energy remaining for the Right to heave up one final contender to counter this narrative.

Trump can be a boor at times. People on the Right know this, but they don't care because at least he is a fighter. Christians who've watched Merry Christmas morph into Happy Holidays, so the commercialism can be kept without the actual reason for the celebration are thrilled to have someone restore their holiday. People who watch athletes who earn millions of dollars to play games and then bitch about how unjust America is are gleeful to see someone call out this gross hypocrisy. Donald Trump didn't create these festering conflicts, but he does reveal them, and for that reason he is a hero to a tribe who had no one fighting for them.

This marks a fundamental change in the culture war, yet it remains to be seen if Trump is an outlier who represents a futile last stand of a forgotten America shrinking into the past, or the rebirth of the ideals which spawned this nation in the first place. As ever, it is up to the American people to determine which, but what is clear is the energy on the Right to speak up for their culture and beliefs has never been stronger, and for the first time in ages, people on the Right are starting to at least consider fighting with full force to defend and promote their beliefs just as strongly as their competitors.

Since I've been on the vanguard of this movement for some time, it's entirely possible that I overestimate what is happening, but the Internet has created at least a momentary opening for a dissenting counter-culture to emerge. Although it is sometimes crass and often irreverent, look to the less frequented corners of the web and you'll see people describing their resistance in seeking to reclaim positive White identity and look upon our history as a source of pride rather than derision. People make jokes, some of which are awful, but many of which are funny, and free speech and debate are existing beyond the false censorship regime of "community standards." We see a vigorous debate of ideas about how we rebuild our culture into one.

Many of these conversations are hard and there are no sacred cows. We talk about race, about religion, about how people are rather than how we're told we must assume them to be, and we admit openly that this might only be fixed through fighting because of how vast these disagreements are. And yet, despite disagreements, it seems there is a growing understanding that a common culture is needed, and so we naturally look backwards for insight as to what has worked previously.

After years of hyper individualism, collective identity is being considered again on the Right. White people are coming together, admitting we have been made a common enemy by the Left, and taking pride in our people. Christians talk to one another, seeing how their ideals are violated, and work in unity toward more righteous ends. Men want to become men once more, masculine and strong, not restrained and forgotten. And they find women who support them, who lend their succor to such strength, hoping again to rebuild the family that once was the heart of America. For alone, we are far less than we can be together, and it took a beat down decades in the making for the Right to realize that, and the desperation of seeing it all almost lost to encourage at least some to fight back with the urgency required.

A special point about femininity also needs to be added. If one accepts, as many on the Right do, that families are the key to both a happy life and to sustain one's civilization into the future, there is no more important issue than reconciling men and women to one another. Where feminism set us apart as adversaries and told women their own value was in what they produced for the economy, a rising wave of femininity is reaching young women to let them know mothers are every bit as valuable as working women, and there are men who want such wives and such partners. The Right is learning to connect people organically, as the Left can only motivate through disconnect and envy. This could be the foundation of our new culture.

From this vanguard and with books like my own humble offerings, those of us who are younger and more willing and able to fight for what we believe are reaching toward those communities who share our beliefs but have long fallen out of action. Admittedly, the challenges of reaching older people with more to lose to enter a cultural brawl are considerable, and there are as many rejections as success stories, yet as these older folks consider the future their children and grandchildren will experience and remember their own past, they too are coming along. Trump is a harbinger.

In this moment now where the two sides remain at relative parity, people who lean Right are investigating the future. And when they examine the trends and demographics honestly, key figures are concluding that the time has come to push these conflicts. There is a window, extended by each Republican in office who understands the subtext, but ultimately America has about a decade to push hard right or the likelihood of success will decrease sharply. Because the future as a majority minority country will not be one driven by liberty, but instead by a purer, cruelly indifferent and involuntary collectivism.

I base that analysis not on idealism, but the realism of what has happened every time the Utopian thinkers put everyone together and trust the state to make it work. It never does because culture is what keeps us afloat. It's what binds us, and through whatever forms of identity it takes, the only successful America or should it come to that, parts of America to survive, will be those that find this essential unity.

The Left and Right agree about little in these United States save that the enemy is wrong, and they are not going to give an inch to the other side. Although apolitical moderates will bemoan this intransigence, the preceding chapters have all been written to demonstrate that the radicals are correct as there is no middle ground between such diametrically opposed viewpoints. When suggesting a civil war is in the offing, people will not want to believe such a conclusion. It is my hope that these many examples have shown just how many divisions exist and how irreconcilable they are, so you will take this prospect seriously for yourself and your family. There is a very high likelihood this time, things just won't work out.

Chapter 31: Other Potential Conflicts

As much effort as I put into prognostication of what I genuinely believe to be an incredibly comprehensive analysis of why civil conflict will accelerate in America, something you should share with others for both their own protection and so I can continue sharing my bluntly honest reflections with you, is that the longer it takes for this to start, the more likely it seems to me new directions of potential conflict will either emerge or re-emerge in addition to those four already identified in ideology, residency, race, and culture. Three such examples follow, including globalism vs. nationalism, Christianity vs. Islam, and the rising role of artificial intelligence.

Globalism vs. Nationalism

Certain people view the conflict in America as part of a larger civil conflict racking all Western Civilization. In this analysis, the struggle we see playing out across different nations primarily in Europe as well as here are efforts by the people to reclaim sovereignty over their lands from transnational institutions. While we are jointly constrained by involvement in entities like the UN, NATO, the World Bank, IMF, WTO, and others, the situation in Europe is particularly pronounced by how the European Union, which originated as an economic project, has basically come to constrain the rights of many nations on that continent with little democratic oversight or accountability.

A clear commonality between America and Europe, which is not seen elsewhere around the world save for other predominantly White countries, is the massive influx of migrants from the Third World who are remaking what it means to be a member of those nations. Where America at least had some degree of ideological flexibility to accommodate these waves and has been somewhat insulated by the reality that Latinos, our largest migrant group are Christian, Europe has been flooded with people who are mostly Muslim, come from cultures where violence is rampant, and as previously much more homogeneous societies, have struggled with how to integrate these people.

News stories increasingly reveal that Europe is failing in this task. Governments and other transnational institutions try to cover the true costs of such immigration by actively refusing to enforce laws on the so-called refugees, instead levying fines and prison sentences against citizens who speak against this invasion. It is an incredibly sorry state which happened very rapidly, led by the efforts of Germany. The resulting spikes in crime and vandalism are creating such discord that the European Union is splitting into two camps.

The first camp is those who primarily lean Left who want to bring in as many of these migrants as possible, often making a humanitarian case for their entry, and who generally support larger government, globalist governance, and who argue the low birth rate of Whites which is even more pronounced in Europe than in the U.S. is needed to ensure the survival of their countries. Worth remembering in this scenario is that many parties that nominally lean right support these policies as European politics skews heavily toward socialism, as evidenced by the "right" Christian Democrats who seem to be neither Christian nor democratic leading this charge.

The opposition are those who think European nations should stand up for their own citizens and not seek to replace their native populations, but instead repel these invaders and work to encourage their own birth rate to rise. Most perfectly typified by Hungary, this position has far more support in Eastern Europe although Italy and Greece have recently moved in this direction. Although these conflicts are most tense in Europe, it's worth noting other prominent countries like Japan also support the nationalist position that their country should be for people of their ethnicity.

These complex issues are part of an ongoing global disagreement between globalism, the idea that there should be a single international consensus that is monitored and maintained largely by transnational institutions, corporations, and a set of ideas whereby governments conform to common standards which emphasizes the sort of bland multiculturalism of the Left, and the revolting citizenry of countries like Britain whose bold statement of self-determination in voting for Brexit is being actively undermined by their own nominally conservative government.

America is at the heart of this battle as our military and our government, with increasing determination under not just Obama, but Bush before him, sought to develop this new world order of institutions unaccountable to people.

Trump, as a committed nationalist, is an existential threat to this order, and American nationalism might collapse the global effort. Without American force to uphold these norms and the American market to sustain such trade imbalances, the departure of the United States toward isolationism or non-interventionism is causing shock waves worldwide.

It's possible such activity might sufficiently embolden nationalists elsewhere to launch formal resistance against their governments, where they cannot take over through democratic means. The shifting alliances we would see as a new order emerges could cause global conflict that would inevitably impact our own civil concerns. Conversely, events here can just as easily set off shock waves elsewhere, which is why many analysts think an American Civil War would be but one campaign in what would necessarily become global conflict.

Pervasive interconnections might explain why such fears exist about Russia on the Left, even as China is a much more pressing threat. As a Right friendly, pro-Christian, nationalist regime, despite the antipathy the Deep State holds for Russia, more people on that the Right are coming to look fondly at Putin, and against the traditional NATO allies who are overwhelmingly socialist, and whose defense seems somewhat comical considering they are undermining their own nations with poor domestic policy. The Left, naturally, believes the complete opposite, and watch for their embrace of China with a communist system to grow in coming years.

Christianity vs. Islam

Fifteen years ago, the possibility of a clash of civilizations between the nominally secular West, but under-girded by Christianity, against the radicalism of Islam seemed not only possible, but likely. One could argue such a contest has already happened, and we have learned that Islam is resilient, and the West has neither desire nor the capacity to undertake the sort of wholesale changes needed to change the Middle East. So, trillions of dollars and millions of lives later, it seems like exhaustion has led to détente overseas.

Yet, we have entered a new phase of these struggles, as Islam is gaining footholds in various countries in the West. More a problem in Sweden and the United Kingdom than in America, this potential battle still bears watching domestically because Islamic activists have insinuated themselves into the leftist coalition. Although such a regressive set of beliefs would seem incompatible with the progressivism of the Left at first glance, the embrace has gone far more smoothly than one might expect for several reasons.

First, Islam tacitly embraces this idea of taqiyya, a concept whereby deception is strategically practiced to achieve the desired long-term end, which is always the conversion to the one true belief system—including both government and faith—of Islam. To the Left, such a combination of state and religion is ideal as it removes the existential threat to the idealism of those who believe in higher ideals absent state authority, long enshrined in the West, but chipped at relentlessly for the last three centuries.

The Left also values Muslims as allies because it allows them to paint the current authority figures as oppressive as they logically question the wisdom of bringing in such a foreign culture. Islam attracts forces prone to using radical violence as the means to accomplish their ends. Sharia gives cover to create extra-judicial authority that could replace the state, as it has done with Courts in England. There are parallels in the United States with sanctuary cities acting in opposition to the Federal Government.

Such an alliance of convenience seems likely only to end with the Left having to choose between the control aspects of Islam or the progressive expression of the out-groups in their coalition such as gays and feminists. But if history serves as any guide, those who support socialist ideals for cultural reasons will be among the first sacrificed to realize the totalitarian ideals. It happened in Russia that way with the Bolsheviks purging the Mensheviks who didn't conform. As we watch those feminists walking around with burkas, such a pattern looks likely to recur. Just as the USSR had to abandon feminism shortly after its formation to sustain itself, the Left will likewise require a rising desire for morality in order to survive. As this manifests, expect them to look toward Muslim doctrines to provide justification. Given that Islam has already made inroads into the Black community, such a switch could be managed.

Should such a conflict arise, Christianity will face an uncomfortable choice. Where Christians prefer to remain apart from politics and identity issues, trying instead to endorse some form of ecumenical universalism, a new spate of Christian murders, as would invariably result from a larger Muslim population, might incite a holy war in America. Just as the various jihadi efforts to invade Europe finally spurred the counter reaction of the Crusades, we could very well see a more nationalist Right in America persuade some Christians to accept the need to fight for self-preservation and restoration of the land.

What we've observed on the Right recently is the inherent assertiveness of a nationalist ethos is trickling across its constituent groups, so it bears watching to see if ideas like Christian Identism or some novel Crusader ethic emerges. Given the perpetually declining attendance of mainstream churches, driven perhaps as much by their tacit surrender in the culture wars to the inclusive agenda of the Left, I suspect a movement of preachers who can speak forcefully to reclaiming America for God, good, and glory would find much support.

One factor which has severely restrained Christian self-defense on the Right is a heavily promoted and widespread belief that the End Times are upon us. As such, many Christians have chosen retrenchment instead of engagement, and an absolute focus on virtue with the expectation coming calamities are the fulfillment of prophecy. Sometimes called Christian Zionists, these people focus their efforts instead on Israel, and have largely absented themselves from other political contexts, instead focusing on dispensationalism as a survival strategy. Perversely, the worse things get, the more this movement will encourage inaction and retreat into a life of prayer.

Artificiality vs. Humanity

One conflict in the future which has the potential to unmake existing alliances and change the dynamics entirely is the rise of artificial intelligence and automation. The fundamental assumption of this book is such technology will be rolled out slowly enough that machine intelligence will not present a fundamental threat to mankind in the near term, but this assumption becomes less probable the more time elapses.

Such a topic is almost beyond the scope of this book, but I choose to include it here because if one looks thirty years into the future, assuming no major disruptions, it's impossible to imagine that the role technology plays in our life, and what agency it is given will not be central questions in our society. Great amounts of money and research are being invested today to realize and exceed the current limits of computing.

Those who support the development of advanced artificial intelligence tend to lean Left by our current standards, though not exclusively so, as they envision a day where the fundamental division in society might become organic beings versus artificial ones. Some support this movement because they believe machines, driven by logic, will do better at managing humanity than we could ever do for ourselves. Others back the development of the mechanical man in hopes of cheating death by uploading themselves into either units or some sort of virtual reality.

If the day should come when humanity's fundamental needs change because of the way we interact or integrate with machines, so too will politics, economics, and culture change. Those on the Right who follow these trends see them as the ultimate perversion and subversion of humanity as unique beings and will probably be the loudest cautionary voices.

Absent effective artificial intelligence, automation will continue to be incredibly disruptive and invasive. So long as we continue our status quo trajectory of adapting ourselves to advancing technology rather than the alternate approach of appropriating new devices to our desires, something we struggle to articulate in this divided cultural setting, such advancements are likely to only further separation between people as we increasingly find ourselves engaging in worlds which are virtual.

The consequences of such could include humanity becoming so isolated that the conflicts we have discussed previous to this issue subside and we just see a bland future where our needs are met, and we are controlled by a formula or those who write it. Such a dismal future scares me personally more than any war or battle, but we can already see hints that many people might welcome such a future as ultimate peace by embracing what essentially reduces life to death, and creativity to the efficiency of ones and zeros.

Absent a collapse that sets humanity back to a more basic technology level, please be aware that such questions will need to be answered in our not so distant future, and poor choices made then might be the death of our species. It's a dismal thought to share, but given such a monumental challenge, this only adds to the import of resolving those conflicts now. Because if we stumble into these challenges unprepared, the consequences might be fatal.

In sum, the future will have conflict just like the past. What it will look like no one can say for sure, but we can speculate and offer some ideas. Whether these will resemble reality or not is impossible to say, but I imagine six possible ways the next twenty years could see this cultural civil war resolve.

Section IV: The Scenarios

Although there are innumerable variations about how this conflict could play out with outcomes representing combinations of the basic forms below as possible, there are certain commonalities we can imagine which should represent the different available options. These are:

Submission: *If the status quo continues, given the demographic trends, or if the Left can accelerate these, they will achieve victory and the future will reflect the diverse multicultural vision of the coalition of the ascendant which will likely slide toward decay and totalitarianism.*

Militarism*: If the current revolution of the Right into government expands or is followed by some effort which effectively uses government authority, perhaps with military assistance, to take control and forcibly rework America toward a rightward vision charged with restoring culture and averting the demographic crisis.*

Decentralization: *The threat of civil conflict could so frighten both sides that a national movement might arise to reduce the authority of the Federal government, and states are invested with greater authority to realize the widely divergent agenda of the respective factions.*

Separation: *With irreconcilable differences threatening active conflict, prompted by currently accelerating trends where the Left and Right are trying to live separately from one another, an idealistic proposal might be forwarded to split America into two or more countries along cultural, political, and/or regional lines.*

Secession: *In opposition to the Federal government, states or even cities may actively revolt and seek to claim their independence from the United States, with likely actors worth watching being California for the Left and Texas for the Right.*

Collapse: *Either a lack of confidence in the government, the failure to address escalating violence, externally induced conflict, or some other disaster scenario collapses access to basic service sufficiently that America splinters into anarchy with only highly fractured remnants surviving.*

Chapter 32: Submission—Victory for the Left

Politics has long been observed to take place downstream from culture, which makes perfect sense. People build their political approaches to realize the ideas and norms which they value. The Left fully dominates culture through mainstream media, controls education from the formative years through graduate degrees, and is relentless in protecting those prerogatives. They have never been more vicious with their insults and slander, and have never gone so far to remove the voice and even the ability of people to sustain themselves who speak in opposition. Such power should not be underestimated, and it is the greatest asset of the Left.

Until 2016, the odds seemed incredibly likely the Left would simply win the cultural war brewing in this country by default. Although the Right certainly had different ideas and some niche institutions promoting these, there had not been a Republican in this country who would offer more than token resistance to the basic program of the Left. The Right had fallen into a pattern of allowing the Left to use government and its resources however it chose to promote their ideas, and to ideologically refuse to use government to resist these developments. Furthermore, the Left was not just stacking the country with people who would be sympathetic to their views by a two-to-one margin or better, but supported policies to ensure this America did not just look different but would act differently as well.

Any sane Republican, which most actually are outside the media bubble, could look at the demography of both the legal immigrants, the many people coming in through the chain migration process, and the illegal immigrants who were being set up for another amnesty wave and see these people would be loyal Democrats. Yet, establishment Republicans have such a pronounced fear that the media might label them as xenophobic, or worse, racist, that they refused to speak common sense. A few exceptions existed, primarily in rural areas, but most Republicans decided not to speak on these issues and instead signaled the complete opposite, choosing to prioritize immediate expediency ahead of addressing a problem that was getting worse each year. This went on for decades.

Which brings us to today. We have not yet reached the demographic tipping point where the Democrats or those to their left will have an unbreakable majority, but it will come in about twenty years. With the Left in power, that number moves forward as their immigration policy of taking anyone and everyone further advances their numbers while also allowing them to polarize the electorate to continue flipping states. They are unapologetic about literally turning the nation into an entirely different set of people, abandoning former allies like union workers to get there, as ultimate power is in reach. I see two ways they could reach their goal.

The first would be if the political hubbub dies down and people go back to something more akin to the old status quo. Maybe they will find another good ol' boy to run like they had in Bill Clinton or Jimmy Carter, one who will say the right things and make sure people in Middle America feel good enough that even if they aren't in love with the candidate, their defenses are lowered slightly, and we continue quietly along the track we were on before Obama and then Trump.

We would be promised an America for everyone, and the political correctness would be dialed down just a notch or two, with the most strident people in the far left put back into the closets at every university and nonprofit. The emphasis would shift to something non-controversial by the media like economic growth, or perhaps a war against some irrelevant but resource rich country might be undertaken to unite the country in a reflexive "rally around the flag" moment. Whatever distraction is used, the Left could find politicians who make America feel comfortable and buy time for their longstanding strategy to reach final victory.

It's well understood historically that the rise of the radical Left is usually pushed through idealistic professors in universities or other actors who are at the margin of society, or who have social capital, but represent a small numerical minority. Conversely, for the radical right to rise, the historical pattern is almost always to do so in response to fears of what those on the far Left will do to people in the center, as well as those with resources. As we see today, a revolution by the Right has a populist character, whereas that by the Left tends to be more elitist—driven by actors who hold institutions of value.

In as much as the Left can accomplish the dual challenges of holding together their disparate coalition of barbarians at the gate as well as keeping the full intentions of their plans from public scrutiny, such a strategy remains eminently viable. If the radical leftists step away from public sight, and they present their policies in moderate economic tones like supporting more socialized medicine, the heat level will drop, and the Right will relax enough to go back to the political warfare we used to recognize. The Left may win, or they may lose these specific battles, but it doesn't really matter in the long-term consideration so long as they continue to control culture so thoroughly, because every few years, they can reliably bring more people to their side whose indoctrination they control and for whose entrance they will work.

Latinos are the best example. Their population in America has jumped by 50 million since 1970, which means an advantage of 16 million more Democrat voters due to immigration and amnesty policies given current voting rates. Nationwide, that means about an extra 5% was added to the electorate in total, and as much as 10% to the voter rolls, provided these people turnout. The pattern holds for every other immigrant group, who not only add when they arrive, but have children at far faster rates, where we now have more future Americans who will be minorities. If voting were split equally like Republicans dream, perhaps this would be less important, but the most rightward leaning minorities vote at least two-thirds for Democrats, so we know what that future looks like. America will become much like Europe is today—mixed ancestry and socialist politics.

How far Left they go after taking power will be a question only constrained by what the Left chooses for itself, with the battles of that future in a secular urbanized country being between the socialist Left and the communist Left over just how much government can intervene in our lives. It is almost certain liberties will be reduced, free speech will be constrained as in Europe in favor of political correctness, and at some future point, when the government feels they have a sufficient majority, they will accomplish their longstanding dream of functionally disabling the Second Amendment.

Predicting these outcomes does not require a great deal of imagination because we have already seen Europe walk this path, and we see the consequences today. The only groups who can be publicly sanctioned are the shrinking majorities, their traditional views, and anyone who questions the authority of the government. It's incredibly ironic that we supposedly fought a Cold War to prevent communism, and yet, western Europe is walking that path on their own at the very time their eastern neighbors are protecting their nations.

It is a brilliant strategy and should nothing else happen and America stumbles along the path it currently walks, it remains the most likely of all outcomes to happen. Absent some novel resolution of the cultural conflict where the Left currently seems most agitated, they will eventually win victory as demography is destiny. There will be more people who share their beliefs, and for the people who want peace at all costs, this will be the ending they will reach. It may be more moderate, or it may be more extreme, but it will certainly see a more powerful, more centralized, and much larger state, perhaps as part of a growing global consensus to organize even further.

Such a world might be more peaceful as the conflicts between nations, at least the major ones, will be reduced, but the unspoken cost will be the sovereignty of citizens everywhere. Governments will answer to the elites who bankroll the cultural institutions, just as they do today, and the society which will emerge though nominally leftist, would likely feature an upper class who determine the party line and are extremely wealthy and powerful. They would live differently than others, just like the limousine liberals of today who take flights spewing fumes into the air to attend conferences on global warming. It would have more market elements, but the old Politburo would recognize their kin.

The second way the Left could win is if they manage to unseat Trump now, through means legitimate or illegitimate, and the radicals who are currently raging against the Right are able to disrupt the incipient nationalist movement before it gets started. For all the support Trump has among Republicans, which is borne out by polling which explicitly states how strongly they want their candidates to back the President, the institutional Republican party remains largely in the hands of donors ambivalent at best and hostile in many cases to the nationalist ideal. Furthermore, absent the rise of some unknown figure, there is insufficient institutional support behind Trump to expect that if he vanishes from the scene the Right will continue its current momentum.

The far right has tried to organize, and while it has been able to influence Republican elections enough to get someone like Trump through the primaries, the constant media scrutiny which manifests as a fatal combination of censorship and propagandizing, has marginalized and limited its effectiveness. Ironically, Trump's success has made putting the heterodox ideas that pushed him forward into the public sphere even more difficult and costly, at least in part because of the unwillingness of so many on the Right to refrain from their usual and incredibly self-destructive pattern of signaling against their own potential allies to curry media favor.

This matters for the Left in taking victory, because if their radicals act decisively enough and are given the fodder which we know the Deep State will either provide or create, if the people are driven by the steady drumbeat of accusations, no matter how farcical they may be, into removing or more intelligently, defeating Trump, the Right will collapse in on itself in a series of recriminations between sides which don't trust each other. The more legitimately the Left is seen to have acted, the more the Right will blame itself, which is something they have probably considered carefully and that's why these show trials continue unabated like the Mueller investigation.

An impeachment, though very popular with the Left base, would seem unlikely to succeed given the current and

334

short-term future makeup of the Senate, and while the activists from the Left want to see this at any cost, the hands running the ship remember well how the GOP's efforts to do the same to Clinton backfired massively. Instead, they probably will look to tie government into gridlock, especially if they gain the House, and to find whatever allies will help to undercut Trump for 2020.

Although they're supposedly apolitical, keep a close eye on the Federal Reserve. Their continuation of raising rates will restrain the growth of the nationalist economic plan, and historically, there are many reasons why the Fed has acted in ways which have largely proven helpful to leftist Presidents. The banks like globalism and it's worth remembering how much money they put into these efforts.

As a last resort, it's worth considering how the Left might still snatch victory should Trump prevail, and the Republicans maintain or expand their majority. The activists, if unable to regain control of the Federal government, will almost certainly be able to maintain their cultural monopoly through tying things up in the court system and with their allies in Congress. Look for the Left to push power to local governments and friendly states and simply ignore Federal mandates. As they become accustomed to such autonomy, and as the media covers for these actions, it's possible they could try to take control directly through refusal to recognize this government.

Later scenarios will cover this possibility in much more depth, but as leftist versions of these will certainly feature some elements of inducing submission from the

Right, they are a chancier proposition that might just end up being pushed due to the impatience from the radicals on the Left, provocations from the administration, and the genuine belief among the Left that they are fighting tyranny. Ironically, their own vehemence is the only cause likely to make their prophecy true.

We close the submission chapter with a few thoughts on what victory for the Left would mean for those on the Right. It would mean the erasure of our history, where statues will all be gone, textbooks will all be rewritten, and could go so far as to see ideas from the Right banned in the future. A subtle approach would be to rework the institutions of the Right like churches to teach the Gospel of Marx, such as we frankly see already happening in churches where the Left has successfully subverted the hierarchy. Less subtle would just be to ban ideas, and in a technologically more advanced state, it's entirely possible the censorship regime could become absolute. Those who resisted would go down as terrorists, probably in small bands, or live out quietly as a tolerated few with scorn and derision in the country, at least until their land is taken for probably tax reasons.

It's not a happy future for liberty or true choice, but it would have peace and unity at the cost of expression. Superficial diversity would be everything, and this America would love experiences, but I doubt it would have any meaningful unity, and we would settle into simply being rather than striving. Utopia…indifference.

Estimated Likelihood: 40%

Chapter 33: Militarism—Victory for the Right

The central thesis of this book is civil conflict has risen because the Left deliberately worked to destroy the common culture America once enjoyed, instead encouraging cultural division and working steadfastly to change the demographic makeup in America to validate their cultural alternative as the new norm in such a way as to ensure a permanent majority for their ideas. The chapters on demography and culture were put in place to illustrate the current and continuing success of their program, which means if the Right is going to succeed, it must act decisively to change these patterns.

At first glance, it would seem like the Right should be able to act to preserve its interest, especially as it controls all three formal branches of government, as well as represents much of the military. In the numbers game, although the Left probably has more people, the electoral maps being what they are and with hardening racial voting patterns, the Right also has the clear preference of Whites who remain the indispensable voting bloc to win national elections. But these numbers are constantly diminishing to the detriment of the Right, and the current majority will vanish within a decade, perhaps permanently.

A major reason for this book is to make these facts clearer for those making policy, but the continuing delusion on the Right is its own idealist fantasy that anyone is just as likely to embrace conservative, traditional, or individualistic ideas stands squarely in the way of the reasoned approached needed for survival. While there are undoubtedly millions of Americans across a number of different cultural, racial, and socioeconomic lines who choose the ideas of liberty over dependency and support the Right in defiance of the trends, the idea that these virtuous few are the vanguard of a much larger group just waiting to be converted with the right opportunity or sufficient prosperity has no historical basis or solid evidence today.

In truth, history shows people usually elect to act upon in-group preference, which is why the Left has grown and the Right has shrunk. Furthermore, given the option between being given a skill and a good, people have shown time and again they will vote for those who offer an easier solution to the one which requires more effort. Couple this with the fact that the immigrants that the Right is trying to convert come from cultures where the patronage system is much more common than the opportunity model it favors, and you see why success at converting enough immigrants is unlikely.

The historical counterbalance which the Right once held was the school system. If the Right in America controlled the universities and the public education system, there would be at least some likelihood people could be converted to a common cultural position more akin to what we held previously. However, as the Left has a near monopoly on what is taught, the published textbooks, and what mass media reinforces, the Right's ideological unwillingness to use government to fight culture amounted to a surrender which disables the Right's ability to win a cultural battle.

Given an infinite amount of time, it would not be impossible to imagine alternatives to express culture arising on the Right, and this is already happening in technology as well as through home schooling. However, these are largely platforms being selected by people who already share certain sympathies, and without mass adoption, will remain more a means of internal organization within the Right rather than any real opportunity for growth. To win back the culture, if it could be done, would take fifty years by means of competition and subversion, and the Left will win this war by demographics in twenty years. Therefore, such tactics cannot succeed, even though they have value as being an alternative to sustain those with conventional beliefs today.

So, we come now to the unhappiest conclusion with which the Right is wrestling, or at least it should be: To preserve our culture, ideals, and history, some form of government intervention will be necessary to change the trends of what America will look like tomorrow. Willingness to get involved in reshaping the public sector in a major way will be required, and any such actions will be extremely contentious and could potentially be met with violent resistance.

Hints of this are already arising as the relatively anodyne measures suggested thus far from the Trump Administration have caused a disproportionately shrill backlash from the Left, spawned as much by the media and the nonprofits as genuine discontent. Should the GOP have the gumption to back even more forceful action, as would be needed to reverse the trends this book unapologetically shares, it will have to do so over major public objection creating massive polarization and certain media outcry.

Immigration is the first issue which must be addressed. To reverse the demographic trends, the United States would need to enact a moratorium on incoming immigration from all sources. While rationalizing the system to move toward a meritorious basis and removing the family chain migration situation, these actions, while they may improve the quality of immigrants for the future, will likely do nothing to stop the leftward shift immigration generally encourages, especially in the ongoing absence of common culture.

Trump's current plan would only buy a little more time given birth rates of existing immigrants. America would also have to step forward and seek to actively deport illegal immigrants in this country, triggering a mass exodus which would be incredibly unpopular in the media, though perhaps not with the people themselves who could see this as a valid security concern. This action will add a little more time to the clock, but the next steps are harder still.

America would do well to look at recent immigrants who have not yet achieved citizenship status and do whatever it can to remove these people from the country if the Right is going to endure. The nicer way to do this would be to remove anyone who ran afoul of the law, something which could be much more strictly enforced or for which new laws may be written. A more effective, but less nice way would be a blanket removal and revocation of green cards. This would go much further in offsetting the demographics, but would very possibly cause a leftist revolt, which is why it likely wouldn't happen unless the Right embraced a path which considers conflict preferable to submission.

The other potential area worth considering which has more carrots than sticks is family planning. While America will almost certainly not consider race-based policies to the benefit of the majority in any scenario before an actual breakdown, countries in Europe have had success in raising the birth rate in their own countries with smart inducements. Given the numbers we saw about who had children in wedlock, imagine if America enacted a family planning policy whereby married couples were offered subsidy to have children and instead single mothers were not given any support. The Left would cry and beat their chests that this was attacking children, but the reality is this directly strikes the moral peril where the state basically is serving as surrogate father to single mothers, a group which overwhelmingly votes Left and is feminist.

I doubt Trump would go this far, but a surprising number of people on the Right would also support policies offering financial inducements for lower income people to obtain permanent vasectomies or tubal ligation to control population growth. If the state decided to pay people not to have kids who couldn't sustain them, refused to pay these people when they had them, and instead worked to actively rebuild the nuclear family by giving two-parent families support on a race blind basis, it would be a win for the nuclear family and might markedly impact demographic development at the same time it marked a stand in the culture wars.

The reason I doubt the Right would ever do this, however, is because they would not want to face the opprobrium from not just the Left, but the many Christians who experience profound discomfort in the government intervening in natal policy. The reality is the Federal Government has already been doing this for years, subsidizing poor people who were poor candidates to have children, but their basic belief in the sanctity and joy of life is likely to constrain how far the Republicans would look down this road.

Still, family planning should be considered because along with immigration, these are the two policies that would allow the Right time to shift the demographic future and begin enacting their own cultural vision. They would be highly contentious, but less dangerous than the breakout of full-scale conflict. It's worth considering the Left may be correct in their analysis of why the proposed border wall with Mexico is so popular with Republicans. We do have a sense of who we are, and whether you define it ethnically or on strictly civic terms, we end up realizing outsiders will destroy the America of our legacy which is now on life-support.

The problem is the Right likes to be right more than it likes being effective. Such morality would be a positive in a healthy society and a normal situation, but their live and let live attitude has proven fatally reckless in allowing a culture that is the inverse of all we once were to not just take root but overgrow all else. And all the paeans about liberty and individualism, made beautifully and eloquently, will only fall on deaf ears against a rising tide who simply wants government to do things for them.

While such policies would need to be part of the mix for the Right to restore the republic or evolve a new model which could restore the lost culture and preserve the liberties they so value, the level of resistance and violence they will attract will be directly proportional to their probability of success. The media knows this, and will make it impossible, especially considering the omnipresent slur to call all Republicans Nazis, to enact these measures without either a fight, or such anguish from moderates in the center that should Trump, or any future Republican try to move in this direction with this electorate, there would be an uprising and the Left would be given back power.

We see the truth of this assessment in how delicately Trump walks a civic nationalist line, actively working to integrate all Americans into the mix, even as watching one of his rallies makes clear those who support Trump fall neatly into the teams this book identifies: Conservative, rural, white, traditionalist. To his credit, he works tirelessly to do things the nice way, stressing opportunity and economic growth, and has avoided social issues to build the base, but unless future elections demonstrate a defection from one of the leftist factions, it should be clear this will not be enough to sustain these policies beyond his Administration.

Many on the Right know this already and so the conversation has shifted to what can be done to preserve our values. And it comes down to a bit of a terrible choice, assuming all else listed above is correct: Either the form of government can be preserved, whereby we will have the letter of the law but lack the people needed to give it meaning, or someone at some point has to do something to have the government take greater control, assuming more authority to undertake action to protect the liberties enshrined even as this would functionally mark the end of our democracy as we know it.

This chapter is labeled militarism, because whether it is from the rise of a populist movement arising to forestall a leftist insurrection, whether it is a security state designed to protect against perhaps the threat of terror from Antifa or other leftist networks, or if the military itself takes control in response to corruption from the Deep State, either independently or in conjunction with Trump or another nationalist figure, the Left has control of so much in America that the most likely way whereby the Right can keep control of the government long enough to change things would have to be through some sort of a coup.

I know people aren't ready to hear this, but it happens a lot in history. Often, the coup happens when the previously elected authority chooses to expand their power to fulfill their popular mandate, using the newly taken powers to get past the institutional actors who represent the countervailing party. Such action is often popular, and historically, have been the results of most democracies where the inefficiencies of the government result in such public discontent they support strong leadership at any cost. When a country hits the point where two or more sides are so at odds there is nothing left to reconcile them to one another, one side, usually the Right, takes their shot at assuming control directly.

Trump once quipped he could shoot a person on Fifth Avenue and not lose support. I do him no favors by telling him that so long as he represented the culture and beliefs of those Americans who put him in office, he is almost certainly right. Because after sixty years or more of compromise after compromise with the Left, where our culture was given away, our country transformed, and where middle America has endured lectures and scorn about our supposed evils, there are more than enough people willing to support him down this path rather than live through another leftist.

Look to polling of not just the Right, but also the Left, of how happy they would be to see an exemplar of their side assume a third term. The Democrats would have voted in Obama one more time, and the Republicans will ride or die with Trump. The intelligentsia will scorn such polls and bemoan the death of civics, but as this book has shown, this is only because most are leftists who realize the status quo now defaults to a victory for their side.

If the Right controlled government for a generation, embracing a deliberately reactionary tack, it could deconstruct the Deep State and the cultural apparatus. Such actions would inspire massive resistance, especially at first, but also much support. If coupled with revelations about scandalous actions from those folk, public opinion might shift far more quickly in favor of these actions, and with the rise of a state-run media, the message shift could do much to acclimate people in the center to the new regime, if prosperity and a reasonable degree of personal liberty were assured.

It's not something the Right would like to do, but whether they will consider it depends on how scary the Left appears, and just how far they are willing to lie and push to remove the legitimately elected regime. The more they radicalize, the more they provoke, the more likely this reaction becomes. I don't rate this outcome as probable, but history has shown it possible, and such action would represent the most peaceful path to victory for the Right.

For the Left, it would mean being branded as terrorists and seeing all they have built torn down. They would prefer to fight rather than see this happen, but if the military and law enforcement worked in concert, absent foreign intervention, it is likely such resistance would quickly be quelled, and they would either emigrate to Europe or Canada, or organize to make a stand in numbers somewhere like California.

Estimated Likelihood: 15%

Chapter 34: Decentralization—The Unhappy Compromise

Did that last chapter shock you a bit? I imagine, unless you're a hardcore activist who discusses things like this somewhat regularly, the idea that the government of this country which has endured for over two hundred years could be removed was probably at least a bit unsettling. And yet, when a government ceases to serve the interests of its people, or its people are irrevocably indisposed to one another, these fights happen. Our own history with the Civil War emerging over issues between Northern dominance and Southern autonomy offers proof of how quickly things can devolve.

However, we live in what is generally a less violent and far less self-sufficient time. People in America before last century were much hardier and able to live on their own, a situation which only remains true for a few country folks today. People almost universally say they desire peace, and I firmly believe most Americans, at least half of whom are religiously apolitical, read things like this book with shock and horror that their fellow citizens would contemplate such things just to realize their ideas. Whether the idealism of the Left or the realism of the Right, both seem equally obscure and insane to the person who just wants to pay the bills and raise a family.

Political types, for all the nice things they say about such people publicly, often see these folks as people whose opinions don't count because they have taken themselves out of the game. For as much as we applaud democracy, it bears remembering America is not Britain today because 3% of the American people were pissed off enough to launch a revolution against the Crown. We are habituated to think 50%+1 makes policy, but that only remains true so long as those who are more passionate accept the system. The truth is, sufficiently motivated, any 5% of Americans could collapse the system at any time. At present, evidence suggests each side has at least that number of partisans or more, with each side growing, to push their cause steadily toward the abyss.

Assuming one does not want to see such carnage and unpredictability disrupt all they have worked to achieve; how can it be stopped? One solution is to separate all those who think one way into one area and those who think the opposite into another and let them go their separate ways. We'll talk about that next chapter, but the only way to potentially reconcile the Left and Right in America without destroying this country is to find a way for each to find expression without the one imposing on the other.

This problem is not new in America. In fact, the recurring problem in American history which transcends the Left/Right division is between different cultures wanting to realize their own unique expressions and yet being able to co-exist. The first century of our existence was a nonstop struggle between the North and South, where states had to be admitted in equal proportion of free to slave, and where protectionist industrialists in the North butted heads with agrarian free traders in the South. So long as the individual states perceived themselves to have enough freedom of action for the union to remain of benefit, they could work in concert to expand this country across the continent. But as one side sought to impose their views on the other, which is what the North essentially did in the Civil War, conflict became inevitable.

That was the bloodiest conflict in North American history. Historians estimate 620,000 Americans perished during that war on either side, compared to an estimate of 644,000 Americans in all other domestic and foreign wars combined. It's worth remembering the implied costs that arise should brother come to arms against brother because one side falls so in love with their beliefs they decide to force it upon others. The casualty numbers would almost certainly be much higher today given our much larger population.

Yet, the Northern victory had a major consequence which accelerated to today, for good or for ill. The United States now has an incredibly powerful Federal Government. The states have not exercised their sovereignty in such a meaningful way since that time, and in addition to the legal authority, the actions of the 20th Century gave the financial backing to the Federal Government to allow it carte blanche to undertake as expansive a social welfare and warfare state as could be imagined. With the rise of so much power in one location, the temptation to use such power to push one's views over the whole of the country has proven irresistible.

As we have two more or less equally divided factions playing tug of war over DC, whenever one side wins, they impose their views on the other. The Left started this game, but it's fair to say the Right is now playing, and if this remains the game, one begins to see that someone must win. Or, if a winner doesn't emerge, the two sides might just escalate into a brawl like you would see on the playground.

Can that be changed? It seems like it would be difficult to accomplish at this late hour, but history also shows us America has worked best when there has been space for different forms of cultural expression to each occupy their own political space to ease tensions and increase happiness for the people where they live. If Americans came together in huge numbers, which would frankly require intervention by people who would prefer not to care about politics, and demanded DC allow states to go their own way without forcing a one size fits all solution, much would be done to alleviate the pressure.

To make this happen, politicians across party lines would probably have to agree to cede legal authority back to the States, to rework the Fourteenth Amendment and interstate commerce clause used by the Supreme Court to justify so many of the existing Federal Agencies and elevate the Tenth Amendment which explicitly and unambiguously reserves rights not delegated to the Federal Government to the respective states.

The Left would have to agree to dismantle the welfare state, instead transferring it to those states which wanted such provisions, and the Right would have to give up the enormous military apparatus it tends to support. Many Federal agencies would be disbanded, all would be reduced in size, and a new national consensus on immigration would still be required, which given the import and vast disagreement on that issue, would be hard to envision. Yet, if such a consensus emerged, and the taxing authority was transferred to the states, it's possible we could have many Americas co-exist in something nominally like what we have today.

Assuming all this could be done, one could ask what might keep these disparate states together where you imagine a California that looks communist working with Texas swinging hard right socially and toward free markets. I'm not sure it would hold together, frankly, as you would see regional blocs emerge based on common beliefs and culture. But the path toward peaceful dissolution where people move voluntarily to be in places that better fit their mindset would at least allow more people to live according to their beliefs, including the many who just don't want to see politics become a fight.

It's also possible the good fences makes good neighbors policy could cause an age of American renewal. Different systems benefit different modes of thinking as well as different industries, and the advantage of having different legal opportunities could create more commerce and advancement within the country, where the benefits could increase political satisfaction. If one were unhappy with their state, they could simply move, and a fight would theoretically be unnecessary.

The best thing about this approach is that even though Congress would be the most likely method to realize the radical decentralization described above, the Constitution itself prescribes at least two other ways a major reorganization of the government might be achieved. The first would be at the request of the States whereby a majority, each of whom has their own gripes with Federal authority, could meet to consider amending the Constitution. The other option is the people themselves, through Article V, could, convene the state legislatures, holding conventions, to consider a new form of government for America.

Activists on both sides have occasionally looked at the viability of such an approach but have refrained from encouraging this too publicly for fear of what the other side might propose. The Right, much more likely to be able to use this path due to having control of nearly the required number of state houses, fears Leftists would seek to abrogate the Second and Tenth Amendments. The Left would be just as fearful about how the Right might use such a convention to propose new amendments to restrict centralization of power, but perhaps as tensions rise, an unhappy compromise might prove sufficiently appealing to the rest of America that they could demand such a resolution.

It's worth noting that between the onset of the American Revolution and the complete ratification of the Constitution, fourteen years elapsed. From the Treaty of Paris which ended the Revolutionary War in 1783, it took another four years to draft the Constitution, itself an uncertain compromise agreed to only after the failure of the far weaker Articles of Confederation, and then over two years for states to ratify the new compact into law. Building a new government is hard. Re-purposing an existing one might be even harder. Yet, we owe it to ourselves to explore all opportunities to realize paths which limit bloodshed. Because should it come to a fight, we don't know if the outcome will be better, but we know for certain many people will suffer and die.

The political types will not go for this of their own accord. The moderates are too entrenched in a system where they have power and prestige and will not want to devolve power. The Left, specifically, would resist this idea as their basic idea of centralizing power, which is happening not just at the national but international levels as well, would be jeopardized by a devolution of power to the state level such as being suggested here. But the Right might listen, and there would be many, hating the suggestion that power most likely must be taken to protect their culture, would consider the notion as libertarians and constitutionalists have for years. The problem is that the likely sticking point would end up being immigration, unless some novel compromise were worked out there.

But it would be quite a scene and perhaps the only way America could be fixed, if the people of this country could agree to hit the reset button without having to use conflict, accepting there would be many Americas instead of one. I am not an idealist by nature, but I think many people would give this a chance, and if everyone gave up some, perhaps we could all get much more. That said, you'd still have people in states more closely divided mad at one another, and the number of people who would have to move to make this work for what would ultimately be a compromise could pose an obstacle.

If conflict goes on long enough without decisive results and without descending beyond the brink, it bears watching if a popular movement around decentralization could succeed. The problem is that it remains a concept without any institutional or organizational support and counts on people whose very instincts will be to run from politics or hide in one camp or the other to do the complete opposite. Possible, but highly unlikely.

Estimated Likelihood: 3%

Chapter 35: Separation—A Mutual Departure

If this book has demonstrated anything, it probably has shown that there are two very divergent versions of America. I suspect leftists would argue I don't do justice to their vision of the future given my own biases, but I'd freely concede as I think they would agree we want to see very different futures. Right now, we're trapped in conflict because of the presumption one side will win, impose its views, and the other will lose.

But as the two sides have rough parity with one another, and each agrees the other is manifestly unfit to lead the country, it's not impossible to imagine a day will come when serious discussions are held about splitting America into two or more sections to enable these visions to go their separate ways. Unlike the previous chapter which aimed to hold the country together, driven perhaps by the wishes of the majority, this chapter supposes that the political types will decide to forge their own solution and recognize that each is more likely to achieve their ends within a state of their own than in the outcome of conflict to control the whole country.

America is already a highly regional country with distinctive cultures, so the fault lines upon which a new map may be drawn are not so difficult to imagine. What makes this hard, however, is that vast spaces of the country are occupied by people who lean to the Right, but the population centers lean to the Left. While one could imagine America, in theory, having coastal republics of the Left that traded for goods with inland powers who leaned Right, having such complexity would be almost impossible to manage in terms of an organized separation.

Consider all the questions of who would own what, what systems would remain in place, and how information would be transferred. Such concerns ensure that with few exceptions, states would almost certainly remain intact in a planned division scenario. If we ever went so far as to seriously contemplate separation, which I admit is more likely a theoretical exercise than one the sides would willingly contemplate, it also must be considered that the Left and Right will not want to live near one another and will require some separation between their holdings.

With these factors in mind, let's look to history for two examples. The first is one of the most complicated separations ever effectuated in the British division of India, then sometimes called Hindustan, into the states of India and Pakistan based upon religious lines on the authority of the local prince. Such separation was mostly peaceful but has kept some of the most dangerous flash points in the world like Kashmir where disputed borders at the point of cultural overlap serve to generate constant enmity. There are few examples of countries who like their neighbor less, yet peace has mostly held. Interestingly, the area of East Pakistan, now called Bangladesh, was a much smaller Muslim exclave, but whose proximity to India has drawn it more moderately into the orbit of the larger state. Such an example matters because of how we might draw America into two or more parts.

There was a time when it was imagined this continent would be settled by two great countries. One would be the United States of America, based on the Atlantic Ocean, and other would be a newly settled Columbia, stationed on the Pacific. Before the advent of railroads connected the country more thoroughly, such a vision had many adherents, and even today, we see the west as a very different animal from the east, with a relaxed culture, much more urban, multicultural, and supporting the Left in far greater intensity.

By contrast, when we look at where rural folk live, where traditional values are supported, and where Republicans are found, we see the South, Midwest, and increasingly even parts of the Northeast properly are coming around to support the Right. My prediction is that these trends will accelerate as voting patterns come to reflect more explicitly residency and race. So, while there will be the establishment corridor of big cities that votes leftist, everything east of the Rockies is essentially Republican territory.

Why not use such trends as the basis for an amicable split? The Rockies make an excellent geographic barrier to ensure both sides relative security. The United States would continue as a much more conservative and traditional nation, shedding the states of California, Oregon, Nevada, and Washington. There would be disputes over much of Idaho, Montana, Idaho, Arizona, New Mexico, and Colorado, but given the evolving demographics, it seems most of these states will fall into the Left's orbit anyway and

357

could be given over in exchange for the recognition the great cities of the Northeast would have to become part of the Right leaning America which remained. If drawn by state, it seems the cleanest line might be to have Idaho, Utah, and Arizona represent the western expanse of the leftist state based on Columbia which would almost certainly have a less offensive name.

For convention, let's call their state Pacifica. Pacifica would have ample supplies for self-sufficiency, would likely have good relations with both China and Mexico, and would attract many of the Latino population as well as white liberals from the Northeast, Chicago, and other cities. Departing conservatives could be resettled in Montana, the Great Plains, and if still held, Colorado and New Mexico. Pacifica would be free to pursue policies as leftist as they wanted, have an open borders policy that would attract many more Mexicans or people from abroad, while the Heartland would be able to continue with its own sensibilities.

In this scenario, the biggest challenge for America would be in how the biggest cities of New York, Chicago, and Philadelphia adapted. I suspect there would be many people who chose to immediately depart for Los Angeles, San Francisco, Portland, or Seattle. Those who remained would be absorbed and hopefully included in a new form of civic nationalism which would have time to grow in this new state which would be alleviated of many of the demographic pressures being most heavily forced by the West Coast and would possibly even serve as an attraction for a new wave of European immigrants, nationalists by inclination seeking to leave their globalist-oriented countries.

This would resolve the seemingly irreconcilable conflict between the two factions by giving each the opportunity to have a state of their own. By reducing the separation to a split between two countries, it would ease the bureaucratic nightmare of trying to work out who owns what, and based upon the precept of natural borders, there is no better way to divide America than along the continental ridge. In many ways, this would seem like an ideal solution to an unsolvable problem, except for a few small details. Even though the lines broadly speaking would put more leftists out West and rightists in the East, there would still be anywhere from 25-40% of people who would need to either move, adapt to a new philosophy, or accept having a government that is hostile to their values imposed upon them.

In terms of raw numbers, that means millions of people. Just to put how vast the numbers of people involved are, consider California which has just under forty million people. If we assume just one in four leans right, that means ten million people would be expected to either give up their homes or their beliefs for a settlement. In many cases, these people will live in areas where most people think as they do, such as the area known as Jefferson in the north of the state which is thinly populated and consistently votes Republican. To make such an arrangement for peace means asking these people to either abandon their homes, pay for their resettlement, or accept a hostile regime.

For families who have lived for generations in a given area, it would be a nonstarter, so even the best thought out separation would instantly lead to insurgency actions from adherents choosing to defend their homes and remain behind enemy lines. This problem, which we're going to get deep into during the secession examples, would also happen in a separation scenario, but would likely be squashed much more quickly by the dominant regime in the designated area.

The question is whether America would accept having to move potentially upwards of 50 million people to realize political peace, especially when each side thinks they have a decent chance of winning a battle to claim the whole country? I'm not sure they would, not only because of the anger it would generate with their own partisans, but also because of the inherent risks of having neighbors whose views run directly counter to their own.

From the Right's perspective, having a communist state which could serve as the foothold for Chinese influence in North America sounds like an invitation to a future war, not just against Mexicans and liberals, but potentially millions of Chinese with advance positions and uncontested dominance in the Pacific. Such thoughts could be fantasy, but a state made from shunting the Left apart would inevitably have such an ideological character, these doubts would become dogma.

From the Left's perspective, they would naturally be paranoid about an America based upon old values seeking to restart manifest destiny, taking back the reconquest as it once did in earlier history, and building upon a nationalist vision which would likely emerge to seize more living space and reclaim the entirely of America. Whether such visions were real or not, their propaganda would make them seem such.

These problems only accelerate the more narrowly you divide America. It's tempted to look at splitting us into multiple countries, based on cultural regions like New England, the Mid-Atlantic, the South, and what not, but while these areas certainly have unique attributes to bind them, given the reason for such divisions is ideological rather than regional, such lines would prove even more contentious and fractious for future fighting.

People on the Left and Right both know that and given that they are driven as much by idealism as realism, the political types seem much more willing to look toward solutions that allow them to take all of America if possible. For that reason, I rated the slow seizure plan of submission to the Left and quick seizure plan of militarism by the Right as far more likely strategies, requiring the consent of a much smaller group of people to enact, and see them as the more peaceful paths both sides will likely angle toward.

Both this chapter and the preceding ideas about decentralization represent an effort to envision how America could try to split the difference and peacefully separate without going down the path to change government. But what they reveal is that it is much easier for government to make someone do something than to ask people to do things.   Given that reality, which exists in our divisive environment, it seems the separation scenario is among the least likely of scenarios.

Estimated Likelihood: 2%

Chapter 36: Secession—A More Orderly Breakup

Whereas the first two scenarios presume one side acts so decisively as to gain, or inversely, acts so indecisively to cede complete dominance, and the second two scenarios are based on a cooperative approach, both the secession and collapse scenarios presume neither side can take control nor in most cases are the actions organized. Much like the evolving situation at present, there are actors affiliated with either banner, but whether at the state level or below, it is quite plausible that we will see lower levels of authority seeking to invalidate those above them.

If politics can be managed to a point where one party can so dominate the Federal Government, and should those in power act in such a way as to make their power more permanent and sufficiently incite those in opposition, then there will be such energy for states to look to different paths as America hasn't seen since the 1850's. Although the governments of states will likely be loath to walk down such a road, many states allow for public referenda on these issues, and we already see hints of what could follow.

Although it is presently being held from the ballot due to the State Supreme Court of California wanting to review the legality of the proposition, California already has a ballot initiative to split into three states. Given that the proposed borders would produce three Democrat states, it's unlikely the Republicans in Washington would ever entertain such a gesture, but there are other secessionist movements out there as well. Jefferson, for instance, has been working to separate the conservative counties of Northern California from the progressives in the rest of the state who lord over them. So, even though formal secession hasn't yet hit the ballot, ideas about Calexit as it might be called are already proliferating.

During the Obama regime when the Left seemed to have a stranglehold on power, a vibrant sovereignty movement started gaining traction in Texas. So long as none of the mentioned factions gains undisputed dominance, such a movement will likely be restrained. But if Texans retain the same makeup over the course of another decade of Democrats in Washington, the calls for secession that are now a faint whisper could become a rebel yell. The billboard recently posted in Texas telling the Californians to keep driving if they left their homes is demonstrative of how pronounced this mindset has become.

The question about which side would continue walking a path in opposition to the Federal Government depends heavily on who controls what. If we accept the supposition that Trump is likely to win in 2020 as much because of how the radical Left is alienating the center as anything else, it seems the window where the secessionist impulse should strike for the Left would be in the early 2020's. Should they pass through eight years of Trump without becoming fully unhinged, given the historic pattern where voters switch parties periodically, and presuming the absence of a nationalist of equal or greater fervor than Trump, it would seem plausible a change of party would happen in Washington which might quickly flip the calculus.

Remembering that inaction by the Right results in a default victory for the Left by demographic means, if eight years of Republican control proves insufficient to address the systemic disadvantages they faced in immigration, demography, and means of cultural promotion, another chance to correct these at the national level seems unlikely. Patterns driven by demography predict states like Arizona going blue, and states in the southeast following the example of Virginia, a state which was once guaranteed to vote Republican, but has now slipped away. The acceleration of these voting habits will require a shrinking Right to decide if they should attempt to remove themselves, which very well might be inspired by a new social justice regime that one can imagine being created by Leftist regimes post-Trump.

In some ways, secession, unless it happened in a sizable bloc of states, would represent a strategy born of desperation. While California and Texas are large enough to think this way, given the number of people each possesses and the natural resources available to sustain an internal economy, most states would have to band together and that sort of interaction seems unlikely while the Federal Government still exists. The only exceptions I can imagine where a sense of common identity might allow people to at least think this way are the longstanding regional divisions like New England or Cascadia. But except for Dixie, which would now just be the Deep South, Tennessee, and

Arkansas, it's hard to imagine the contested states elsewhere taking secession seriously.

When we think about who is most likely to attempt secession, it seems the path is easier for the Left than the Right. Because of their radicalism, distance from the capital, and having the option of ballot referenda which many states in the eastern half of the country do not, signs again point to the Pacific Coast as where either individual states or a group of states might elect to leave the union. I could imagine California acting alone or perhaps in concert with Oregon and Washington. While these states certainly have many who would oppose separation, the urban majorities would drive support upwards, and if the Republicans were undertaking the immigration policy required for the survival of the Right's ideas, these states with potential neighbors in Nevada and a future left-leaning Arizona might be inclined to go along.

It's highly doubtful that a Federal regime effective enough to contemplate full immigration reform will simply permit California to walk away. To allow the dissenters to simply remove part of the country would threaten the potential dissolution of the entire country along ideological lines, which in a disorganized way, could inspire places like the Northeastern corridor to look to further divide the United States. To prevent that, the Administration will likely have to act, and how different parties would behave in a secession crisis is difficult to guess. Would the National Guard, who leans right, fight for the Governor(s) out west? Would the military be willing to put down any civil unrest and impose martial law?   What sort of resistance could follow?

As idealistic as it sounds, a popular secessionist movement which featured a campaign of nonviolence was incredibly successful in India.   If certain states were to simply refuse to recognize Federal authority, accept occupation in response, but have their people engage in a general popular strike, a prolonged standoff which doesn't result in violence could galvanize popular support to let them go.   Although another imperfect example, the recent Arab Spring protests which were successful in Tunisia and for a time in Egypt, shows the model the nonprofits have perfected around the world, often with ample CIA funding.

The problem is that should secession be declared, wherever it happens, it's quite possible there would be skirmishing between partisans wanting to stay in the United States and those wanting to leave.   Such disagreements would probably start at the public level of having rallies and counter-rallies, but as we've already seen at events at Berkeley and other places, such contests are already descending into low level violence.   How much more pronounced will the violence become when passions are elevated to the point of proposing a new separate government?   It would only take one incident getting out of control and becoming the equivalent of a street battle to potentially set everyone on edge to such a degree that armed factions would arise in self-defense.

Given the many divergent interests and groups in a big state such as California, organic factions based on neighborhood, race, and ideology will form to ensure local protection, often in concert with the local administrations which will probably start declaring themselves loyal to Washington or Sacramento, in accordance with the ideology of their region. Just as West Virginia declared itself separate from Virginia in the original Civil War, everything from north of San Francisco to the Oregon border would likely declare their own separation as Jefferson, and seek representation as the true government, or a legitimate splinter government for their region. A confused mess with panicked people would result, where every choice available to the Feds would have problems.

Should the Federal government push the issue further and arrest the offending governor, would that lead to a mass insurrection? Would that be allowed? Could you imagine Federal troops or law enforcement firing at either State officials, or perhaps a state militia formed of volunteers who believed in the cause? There would be so many actors and so much chaos that one must imagine radicals willing to go this far would exploit such an opportunity to raise the stakes.

Consider the historical context of how secession played out in the past because it might prove relevant. After Lincoln was elected in the contentious four-way election of 1860, backed by Republicans who demanded at a minimum that no new states be admitted as slave states, it was clear a crisis was brewing about an issue key to Southern interests.

Before Lincoln could even take office, seven states in the Deep South declared their secession, and these states would form the core of the emerging Confederacy. They had hoped to peacefully exercise such a right, as New England itself had considered in 1814, but for which there had been no precedent. Although politics worked at one level, there were contradictory efforts to reconnect the Union or at least redress grievances for remaining slave states. So, while the Confederacy was coming into being, there was also a Peace Conference launched in February of 1861 between states like Pennsylvania, Maryland, Virginia, and Kentucky, which even offered up a compromise to seek to forestall conflict.

What they found is that neither side could agree to what the other would offer, and that the temptation by the Republicans newly come to power in the North was to fulfill their mandate. At the same time, the Democrats then in the South could not accept further limitation of their future prerogatives. Cooler heads might have prevailed in time, but with the attacks on Fort Sumter in South Carolina, where Confederate Forces began shelling the Union garrison, positions hardened, and existing loyalties pushed toward conflict. Holding peace together was harder than keeping people from a fight whose onset had been delayed nearly thirty years by unhappy concessions and compromises.

In many ways, our situation reflects what our ancestors experienced, except where they had the clarification of having discrete geographical locations mostly united behind their remaining or exiting governments, our affiliations are cast far more widely as we live among one another. But the similarity of having an unstable political situation, two diverging cultures, and the ease with which a radical group could provoke the two sides to begin taking actions from which there would be no simple return is striking.

When a compromise was available before guns started firing between the Union and the Confederacy, people rushed to support their own partisans, and I cannot imagine Californian secession any differently. It could happen when Californian partisans try to seize a Federal asset. I doubt they would be so bold as to attempt the Marine Base at Camp Pendleton or any of the Naval Facilities in San Diego or San Francisco, but we've seen right-wing people already occupy Park Ranger and Bureau of Land Management Offices in rural areas. A symbolic seizure of a real asset is one thing which could happen.

Just as likely, proactive measures taken by the Right against leftist traitors, as they would then be deemed, could see the tension level rise quickly. In areas where there is relative parity between the two sides, these would seem the potential hot spots, and once a fight breaks out using more than just words, one movement or both will have martyrs whose sacrifice will unleash waves of fury. It took four years of fighting across an entire nation once we went that far last time, it could do so again.

One thing we realize is that once a state seriously walks down this road, one of three things will happen: Least likely, the state will just be able to walk away, and a peaceful separation would be affected. The nonviolent approach highlighted earlier might permit such an outcome but given the number of opposing partisans who would prefer to stay and the likelihood actions undertaken by them against the nonviolent crowd would prove able to transform the activists into violence. Given the existing polarization, it's hard to imagine sympathy could do anything but split along whatever line is primarily driving the conflict.

Considerably more likely is the Federal police or other units would be deployed to assure order. As this happens, a question will arise if California or whatever other state acts will continue to resist, or if such actions will cause other states to question the legitimacy of the DC government. During the Civil War, the fighting outside Charleston is what flipped Virginia and North Carolina firmly toward the Confederacy, and heavy handedness from the national level would have many other left-leaning states, including those closest to DC, on edge. Putting down revolts out west might very well expand quickly to a nationwide insurrection.

Such action could lead to the formation of two distinctive sides with states declaring in support or resistance of Washington. Our scenario has the Left in insurrection, but the broad strokes of the argument work just as well for Texans against a socialist. The question about what the military does becomes essential. Does it hold together? Does it support one side? No one knows, but commonly held speculation on the subject suggests the Republicans would have much better chances of keeping units from deserting given the leanings of most veterans.

Then, the question becomes whether the opposition would continue to resist, and live in protest, or would they raise forces to start fighting? As a local problem becomes the inescapable issue, a fight in one place that leads to a shooting in another could set off the entire country. With different areas descending into chaos and national authority stretched beyond the ability to easily enforce its mandates, if the sides don't align neatly, then while secession might be announced, it will likely fall into a much greater collapse.

Secession is the attempt to break away in an orderly fashion, and while not impossible if everyone agrees to avoid violence, it would take the best of all worlds for events to play out so neatly. Political idealists may well propose this solution without considering all these consequences, instead simply asserting that separation is a logical way to address grievances held by their majority. But considering how many people get dragged into a solution they don't want, secession has the same fatal flaw as separation, which is that people would rather win than settle.

But, when you fight for everything, sometimes all that is left after the fight is nothing. In many ways, secession is a desperation play, but if either the currently rising angst of the Left or the coming demographic crisis of the Right make enough people worried, we could see this be the starting point of a much larger fight, which will most likely descend into some level of collapse.

Estimated Likelihood: 5%

Chapter 37: Collapse—Any Miscalculation

For their many differences, each of the preceding solutions assumes some recognized authority figure(s) remain and can provide enough support to and from their people to be useful and relevant. A collapse covers any other scenario where all levels of government break down, or at least devolve to such a localized level that people are unable to rely upon basic goods, services, or the rule of law.

Our society operates on a most interesting contradiction. We are incredibly efficient because we are very specialized, but any system so precise requires a great deal of management to assure all the moving parts remain in motion. Having worked in the field for a few years, I observed the logistics alone of how many people, how many services, and how much infrastructure is required to get any item from point A to point B. We count on all these unseen actors doing their jobs as they always have for our survival.

Consider the food supply chain. The producer needs goods to work the ground or handle the livestock. Labor must show up, and then for cities to get food, the decision must be made to send it out for money as having greater value than the food itself. Trucks are needed to transport for further refinement or packaging, counting on open roads, protected by police, not subject to interdiction by partisans. The roads need to be open, the refrigerators working, and gas readily available. Assuming all of this, then food shows up at a supermarket, hopefully still open, and a person in a city gets fed.

Can you count the number of things that have to go right for society to continue? Because the one thing we all know is that when people aren't being fed, nothing else is going to matter, and people will not go to work. The same will be true if the roads are split, the power stays out, or any of a host of other natural or artificially provoked challenges emerge. The moment the government proves incapable of handling a crisis at the regional or national level, whether it be politically inspired or otherwise, a breakdown scenario will occur where survival instincts will kick in and survival will become a very local proposition.

It is generally believed that emergencies will bring out the best in people. Historically, America has been fortunate in that disasters like hurricanes and earthquakes have brought support and external resources to resolve crises. But should the crises occur in response to political polarization, it's very possible that the government will only exacerbate tensions by getting involved, further spreading the breakdown.

To describe what will happen is impossible because collapses happen quickly or slowly. Areas with greater trust and homogeneity should have the advantage of people being able to pool resources and abilities together more quickly, and with less discord for common benefit. Those who act quickly will put themselves in a better position as will those who have prepared for days of uncertainty such as these.

From the rural perspective, the advantage will be having access to more food, enjoying a major security advantage of low population density, and living in communities primarily where people know one another well enough to avoid direct violence and not having the consumption problem. The disadvantage is basic services will be least available here, so those most reliant upon civilization to survive will be among the first impacted.

From the urban viewpoint, it's likely any government aid made available will first come to these locations, if it does arrive, but the challenge of having more people needing to consume food, water, and energy than might be arriving will quickly lead to conflict. Furthermore, the proximity of multiple cultures could prove to allow for some sharing of skills, but given the pressures, will more likely lead to violence as the more pragmatic types establish zones of control to hoard resources.

In a collapse scenario, the cities are likely to prove the most dangerous places because when all encounters are uncertain, being around people one doesn't know is the greatest risk, and though cities will likely rally to protect themselves, how well they can work to ensure they will be fed is a very difficult question. A happy answer requires the participation of actors over whom the cities have optimistic expectations, but no control.

The suburbs end up being the front lines between two different war zones, where people escaping the city will probably head to first, where country folk will make sure threats are contained, and where the larger numbers of the city will come out to gather resources they need once they exhaust the wealth which will be in gentrified areas.

Just as the needs for survival are locally driven, so too will be the authority figures that emerge. In some places, government will organize smartly and sharply to meet the basic needs of people, where local assets from national agencies may hold things together easily. Other places will hold together less easily but will still manage based upon community cooperation.

There will be other places where citizens themselves probably take control by force, especially in rural areas where such organizations exist as to manage these ends, and you could see outposts and militias emerge. Some might even cooperate to establish control over larger areas, and the military's own planning of what an American breakdown scenario looks like includes the reign of such warlords.

The premise is simple: People will do whatever is necessary to satisfy their basic needs of security, shelter, food, water, and warmth. If someone manages to control access to these in a given area, that person or group will control the area, and will be able to expand their influence to the extent they can meet these needs for others. Whether through appropriation of existing resources or community planning to cover future allocations, those who can provide these services will be in charge.

They will remain such if they have the force to defend themselves against other potential actors and will be co-opted if they do not. For a time, all authority will revert to the hard authority of whatever one can hold through force, and justice is likely to become severe. Theft could become a capital offense when supplies are limited, and people working against the common good, as defined by the majority in each area, will likely be exiled or worse.

Sometimes people say the terrible thing about imagining the coming civil war in America is you wouldn't know who is on which side, and this is entirely true. Quickly evolving conflict seems much more likely to devolve into uncertain lines than clear adversaries, where we know the four factors of ideology, residency, race, and culture will determine who teams with whom initially, and who looks to befriend whom., But where such divisions may spawn hundreds or thousands of parallel and contesting efforts, most of these efforts will try to employ their ideology or identity in the most basic of goals: Survival.

For those who become larger upon the success of meeting the needs of their people, or promising enough resources to inspire others to successfully usurp power, they will likely seek to expand to amass resources, personnel, and control over a given area. There are so many variables that any more concrete predictions would simply be guesswork but look for places with many weapons like military bases to serve as hubs.

Perhaps I am too cynical in my estimation, but I think this war would be one where people shot first and asked questions later. People not already known will be assumed to be the worst of possible applicable stereotypes, and for that reason, even as the front lines will be jagged as hell, any of the maps which show the split between Democrats and Republicans is likely to show at least where the starting lines will be for this fight.

Given such a dismal outcome, one might wonder why people would consider a civil war at all, but the answer is because they imagine they can avoid going down the road where it all falls apart and can find victory over the other side before authority is lost. In many ways, radical politics counts upon the idea that so many people will not want to see the destruction of their basic material comforts that they will support any authority over no authority, which is why the cultural insanity of the Left goes unchallenged and why a coup by the Right might get popular support. Because a hard reset would go beyond politics and force people to just face a survival scenario.

And yet, there are those who consider this outcome better than defeat, and there are quite a few Americans who believe an uncertain fight is better than an ignominious surrender or defeat. For people who live in the country, there are a number of people in certain regions who think they can survive and be happier if they can simply walk away. The far right calls them balkanization advocates, and however people believe things will happen, regional movements designed for self-sufficiency are on the rise.

Conversely, there are leftists who think a broken America is an opportunity for them to bring in foreign support to advance their ideology or identity, and certain groups might try to take advantage of such scenarios. It's even imaginable that people on that side could work as subversives in the interest of a foreign power like China to advance a shared interest in exchange for promised support.

Why would people do this? The breakdown scenario is the only one which resets the rules and puts everything into play. If a faction thinks everything is so broken or upside down that it can't be fixed, they might argue a reset toward nature is needed, as I know some on the Right believe with the cultural extremism of the Left. Or, they might just see such a reset as an opportunity to impose policies people would never support by common consent, and for which there would never be a popular movement.

Is it crazy? I guess it depends upon how you ask the question. If you were to ask if taking down a country to push a political ideal is good, most people would answer negatively. Yet, if you knew the politics of your county ended with your erasure, marginalization, or imprisonment, might you decide the cost of what battles happen today are worth having some future? Given how much fear has arisen about what the other sides intend on all sides, people are asking that last question with much more intensity, which is why you might just hear someone say it would be better for us to get this fight over with now.

As a country, America is fundamentally broken. We do not know what we want to be. We have two or more competing and opposing visions. Without unity at our core, these conflicts will only increase, and as they do, polarization will continue until either one side wins or some new arrangement emerges to resolve the differences of Left and Right in a third alternative. Honestly, it looks like the fight is coming, and as bad as it would be, I can only hope that if such a conflict occurs, it will prove decisive.

We cannot go on with a political process of one side punishing the other indefinitely and hope to achieve anything but hatred. We cannot seek to replace the existing majority with new people from far away and think people will cheer this insult. People who want government to run their lives aren't going to embrace those who just want to be left alone. These differences are too stark, have gone on for too long, and will destroy everything if they continue to fight long enough.

We stand on the precipice of a collapse because of these questions. It might not happen. One side might win, quietly or decisively, but it's just as possible that we all lose. Because there might not be anything left to save. War is that sort of hell.

To understand what happens when all that is left is survival, there is ample evidence of how rough civil wars become, and the Balkans where campaigns of genocide and regular violence were conducted between all ethnicities and faith groups might give you a hint if you want to research further. Expect mass death, killing, and suffering in a collapse, and your idea of humanity to be forever changed, and not for the better. To survive such times, you will find being prepared is everything, and that's why this book is here to warn you about political violence and civil war coming down the line.

If you know things are coming and prepare yourself and your family, good times will be better, and you might just survive bad times. You might see the world, eventually, look more like you hope. And maybe, even more optimistically, maybe after reading this, you will think more carefully about what a civil war could mean, and why the coming conflict must be dealt with so thoughtfully.

Any outcome is possible after a collapse. Whole regions will be remade in terms of their population. But even these fights will likely still leave us with divisions to be resolved. So absent one final victor after a long campaign, assuming this doesn't become an international mess, that common culture still be must be won for victory to have meaning. The shame is how we seem unable to get there any other way.

Considering how many different paths lead to this outcome, and how disorganized both sides are, this represents a probable outcome for which you must be ready.

Estimated Likelihood: 35%

Section V: Practical Advice

These last suggestions are designed to share useful information to prepare yourself and your family for the conflict ahead. Should things resolve peacefully, the suggestions will only improve your life and preparedness, but if things continue down a more dangerous path, the words contained herein might save your lives. Those who will survive an uncertain future are those who prepare, who actively seek awareness of their surroundings, make sure to make friends and support during good times, and who are part of communities better suited to protect themselves in challenging situations.

Chapter 38: Practical Suggestions

Seek Out Useful Information

Assuming they have good information, most people are smart enough to make intelligent decisions given useful facts and context. If you're reading this book, you're obviously smart enough to follow societal patterns and be concerned about evolution of conflict in the United States and elsewhere. But, to protect yourself most effectively, one must constantly keep informed about one's surroundings.

This starts by becoming a realist. Even if you have ideals by which you live, any person who is incapable of assessing reality is already at a huge disadvantage. It sounds stupid to tell people to base their judgments on reality, but I do so because at least when it comes to politics, people signal so often for the ideals they're taught they must defend, even when those ideals contradict the evidence of their eyes. As a result, we encounter many people living in clear defiance of obvious realities that put them in danger.

One thing you will notice in my writing is that no subject is off limits, no groups beyond discussion, no people with whom I will not engage, and no areas where I let feelings get in the way of observable reality. Like anyone else, I often wish the world were such that good feelings alone would make things better, but I'm not willing to sacrifice myself to the mere hope of placing faith in a government that will do the right thing. I am willing to consider anything, but only if it makes sense for me and mine, and such pragmatism is what is needed not just for survival, but if cooler heads are to prevail.

Because the reality is that while the two ends are screeching toward a fight, the response by the majority in the middle is to stick their fingers in their ears and pretend this isn't happening. Such a reaction is not at all helpful. Sometimes, that means repeating lies that are happier. Other times, that means just living one's life in the oblivious hope nothing bad will happen, trusting life will continue as it always has, while ignoring the sound and fury of politics.

Those people may be proven right. I gave it a 40% chance of going just that way, which might be too pessimistic, but why would you choose to ignore something which could have such an impact upon you? So many people say it is because they feel helpless to act given the scope of problems and conflict, but when the problem seems too big, those who have a good mind and resolve can make the conundrum manageable by taking everything down to the personal level.

Good information starts with knowing yourself and your beliefs. Once that is known, getting to a place that fits those beliefs is powerful, and if you don't know what you should be thinking, it is very vital to find more information.

I read an insane amount of information every day. From sources I trust, I build a worldview, but I also look at ones which frankly irritate me, ones that lie more often than not, and ones where much is disinformation, but some gems can still be found. The media loves to place filters on what you can learn by labeling things fake, but all news is just the combination of facts and propaganda disguised as narrative. The more you read, watch, or hear, and the more you vary your sources, the more accurate your picture of what different people are doing will become.

Reading foreign media is especially useful. Anyone too close to a situation loses a certain objectivity, and there are things about America you can learn from reading how others report on our country, which local sources would never think to share. This is especially true for mainstream sources which basically exist to support the Left in their efforts to remake America. They've demonstrated their clear allegiance to that cause, and have no compunctions whatsoever about lying in the service of that cause.

Alternative media is something else to seek out while one still can. It's amazing how different discussions will look on the Internet as opposed to those on television. The more sources available, the better your perspective will become, as you can see in real time how people dissent and argue with one another. Where the primary media exists to conceal and propagandize, look to smaller voices not getting paid to put information out there, and the story changes rapidly.

Lastly, never believe anything that you can't verify for yourself or which simply doesn't make sense. Whether news stories or books, test the reasoning of the author, and consider more than just the ideology to see if their reasoning is sound.

Once you've done that for politics, every other area where you can become informed is to your benefit. If you're afraid you'll forget, print out what you need or keep books around. Knowledge has always been power, and as the world becomes smaller and scarier, those who have the most to offer in terms of skills and knowledge will be those who have value far more than those with fat bank accounts.

Live Where You Belong

So many people live in places they hate, often with jobs they cannot stand, because they cannot imagine anything better and they fear the unknown. Perhaps they have financial obligations that bind them to a location, or maybe their specialization requires them to work in somewhere less than optimal, but what I want to suggest is that with the uncertain times ahead, where you choose to live has never mattered more.

America's current economy relies upon mobility, specialization, and that in a general sense, everything mostly operates the same everywhere. Cities run smoothly and in concert with the rural areas because of the market and other systems designed to connect the two. In our lives, most of us have never known anything other than minor interruptions to basic services, but a time is coming when one needs to clearly assess how likely such disruptions could become. How much do you want to expose yourself to such risks?

If you are a conservative living in a very blue state, or a progressive living well out in the country, you should realize that as political clashes escalate, you might become a target. It starts with policy that works against your interests but will not relent unless you culturally conform to the expectations of your area. While the old political process will chug along, there's little to suggest the old civic consensus will become stronger or recur. Given such a reality, living in a place that fits your social views seems only prudent, ideally one which can self-sustain.

Because beyond ideology, people look for bonds of trust based on friendship and shared identity. Small towns and close-knit neighborhoods will have an advantage over other areas because people will work together. In good times, this means having a community with resources and energy. In bad times, that energy and those connections will be the bonds that build and protect. It's a better life, but a different one than we're told to pursue based upon career and individuality.

Lest these suggestions seem abstract, I can share that I live this reality, which is why I reside happily in rural Maine. I make less than I ever have in my life, writing books like this which are an honest expression of my hopes, fears, and dreams, and yet enjoy healthy food in a friendly town in as safe a place as I can imagine. We have the beautiful night sky and the whispers of nature beyond friends we see each day, and if I gave up the ability to reach more people in some far-off city, it's because the reality I see coming has pushed me somewhere my wife and I will survive and thrive.

You deserve the same. Whether you share the views of the Right which I believe, or lean Left, the more of us who work with our own but with good sense and humor, the more likely it is we will resolve these issues in ways which are humane and thoughtful. I don't think the whole thing holds together as-is, but alternatives in this book represent a conversation that could be had, an effort not made often enough because people would rather embrace the happy fiction that all is well.

You wouldn't have purchased this book if you were someone oblivious to reality, and all I argue is that families should have the courage of their convictions. With some planning and honest thought about what suits you and yours the best, the economic opportunities have never been greater than today, and you may not have the option later to reconsider where you live, where you work, and what you do.

It can be scary at first, but the other thing I've learned in this life is the fear of either the unknown or of failure are usually far worse than the experience of making a mistake. We learn and become better people from our mistakes far more than our successes, so if it takes a time or two to get it right, better to start sooner. You'll learn about yourself from the process.

Protect Yourself and Your Family

Once you find the right place to reside, understand how to meet your basic needs.

The first is security. Without the ability to defend what you hold, all you may possess is a resource for someone else to take. Part of this is weaponry, but of equal consideration should be knowing your neighbors and if you can trust them. When the entire community looks out for one another, there isn't violence. When they do not, then anyone becomes a potential threat or victim.

Realize security through having a shelter that is sensible. Except for the most adventurous types, this will almost certainly be a necessity for protection from outsiders, from the elements, to store valued goods, and also for comfort. Having a home one can defend and enjoy in good times or bad will be essential.

Access to clean water and food supplies will alleviate other pressures. Preparedness means having food ready to survive at least some length of time, but fresh sources of agriculture or meat will be welcome supplements. The skills involved in gathering and producing food are wise to cultivate well in advance. Even a modest garden or hunting ability will extend one's ability to survive.

Warmth and energy are the final considerations. Having fuel for winter fires or cool places from summer heat will help immensely. Systems that run independent from any grid will be very useful, though potential targets, and especially for those who live in normal climates, being able to depend on readily accessible wood for warmth as opposed to gas or oil which must be shipped in may prove crucial. Weather appropriate clothing is also vital, as well as looking at insulation and passive systems that could survive any interruptions in electrical or fuel.

We take each of these for granted counting upon our economic ability to allow us to purchase these needs. But if things get bad, and commodities get scarce, you won't be able to buy your way out of the mess, so being ready now gives peace of mind, and allows you also to take one final step. When you are part of your community and self-sufficient, then you can be a complete political citizen, able to act upon your beliefs instead of your fears, and to honestly not just assess the larger situation, but your own place in this struggle.

It's worth remembering our ancestors were willing to risk years of conflict and hardship over a series of taxes on stamps, sugar, tea, and being deprived of their own currency. These issues reflected a much larger battle, which we still fight today, which is whether this country will be one based on liberty, for which the Right fights, or to try to realize equality, the ideal the Left dreams of creating.

Whether you share either dream or just dream of surviving to see better days ahead, prepare now and only good can result. This book doesn't argue so much for what should happen as what is likely to happen. Whether you agree or not, I can only say I've made my best case and that I wish you your survival and prosperity.

Post-Script

People sometimes ask me what to do next, and the only advice I can give is to act in accordance with your beliefs, politics, and expectations for what will happen next. There is no precise timetable for when this will happen, or if it will happen, but I note the storm clouds on the horizon look darker each day.

Writing a book is much like a journey, where you know the destination and can look up some of the landmarks along the way, but the surprising parts are always those things you didn't expect to see. After writing this book, I'm more convinced than ever these differences between us will not be easily reconciled, and so I prepare personally, locally, and nationally. I think war is coming.

If you are a nationalist like I am who believes the basic precepts of the Right should be the foundation upon which our culture should be defended, check out www.nationalright.us, and consider reading my earlier volume Someone Has To Say It: The Hidden History of How America Was Lost to better understand how the Left played the last century and perhaps also why I lean Right. I lost my job to defend these ideas, and suffer quite a bit financially, but it's better than living a lie.

My ambition is for the National Right to serve the dual purposes of defending the ideals of the Right to support responsibility, liberty, morality, and identity, to defend against the extremism of the Left, and seek the best way possible to sustain as much of what is good in America as peacefully as possible in defense of this cause. Such goals might sound potentially divisive but given that the Left's radicalism is encouraged most by having no opposition, people need to stand and be counted to make clear what is at stake.

Look for future volumes to better articulate strategies for the Right to accomplish its goals and rebuild our nation around a common culture. You'll be hearing more from me, but who knows what platforms will allow such speech?

Until then, I want to share my wishes and prayers with you for safety and security, in faith that the future will eventually be better, and in hopes this book has given you much to think about.

I close by sharing that it is still better to die as a free man than live as a slave. That's why crazy people are willing to fight, because a life that means something is everything to some of us. Including myself.

God Bless.

Acknowledgments

I intentionally save the acknowledgments for last because I know readers often care more about the work than these notes of appreciation but allow me to say this new career of mine of being a writer, activist, and intellectual is only possible with the help of many people.

Because naming most by name would only cause them difficulty in this political environment, I will refrain from sharing their identities, but will simply say those offering moral, personal, and sometimes material support are much appreciated by both Dana and I, and you make it possible for us to speak for you. Ever since my dismissal from serving as Town Manager, you have been steadfast friends, and we appreciate it.

If you like what you have read and want to offer words of support, skills, or maybe can be more generous, reach me at tom@nationalright.us. I pride myself on being accessible and civil to all. I even debate with respectful opponents! Check out the website and you might enjoy the new podcast **Conversations with Tom** posted twice weekly there as well.

I want to thank the many people who regularly argue with me and who offer their support. My preferred social media is Gab, which doesn't censor like Twitter, and is a place where real conversations happen. Switch over and you can find me at http://gab.ai/tomkawczynski.

Special thanks go to John Young, a man of incredible intelligence, wisdom, and whose writing skills make this manuscript much more readable, who generously offers his time and intellect as editor. His organization at www.europeanamericansunited.com definitely warrants attention and support, and I thank him also for his friendship and encouragement.

I also want to especially acknowledge Bob, Rich, Stephen, and John for their specific comments and help along the way. One could not ask for better friends.

Thank you to everyone else who has reached out and know that your words of support and your willingness to support this writing career and activism is trust well-placed. I am proud to fight for our shared beliefs, to honor our past, and protect the future.

I end by thanking Dana, my lovely and patient wife, whose struggles to defeat Lyme Disease inspire me daily, and have shown me that the way to win an unwinnable war is with grace, perseverance, humor, and the refusal to quit. This wasn't the life either of us planned, but we face it together, a fact for which I am eternally grateful.

May the Lord watch over you and yours as He has my family. Through Him, all things are truly possible.

Like What You Read? There's More Out There!

SOMEONE HAS TO SAY IT
THE HIDDEN HISTORY OF HOW AMERICA WAS LOST

TOM KAWCZYNSKI

Check out <u>Someone Has to Say It: The Hidden History of How America was Lost</u>, a provocative work detailing how the good country of America was deliberately subverted.

Written in clear and concise language with a compelling story sure to appeal to any audience, this story tells how the 20th Century saw America go from a free country to one where socialism has become common, our culture has fallen apart, and why we let this happen.

To understand the future, we must first understand the past, so take a closer look at the highly acclaimed first nonfiction work by Tom Kawczynski today to understand these struggles, and to cut through the media lies and propaganda.

Copies are available through Amazon.com, as well as a limited number of signed copies being available through <u>www.nationalright.us</u>.

Made in the USA
Columbia, SC
23 May 2019